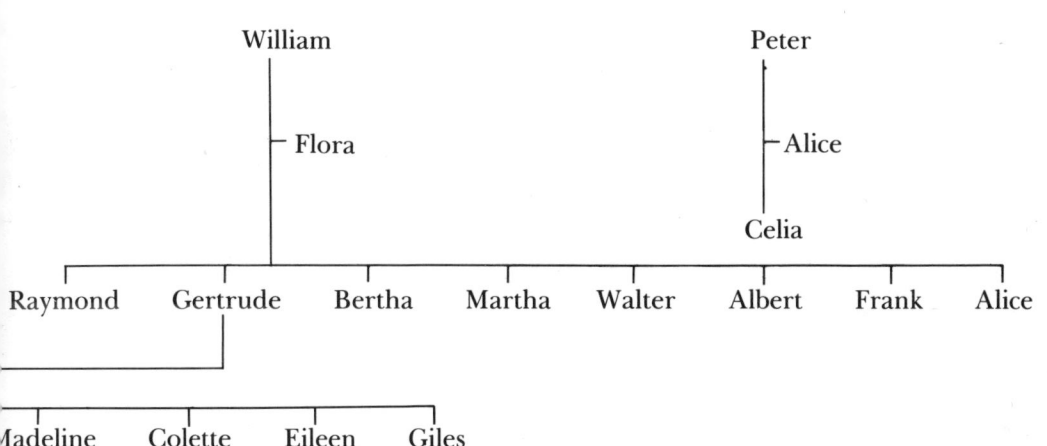

Backward, Turn Backward
Recollections of a Childhood in Northern Michigan

"Backward, turn Backward, O Time in your flight
Make me a child again just for tonight."

Elizabeth Akers Allen
1832–1911

To my husband, Hugh, and to our children,
Wandalie, Harry and Dan

Backward, Turn Backward
Recollections of a Childhood in Northern Michigan

Beatrice Schmitt Henshaw

with illustrations by

Cara Bobbitt Hochhalter

Historical Society of Michigan
Ann Arbor, Michigan

Copyright © 1986 by
Historical Society of Michigan
Ann Arbor, Michigan

All rights reserved. Printed in the United States of America. No part of this book may be reproduced in any manner whatsoever without written permission except in the case of brief quotations embodied in critical articles and reviews. For information address The Historical Society of Michigan, 2117 Washtenaw Avenue, Ann Arbor, MI 48104

ISBN: 0-9614344-1-4

Library of Congress Catalog Card Number: 86-82609

First Edition

Table of Contents

Publisher's Note vii
Preface ix
Acknowledgments... xi
  1. The Big Cork.. 1
  2. Oatmeal Rocks 15
  3. Like a Diamond in the Sky 29
  4. In Fletchers Field 41
  5. Choirs of Angels 53
  6. Turn, Stand, March 67
  7. Of Horses and Men 81
  8. Untimely Beginning 93
  9. Little White Church on the Farm 103
10. Babies from Heaven 115
11. Requiescat in Pace Aeterne 127
12. Unfirm in the Faith 139
13. The Great Improvisor 153
14. Mary and Martha 169
15. Pills, Chills, Spills and Swellings 183
16. Hay Power Versus Gasoline Power 197
17. Daughters of Eve 211
18. Bad Books 223
19. From the Goldfields to the Stockyards 235
20. Fatherless Children 245
21. Historians are Made 255
22. Tit for Tat 269
23. Cheerio, Carry On 277
24. A Brush with the Law 289
Epilogue: "Forward, Turn Forward" 303

Publisher's Note

Backward, Turn Backward: Recollections of a Childhood in Northern Michigan is the second volume published through the John Gillette Publishing Fund of the Historical Society of Michigan. The first was *Fiery Trial,* the story of Michigan's great fire of 1881. It was published in 1984.

The Society's Gillette Fund was established to support the research and writing of Michigan history. Beatrice Henshaw's *Backward, Turn Backward* is an appropriate addition to the field.

Mrs. Henshaw has captured the warmth and emotions of family life, the successes and troubles of the small family farm, and the style and substance of a by-gone era. Her childhood was absent of the trappings of affluence but rich with those aspects of life that cannot be calculated and are, therefore, priceless.

You will laugh and cry with her as you meet her family and follow its history over one generation. Her recollections of another time and place are a valuable record, true history but not found in history texts. It is indeed, in stories like these, recorded lovingly by Beatrice Henshaw, that the history of our world, nation and state are truly found.

At the same time her memories are universal over the ages and not of one era: evidences of parental love, sacrifice and heartache; sibling rivalries and loyalties; the ties of family to home and the inevitable breaking of those ties as one generation supplants another. All those human matters are here.

Mrs. Henshaw has evoked memories of our own childhood by sharing her recollections with us, and for that we are all thankful.

> Thomas L. Jones
> Executive Director
> Historical Society of Michigan

Preface

The rural life I knew as a child exists only in memory. Although the farmhouse where my father and also we children were born is still standing, its windows and doors are boarded up and the stone foundation is crumbling. The big, hip-roofed barn which was meant to shelter the family's livestock for generations remains strong and tall, but its paint has faded and more and more of its cedar shingles are blown off each year, letting the rain and the snow fall into the empty hay and straw mows below.

The chapel which my grandfather built in thanksgiving to the Lord, for saving him from drowning, is gone—only the lilacs and the bridal wreath grow untended in what was the "church yard." The black walnut trees which my father refused to sell for gunstocks during World War I are dead or dying, and where once our horses grazed and we children played, there are only weeds and tangled grass.

It was not until I began to pour over family history and note the dates on old photographs that I realized that the heyday of the small farm was already waning during my childhood years. When there were giant oaks and sturdy maple trees to fell and be hauled to the saw mills and when horse-drawn implements were used to till the soil, the "80 acre" farmer had a measure of self-reliance and independence even though life was hard; he might even be prosperous enough to build a new barn or spend a few dollars for a photograph to celebrate an engagement, a wedding, or an "increase in the family."

But with the slump which followed the First World War

came hard times in Northern Michigan—the small farm became marginal—then almost extinct. There was too little acreage to warrant the purchase of the high-priced mechanized equipment needed to compete in the marketplace. No longer were little luxuries possible, like having the children's pictures taken. Only by supplementing the meager farm income with wages earned at other jobs were many families able to remain on their ancestral acres.

There has been a trade-off of sorts; there are machines to do much of the back-breaking work of an earlier day, both in agriculture and in factories. There are such programs as student loans, unemployment benefits and social security pensions.

Something has been lost and something has been gained, but there is much to do and far to go if we are to reach the "land of milk and honey" which modern technology could make possible, not only for our own countrymen but for all people everywhere. However, if we are to move forward toward the goal of a better, safer, more kindly and self-fulfilling society, we must stop fueling the engines of war and light the candles of peace. That is the dream and the challenge.

Beatrice Henshaw
July, 1986

Acknowledgments

At the University of Michigan, I found myself to be a very small frog in a very big puddle. No longer was I getting all A's (an earlier obsession) but I was beginning to search diligently for answers to the problems which beset our society. It was during the Great Depression and it was Carlton F. Wells, a young professor who considered his first obligation was to his students rather than to the "Publish or Perish Diktat," who encouraged me to write about the rural world I knew, and to express my sometimes unconventional views in newspaper readers' columns.

Many years later, it was a Letter to the Editor in the *Ann Arbor News* written by Harriette S. Arnow regarding the shelter controversy then raging ("... but even if these underground contraptions could shield human beings from nuclear fallout for a time, what about the birds and flowers?"), which emboldened me to phone the author of the much acclaimed *The Dollmaker*. We became friends and often exchanged childhood reminiscences, hers of the hills in Kentucky and mine of the hills in Northern Michigan. It was she who suggested that I submit some of my sketches to the Historical Society of Michigan.

I wish to express my gratitude to them and to others who encouraged me along the way, among them my husband, our daughter Wandalie and my friend, Charlotte Sanderson.

The Big Cork

ONE of my very first memories is that of a clanging and rumbling and shouting on the roof of our farmhouse in the middle of the night. Cowbells were ringing, a heavy chain was being dragged back and forth and boisterous voices were yelling, "C'mon out, c'mon out! We want beer, we gotta have beer!"

My brother, Carl, had been awakened also and had taken refuge under our parents' bed. In the light of the kerosene lamp I could see his head, his eyes peering upward toward the ceiling. Apparently he was torn between the fear that the world was coming to an end and the possibility that he was missing something very exciting.

But I was crying in genuine terror and Mamma was trying to comfort me. "It's all right, it's all right," she kept saying. "It's just that they've been drinking. Papa will make them come down."

But it wasn't all right. A big chunk of plaster came crashing to the floor, my brother's head disappeared under the bed and Mamma was visibly shaken and angry. Plastering was something which took the kind of skill that had to be paid for in hard cash which was always in short supply at our house. "Drink, it's the curse of the world," she kept repeating.

Papa's brother, Albert, had gotten married the week before in Kingsley and had come to our house with his bride for a brief visit before returning to Grand Rapids where he had a part-time job as a church organist and a full-time job at

Jenning's Manufacturing Co. where he bottled vanilla and other extracts. There had been some deliberation in the family as to whether a keg of beer should be purchased in case there would be a shivaree.

According to the dictionary, a "shivaree" is a mock serenade with kettles, pans, horns and other noisemakers given for a newly married couple. In our area at that time at least, the noisemakers were more lethal than pots and pans, and instead of a serenade the shivaree seemed to be an excuse for a beer binge and those who failed to provide the beverage were in for big trouble.

Papa had thought that having the beer on hand might be a good idea, not because he liked the stuff but because he wanted to keep on good terms with everybody. However, Mamma had talked him out of buying the beer, first because it would be compromising her principles and second, because beer cost money. Or perhaps it was the other way around. Furthermore she had argued, since the wedding celebration had taken place at the home of the bride's parents almost a hundred miles away, it was very unlikely that there would be additional honeymoon hi-jinks a whole week later.

However, the groom's friends had little regard, apparently, for the social niceties or for the temperance ideas in our household. Forever after, Mamma maintained that our roof had been targeted because of her outspoken antipathy toward all things alcoholic, whether the drink or the drinker. And she may have been right insofar as the preparations for the late-night onslaught were concerned—not just cowbells but also a ladder, a logging chain and assorted sledgehammers had been brought to the premises.

Even many years later, when offering a guest a legal drink was considered to be a sign of hospitality, Mamma would turn down a glass of wine or whatever with a polite but frigid, "No thank you, I don't like the stuff!" The way she pronounced the word "stuff" carried a monumental value judgment. Papa, however, would accept a "cup of fury" with a nod and a slight smile but as soon as the opportunity presented itself, he would quietly dump the contents over a porch railing or somewhere conveniently out of sight.

Papa didn't like to hurt anyone's feelings, whether it was an over-exuberant host or a drunken driver. After Michigan became a dry state, there was a moonshine still in the woods several miles beyond our farm and many a night, Papa would be roused from his sleep and called upon to hitch up his team to pull a tin lizzie from a ditch, its driver too drunk to keep his car on our narrow road. And when Papa got home, tired and mud-spattered, Mamma would say, "I hope you charged him plenty!"

His answer would be something like, "He gave me fifty cents—that was all he had." Or it might be, "He didn't offer to pay and I didn't like to ask him because I don't think he had a penny left."

To this Mamma would respond a bit caustically, "Well, put your muddy overalls in the wash but next time, make sure you get paid before you pull out the bum!"

Several years after the shivaree, when my brother Carl and I were discussing the "pro's and con's" of guns (he was "pro" and I was "con"), he tried to bolster up what I considered a failing argument with an account of what had happened the night of the big commotion on the roof. According to his version, as soon as "all hell broke lose," Papa grabbed his shotgun from the cellarway where it was kept, loaded it, put a supply of shells in his pocket and rushed outdoors where he took up a position on the raised cistern lid and ordered the revelers to come down. To let them know he meant business he shot into the air, reloaded his gun and warned that he would shoot every last one of them dead if they didn't get off our roof and off our property. He gave them exactly five minutes to do as he ordered, and it worked—one by one the shivareers came down the ladder, bringing with them the cowbells, the chains, sledgehammers and all.

My brother's dramatic tale didn't sound right to me. I couldn't believe what he said about Papa threatening to shoot people dead if they didn't get off our roof. Papa did have a shotgun which he kept out of sight in the cellarway, along with old coats and little-used items like the cherry-pitter and the cider press. And he did use it occasionally to shoot hawks which were preying on our chickens and the raccoons which were raising hob with our corn. But being ready to kill people, even if they were mortal-sin bad, didn't sound like Papa at all.

When I asked Mamma about Carl's account of what had happened her story differed markedly. She said that Papa had taken out his gun and shot into the air once in order to make himself heard above the racket but it was the promise of drinks all around the following evening that brought the young hellions down, not a threat of being shot. And it was actually the groom, Uncle Albert, who treated the shivareers at a saloon but it was Mamma's savings which provided the wherewithal.

It was June, a time when farmers were usually short of funds so the only available cash was her precious egg money which she had been setting aside for a bolt of outing flannel for making diapers and pinning blankets for the baby she was expecting the following October. That a baby had to be shortchanged in order to buy beer was too much for Mamma to accept with equanimity.

Drinking, I learned, was not the act of sipping milk from a glass or a cup. It was "boozing it up," it was "hitting the bottle," it was "guzzling the stuff." It was something that nice people, our kind of people, simply did not do. And it caused all kinds of problems in addition to knocking the plaster off the ceiling and scaring children half to death. Drinkers did shameful things, they spent their last nickels at saloons, they came home cussing and staggering, they beat their wives and children, they lashed their horses and kicked their dogs.

I don't recall that Mamma ever felt the need to bring God or the devil into her anti-liquor crusade. She had practical reasons, enough and to spare, for her intense dislike of the Demon Rum. As for Papa, who also disliked the idea of drinking, he seemed to feel sorry for those who had to drown their sorrows and their frustrations in liquor, as well as for those at home who had to "put up" with the drunkards.

There was a ditty which Papa liked to sing while he was doing the chores in the barn. Mostly he sang two kinds of songs, church hymns and sad ballads. The one he sang about a little child begging her father, who was drinking in a saloon, to come home was definitely a sad one. It went something like this:

"Father, dear Father, come home with me now
The clock in the steeple strikes one
You said you were coming right home from the shop
As soon as your day's work was done.

Our fire has gone out, our house is all dark
And Mamma's been watching since tea
With poor Brother Bennie so sick in her arms
And no one to help her but me.

Father, dear Father, come home with me now
The clock in the steeple strikes two
The night has grown colder and Bennie is worse
And he has been calling for you

Indeed, he is worse, Mamma says he may die
Perhaps before morning shall dawn
And this is the message she sent me to bring
Come quickly or he may be gone."

If I closed my eyes I could see the picture vividly—a shivering child wandering up and down the hills of Petoskey on a bitterly cold winter night, looking for her dear father. At long last she recognizes his horse, tied to a hitching post on Mitchell Street. She hesitates at the entrance of the nearby saloon where "the doors swing in and the doors swing out" but finally she gets up enough courage to enter the dimly lit room with sawdust on the floor. There, sitting at the counter with a lot of other men, she sees her father with a mug of beer in his hand. She tugs at his coat, she tries to get his attention, she calls to him,

"Father, dear Father, come home with me now!"

But he seems not to hear her above the loud voices and laughter of the other drinkers. Meanwhile the clock in the Courthouse several blocks away strikes the hour mournfully.

She goes back to the saloon again and again and although she pleads with her father and tells him that her little brother is worse, he seems to be unaware of her presence as his head sinks lower and lower over his mug of beer and the voices of the other men get louder and louder. And then the clock in the Courthouse strikes three, but now it is too late:

*"Poor little Bennie is dead
And gone with the angels of light
And these are the very last words that he said
I want to kiss Papa Good Night."*

I wept for little Bennie, I wept for his sister, I wept for his mother and I even wept for his father who would never be able to hear his little boy's last whispered "Good Night." And it was all because of drinking which was, indeed, the curse of the world.

How lucky we were that Papa would never go through those swinging doors unless it was to look for Johnny Maloney, nor would he spend his hard-earned money in a saloon. If he had any cash left after selling a load of fire-wood or a wagonful of farm produce and purchasing the necessaries, he would buy a nickel's worth of candy for us children—long, luscious licorice whips or red and green striped peppermint sticks or round, pink wintergreens. When he got home from one of his trips to town we would wait expectantly while he put the horses in the barn and gave them some hay.

"Horses take their time about eating—they don't gobble up everything in a minute. And divide the candy up equally," he'd say with a sidewise look at Carl who was known to try to get more than his share because he was "older, had a bigger stomach and all."

But in other families, like the song said, the houses were dark, the fires had gone out, the mothers were weeping and the poor little children lay dead—and all because of saloons and beer. How I wished for a world where all fathers would come home with surprises in a paper sack.

The day will come, Mamma assured me, when the country will "go dry." To a farm child the meaning was perfectly clear—when a cow goes dry, there is no more milk. But Cousin Celia who boarded at our house the year she taught in our one-room district school, was not so sure that Prohibition would solve all the problems of the country. I heard her telling Mamma that it would take more than closing up the saloons to make things better. "Being poor," she said, "was enough to drive anybody to drink!"

But Mamma only laughed and said, "Then on the wages

you get and what we make on the farm we'll all take to drink!"

As I later realized, the thirty dollars a month which our teacher was getting was not really so much—at the time I thought it was surely enough to make her rich—thirty dollars for teaching eight grades and doing the janitor work, also furnishing many of her supplies!

But it wasn't just her own wages that she was concerned about—she would talk to Mamma about the way the lumber barons had stripped the woods of the big trees while paying the lumberjacks low wages. This being the case, how could the farmers get a decent price for their produce if the workers didn't get paid enough to feed their families properly?

In some parts of Emmet County where she had taught, she said, there were children who couldn't go to school during the winter because they didn't have shoes or warm coats.

Carl and I would hear them talking and I would be troubled and confused by such stories but Carl could always come up with quick answers to the most complicated social and economic as well as religious problems. According to him the blame for drinking could be laid squarely at the door of the local brewery—"burry" to him.

On the shore of Mud Lake near Kegomic (a small company town where a lot of poor people lived) stood the "burry," a peculiarly shaped red brick building, five stories high in the center with four story wings on either side. It was the biggest building we had ever seen, taller even than our church. But instead of the nice smell of burning incense and candles, there was the odor of the fermenting barley and hops. It was where beer was made.

"Why does it smell so bad?" I asked my brother.

"Because it's old, beer's like eggs, the older it gets the worse it stinks."

I knew all about rotten eggs because Carl had invented a game which involved eggs which had gone bad. When we found a long-deserted nest hidden away under the corn crib or in a patch of burdocks, we took the eggs behind the barn where there was a big fieldstone. Standing about ten paces from the stone we took aim and fired and the player whose

egg splattered the farthest was the winner. Of course Carl usually won and I often got splattered.

"But how can people drink the stuff when it smells so awful?" I asked.

"It's because of the devil," Carl informed me. "See, it's like this—you know when you pinch your nose you can't smell anything. Well, the devil pinches a man's nose when he's drinking beer. That's why Johnny Maloney's nose is so red, it's from being pinched so much."

"But how can the devil pinch a lot of noses at the same time?" I wanted to know.

For a moment he was stumped but as always he managed to come up with a fairly good explanation, "It's 'cause the devil is like Santy Claus—he kin be lots of places at the same time."

I didn't like the idea of the devil and Santa being lumped together but Carl's reasoning seemed to make sense. "And does all the beer stuff come from the burry?" I asked.

"Yep, that burry's filled right up to the roof with beer. There's enough of it in there to make jist about every man in the whole country drunk," he answered. Only men, it seemed, ever figured in Carl's important statistics.

The thought of that huge building which he likened to a great big sauerkraut barrel filled to the very top with beer raised some questions in my mind. If the door on the ground floor were ever opened, the beer would come gushing out in a torrent and nobody could get the door shut again. "Do they have to climb up on the roof and dip it out?" I wondered.

"Naw, there's a cork around in back where you can't see it, it's about as big as an ear of corn, pretty big cork. An' when the wagon comes for the beer the driver jist pulls out the cork an' fills up his kegs, then pushes the cork back in again real quick." I'd heard talk about corks in connection with drinking and comments like "He's on the wagon now" or "He fell off the wagon" so it all fit together. And having all that beer with him, a driver might get so drunk he'd fall head first off the seat and get stomped by the horses or smashed by the wagon wheels.

By now I was convinced that the burry was the biggest villain in the wet parade. And after the burry came the saloon which led to the Pesthouse and from there to the Poorhouse, according to Carl.

The Pesthouse was south of town so we seldom drove by it with the horse and buggy but one time when I happened to be with Papa when he was on the way to buy a peck of a new kind of seed corn, he pointed it out to me. It was an old weatherbeaten frame building with its windows and doors covered over with boards and surrounded by a tangle of dead weeds and underbrush.

"That's where they used to put people who had smallpox," Papa told me.

"Did they die there?" I asked.

"Most of them did—nobody was allowed to go in to help them, not even the priest. It was a terrible way to die—thank God there isn't so much small pox any more, the place is all closed up now."

When I told Carl I had seen the Pesthouse and that I was glad there weren't sick people there any more, he had a different story to tell. "Pa [Carl thought Papa sounded babyish] doesn't like to talk about such things to you girls, but that's where they put drunks now."

"But the windows and doors are all boarded up," I told him.

"Oh, that's so they can't get out, you wouldn't want a lotta drunks running around loose, pests that's what they are an' that's why it's called the Pesthouse," he confided.

"But, how can they see in there an' what do they have to eat?" Bad as drunks were I couldn't help feeling sorry for them.

"Jist any old rats they kin catch. An' after they're 'bout starved to death, drunks 're put in the Poorhouse."

Carl always injected just enough reality in his tales to give them the ring of truth. The Emmet County Poorhouse I knew about—it was next to the cemetery where we occasionally put flowers on the graves of relatives. But at least it was better than the Pesthouse, bad though it was. There we would see old men puttering around, hoeing in the garden or just sitting dozing in the sun. Sometimes I could hear them mumbling and grumbling but I couldn't understand what they were saying and maybe that was because they didn't have any teeth like Old Johnny Maloney.

It was to the County Poorhouse that Johnny had been taken just before he died. Papa never got to visit him there but he did go to the funeral, such as it was. There weren't many other mourners, Papa said, and Johnny was buried in a rough pine box in a corner of the graveyard reserved for those who died penniless.

The old Irishman had lived with his wife in a tar paper shack a few miles east of our farm. When he had some fur pelts or huckleberries to sell, he would hitch up his skinny nag, take them into town and with the proceeds he would go on a "toot". It didn't take much to get him drunk and sometimes the saloon-keeper would give him an extra drink just to hear him babble about the things he was going to do when his "ship came in." When he fell off his stool he would be helped out to his rig, his mare would be untied from the hitching post and she would find the way home without directions from Johnny who was conked out on the seat.

One time when the old man had apparently forgotten to secure the rope properly, his horse got tired of waiting for him in the winter cold and headed for home without him. It was in the middle of the night, the snow lay on the ground, thick and frosty, when Johnny's wife, Katy, came pounding on our door. Papa was always a soft touch for people in distress.

After he had changed horses, putting Johnny's tired old nag in our barn to warm up and eat a bite of hay, Papa and Katy set out for town on the lookout for a dark heap in the snow, Papa scanning the bank on one side of the road and Katy the other. Papa had brought along our buffalo robe in case they found him but there was no sign of Johnny on the trip back to town. Eventually, however, they stumbled upon him in a dark corner of one of his favorite saloons and between the two of them, they got him into the cutter where he sat slumped on the floor with his head on Katy's lap.

"K-K-Katy me luv, belave me, I'll b-b-buy ye a rail nice farm, a rail b-b-big one an' begorree, I'll b-b-buy ye a house in town, too," he roused up enough to say.

Poor old Johnny, he was never able to buy her either one. Katy finally left him and after that he went from bad to worse. Early one spring morning the sheriff's man pulled him out of a puddle by the side of the road, his hair and beard matted with mud and his ragged overalls soaking wet. After they sobered him up they put him in the Poorhouse to die.

Johnny didn't have a decent chance, Papa said. The soil around his shack was too light and sandy to grow anything but jack pines and huckleberries and besides, he didn't know the first thing about farming. However, he had been a dandy worker in the lumber camps, an expert with an axe and a cross-cut saw, Papa insisted, but "they wore him out in the woods" and when the big trees had all been felled, people like Johnny weren't needed any more. Then he'd squatted on a no-good piece of Government land, built himself a one-room shack and found a wife.

But nothing seemed to go right for him and the drinking which he had learned when the camps broke up in the spring became his only respite from frustration.

And so it was that he died in the Poorhouse,

> *"With nary a mortal to close his eyes*
> *Or a woman to cross his hands."*

The pine box was nailed shut by the time Papa got to the graveyard so the rosary which he had brought with him could not be entwined around Johnny's bony, work-scarred fingers.

Although I didn't need anything more to convince me of the folly of drinking, Carl had a large stock of stories for that very purpose. One was about the man who was in the throes of delirium tremens (Carl's phrase was "devil's tantrums") and who saw snakes not only crawling up the walls but hanging straight down from the ceiling. And every time the old drunk tried to get away, a snake's tongue would shoot out and reel in the poor fellow.

And then there was the tale about the drinker who had sold his soul to the devil for a bottle of beer. But when he got the bottle to his lips, a snake about a foot long came slithering out and the man swallowed it. The priest was called and a pan of holy water was placed on the floor beside the man's bed and sure enough, it worked—when the man leaned over the side of his bed, the snake wriggled out and drowned in the holy water.

According to Carl, the devil, the Protestants and liquor were somehow intermingled. It wasn't the Catholics who were responsible for keeping the country "wet" because of the wine used by the priest during Mass. It was really the Protestants' fault because not only did the preacher drink the altar wine but everybody in his church as well, lots of it!

The moral was all too clear—the road from the "burry" led to big trouble of one kind or another. But at last came the day when we heard that Michigan had gone "dry" and a padlock had been put on the door of the big brick building where the devil's brew was made. No more would snakes grab their victims or slide down their throats. No more would little children have to wander the streets looking for their drunken fathers while weeping mothers cradled their dying Bennies in their arms. No more would homeless old men spend their last days in the Poorhouse, alone and forgotten.

"But what will happen to all that beer in the burry?" I asked Carl. The stuff, filled to the roof as it was, could still cause trouble.

"Oh, that's easy," Carl answered. "They'll jist pull out that big cork and let it all run down into Mud Lake."

Oatmeal Rocks

IT came in a little pink envelope which was smaller than any other one which was ever put in our mailbox and it was addressed to me, a pre-school child who had never before received a letter. Mamma read my name aloud and the address, R.F.D. #2, Box 115, Petoskey, Michigan, and it made me feel very grown up and important. My brother, Carl, wanted to tear it open for me but I got my paper-cutting scissors and trimmed off the end as carefully as I could so as not to tear the envelope—I wanted to save my tiny pink letter forever and ever, along with my silver dollar which was minted in the year that I was born, 1911.

Inside was a picture of four or five little girls playing *Drop the Handkerchief* on a card with an invitation to attend the birthday party of the young daughter of a resorter couple—resorters being the "rich" people who came north to summer in Bay View on the outskirts of Petoskey. Her name was Arleen but I had never really played with her when she came with her parents in a big, beautiful car to buy vegetables and fruit at our farm.

To me, Arleen with a crisp ribbon bow on her head instead of a halo looked almost like the guardian angel guiding a child across a foot bridge in one of the holy pictures in our bedroom. I had shown her one of our kittens once and she had held it on her lap and stroked it gently but she didn't want to go to the barn with me to see the mother cat in her nest in the hay mow. I think she was afraid of Rover, our herd dog, who always barked and carried on whenever a stranger was on the premises. To be able to play with Arleen in Bay View would be like playing with an angel in heaven.

Weekdays were work-days at our house but on Sunday mornings while Papa, my brother and I were at Mass, Mamma would often have time to bake two cakes, one big one for the family and one little one so I could have a "tea party" when a neighbor girl came to play in the afternoon. My cake would be frosted lightly on top and we would sit at my Santa Claus table, hold our dolls on our laps and feed them bits of cake and sips of cider or mint tea. Parties were to have a good time and be nice to everybody, Mamma said, and that meant that we had to put up with my sister, Madeline, who was two, going on three, and liked to lick the frosting off her cake, drink her "tea" in one big gulp and then ask for more.

But Arleen's party was going to be something different, something much grander than my tea parties, of that I was certain. Carl said her father was "resorter rich" and that meant he was so rich he had five and ten dollar bills hanging out of his pockets. Only a person with that kind of money could afford to buy a Stearns-Knight, a car which probably cost a bushel of money Carl told me. It didn't have side curtains like the Ford which one of the town doctors had, but was "inclosed" with glass windows which rolled up and down so you could get fresh air on a hot day but could keep dry when it rained. It was like a little house on wheels with windows and doors and it didn't need a horse to pull it. And the best part of it was, it had lots of power, as much as fifty or seventy-five horses, Carl said.

"Yah, I betcha he paid a hundred dollars fer that Stearns-Knight, maybe a million. An' they prob'ly eat out of gold dishes or anyway silver," he wagered after I got the invitation.

I knew he wasn't fibbing about the car because I had seen it with my own eyes and I had watched Arleen roll up its window on account of Rover who was yipping and snapping at the tires. So it could be that they had dishes of gold or silver. On dishes like that what kind of food would they have at the party, I wondered.

"Betcha they don't eat potatoes an' gravy an' stuff like we eat," Carl speculated.

"Well, they buy things from our garden," I reminded him.

"But I betcha they have ice cream every day, maybe coupla times a day an' in between, too," he insisted. We made ice cream only two or three times a year—cream was one of the chief sources of our income and Mamma said we must be saving and get our bills paid. Also, it took a lot of work to chop the ice and pack the freezer with the ice chips and the salt.

At any rate, the upcoming birthday party at Arleen's house was something to be savored by day and dreamed about by night. And it was not just the party, I was going to be able to play with a kind of earth angel in her big, beautiful house in Bay View which, on the inside must look like heaven itself. And it had two porches, one upstairs with a railing all around it and one on the first floor with a porch swing on it.

But it was the Stearns-Knight which had captured my brother's imagination. "Maybe you'll get to sit in it," he said enviously.

"I'd rather sit in the porch swing with Arleen," I told him. We had only a rope swing on one of our walnut trees and we had no porches at all. Some of our neighbors had porches on their houses but not a single one had a porch swing. Carl said that was because farmers had to work all the time but resorters had nothing else to do but swing back and forth and look at the Bay or else go for rides in their fancy big cars.

Even though he was much taken with the Stearns-Knight, Carl was scornful of my party invitation. "Buncha rich kids," he said contemptuously. "They wear Sunday clothes every day in the week, never hafta work, they can eat all the candy they want and I betcha they're real stuck-up."

"How d'you know?" I asked him. Carl always thought he knew everything and I didn't want to think of Arleen as being "stuck up" which Carl said meant sticking your nose up in the air.

"'Cause they're rich an' we're poor, that's why!"

I didn't want to quiz Mamma about that because one time when I was helping her to "look over" navy beans, I asked her if it was because we were poor that we had to eat the hulls and the split beans while saving the good ones to sell. Mamma wasn't one to spank or even scold us very much but that time she clapped her hand over my mouth and said, "They make good soup and we don't waste anything in this house."

"You'll have to take Arleen a birthday present," Aunt Alice told me when I showed her my invitation when she came for dinner the following Sunday. She was my mother's youngest sister and was going to high school so she surely must know all about parties and things like that.

"I could take her a kitten," I suggested when Mamma and I were discussing the matter several days before the big event.

"Resorters don't bother with cats," Mamma told me. "Cats are for catching mice so they won't eat up the wheat and oats in the granary."

"But remember how much Arleen liked the kitten I showed her," I reminded Mamma. We had two mother cats and we nearly always had a batch of kittens and when they were old enough to run around they usually disappeared unaccountably. "They've probably found a good home," Mamma would say and this time I told her that Arleen would give a kitty a good home.

"I think that if Arleen's mother wanted her to have a kitten she'd have one already. But it would be nice to take her something good to eat. I could make her some of those oatmeal rocks you like so much," Mamma said. There was no provision for store-bought gifts in Mamma's budget.

If I couldn't take her a kitten, a present of cookies sounded reasonable to me. Her parents were always saying how nice and fresh the vegetables from our garden were.

Mamma had found the recipe for the oatmeal rocks in the farm paper and they really tasted good, especially when she added some black walnut meats which we had in abundance from our row of walnut trees. So it was that about a dozen of the crunchy rocks were packaged in a clean, white shoe box, wrapped in tissue and tied with some bright red cord. It looked very pretty and festive to me and made me think of Christmas.

The birthday girl's house was on the edge of Bay View

which was about three miles from our house, too far for me to walk both ways, Mamma said. It was during the haying season, a busy time on the farm, and Papa was planning to haul in hay the day of the party so the horses would be needed at home. Mamma was needed also to drive the team during the unloading of the hay. Since she couldn't take me herself, she arranged to have me ride with a neighbor lady who was going to town that day, leaving shortly after eleven o'clock. This would get me to my destination around noon, two hours before the party was scheduled to start.

We didn't have a phone to check out the arrangement but Mamma said, "I'm sure Arleen's mother won't mind. Maybe you and Arleen can sit on that nice porch swing and get acquainted."

That, I thought, was a wonderful idea. To be able to glide back and forth on that swing with Arleen and after that, the party—both on the same day! I was overjoyed at the prospect.

I was all atremble with anticipation when the neighbor lady dropped me off in front of Arleen's house. Clutching my present, I dashed up the steps, while still keeping an eye on the neighbor's horse and buggy. It took what seemed a long time before the door was finally opened and there stood a stiffly starched white apron and the whites of two eyes. I stepped back in alarm just as the neighbor's horse was setting off at such a brisk pace that I knew I would never be able to catch up with it. Carl had told me about ghosts who wore bed sheets and carried away children my size, never to be seen again.

"Arleen's party" was all I was able to gasp.

"You shoh is early," the starched figure exclaimed and her voice didn't sound mean or scary. And now in addition to the apron and the eyes, there were two rows of very white teeth. "Come in, chile," I was told as the screen door opened so that I could enter. Now I could see that there was more than apron, eyes and teeth and it was all black from her face to her shoes.

"Arleen and the mister, they gone to town to get the ice cream an' such an' the missus, she upstairs takin' a bath an' gettin' dressed."

In the middle of a week-day was a funny time to take a bath so maybe Carl was right about resorters being different from us—we took our baths on Saturday night in the kitchen. And who was this lady with the black face and hands, could she be some relation to Arleen? I had heard the phrase "colored folks" but I had imagined "colored" to mean many colors, like my box of crayons. But this lady seemed to be just plain black, at least all that I could see of her.

My brother had told me that the devil was black which was from shoveling coal all day and getting covered with soot.

But here was someone in a nice clean apron, not a smudge on the white, so the black couldn't be from coal dust. Besides, she had a big smile and she didn't have any horns but all the same, I didn't want to be alone with her in the semi-darkness inside the house.

"Mamma said could I sit on the swing?" I managed to ask. I would feel safer on the porch and I still wanted to try out the swing.

I was much relieved when she said, "Shoh thing—yu jus' swing all you wants. An' now I be gettin' the party ready but I kin take yoh box."

I shook my head vehemently. And with that she disappeared and I was left to climb up on the swing, still clinging to the present which I did not want to entrust to the black lady. My legs weren't long enough to reach the floor so I wasn't able to get much movement on the swing except for some irregular jerks, nothing at all like what I had expected. In fact, nothing seemed to be working out the way I had envisioned it—Arleen wasn't at home to play with me, a strange lady with very white eyeballs and a very black face seemed to be in charge and Mamma was very far away.

I felt a surge of homesickness, a lump in my throat that I couldn't swallow, and a tightness in my chest that made it hard to breathe. I didn't care about the party any more and I wanted to go home—even the sight of my brother tormentor would have been very welcome. Mamma had told me that she didn't want me to walk back all by myself and that I was to wait for Carl who had volunteered to come for me. But I was almost five years old and if I could pick up nearly as many potatoes as my brother, I ought to be able to walk home alone. I knew the way and I wouldn't get lost.

But what would I tell people when they asked me about the party? And Mamma wouldn't like it if I started out walking by myself! And Carl would say, "See, I told ya, you wouldn't like a rich kid's party!"

I hadn't decided what to do when Arleen's mother, in a frilly pink shirtwaist and a long white skirt, came out and sat beside me on the swing. She smelled like a bunch of lilacs and it was July, way past lilac time. She knew how to make the swing go and she told me that Arleen would soon be home and I began to feel better.

"I was hoping that your mother would bring you to the party and stay awhile," she said. "I would really like to get to know her better, she seems like such a nice person."

"Papa has to haul in hay before it rains and he needs the horses," I explained.

"If I'd known that, Arleen's father could have gone to get you both."

"But Papa needs Mamma, too—she has to drive the horses." I tried to tell her about haying, how the team had to be hitched to the pulley rope so as to lift the slings full of hay up to the ridge-pole of the barn, then send it over to the hay mow so Papa could trip the rope and dump the hay in just the right spot, but I could see she didn't understand about such things.

"Poor woman, I know that farm women have to work hard, gardening and canning, but I didn't think they had to do that kind of thing, and she's so frail looking, she shouldn't have to work like that."

Hearing her say that about Mamma brought another lump to my throat. Mamma never talked about having to work hard, she just kept going all day long. I should try to help her more and not complain about my sister being such a pest.

"What do I see there, all wrapped up?" Arleen's mother asked, changing the subject.

"It's something Mamma made this morning and it's good to eat," I said proudly. "And I cracked the walnuts last night all by myself!"

"Um-m, sounds delicious. Let me take the box and I'll put it on the sideboard where we're going to put the gifts. And I'm going to bring you some books to look at while we're waiting for Arleen. Would you like a sandwich and a glass of milk to tide you over?"

"I'm not hungry," I told her which was true. I had been too excited to eat much of the lunch which Mamma had fixed for me and now I didn't feel like eating. But the armful of books which she brought me made me forget about wanting to go home. As I turned the pages, I saw all manner of wonderful pictures in color of animals I'd never seen before.

And there were even three little pigs and their mother with dresses on—Papa would really laugh about that as our pigpen was usually kind of muddy because the pigs slopped their swill. I hadn't known there were so many books about animals in the whole world.

Time passed more quickly as I pored over the pictures and soon the other guests began arriving. Somehow, they all seemed to look alike, each in a pretty party dress, with matching hair ribbons; most of them had long curls except for one or two and they had braids. My hair was "bobbed" with bangs—Mamma said it was easier to take care of that way.

I looked down at my dress which was "made over" from one of Aunt Alice's. It had seemed pretty enough at home but now it didn't look so good. And I hadn't worn my Sunday shoes—Mamma said I would get them scuffed and dirty, walking home on the dusty road. The party girls were all wearing strap-buttoned patent leather slippers with short socks and I had laced shoes and long stockings.

And then came Arleen with her father carrying boxes and bags. They didn't even see me as they hurried into the house where I could hear them greeting the other little girls, all laughing and chattering. I was still hoping that Arleen would come out and sit on the swing with me for a few minutes at least, but she didn't come so I sat there alone, afraid that I was going to cry.

Arleen's father stopped for a moment on his way back to his car and said, "I'm going to play a few holes of golf now, but when the party's over, I'll drive you to the farm." Then he was off and I was alone again, thinking that nobody would miss me if I started to walk home real fast. But then Arleen's mother came out and took me by the hand, saying as she led me to the dining room, "I want you to sit next to Arleen at the table but first I want to introduce you to her other friends."

Never had I seen anything so fancy—pink and white crepe paper streamers looped from the center to the corners of the ceiling and on the middle of the table a big white cake frosted all over, not just on the top like our cakes at home, and on the frosting there were pink rosebuds with tiny green leaves clustered around the little pink candles. At each place was a miniature lacy-looking basket filled with pink and white candies and on the sideboard were a lot of presents, arranged so that it looked like a mass of ribbon bows. I could see only a corner of my box, tied with plain red Christmas string and I was glad that little of it was showing as it wasn't prettied up like the others.

Arleen's mother "introduced" me and told me the other girl's names but I couldn't remember any of them. Arleen smiled at me and said that she was happy that I could come to her party but then she was busy laughing and talking to her friends and I couldn't think of anything to say. The black lady, they called her Mandy, came in with a tray of sandwiches, little tiny ones, and Arleen's mother filled our glasses with pink lemonade.

I should have been entranced by the beauty of it all and I should have been hungry since breakfast had been so long ago but my throat hurt and I found it hard to swallow. All I wanted to do was to go home but I couldn't just get up and leave; yet if I stayed I might burst out crying and then they would all probably laugh at me. I did manage to eat a couple of sandwiches and drink my lemonade but I shook my head when Mandy wanted to give me another helping.

Then Arleen's mother lit the candles and everybody sang *Happy Birthday*, all except me because I had never heard it before. Mandy took away the sandwich plates which didn't need washing at all and brought in others which had pink ice cream on them but none of the dishes were gold or silver so Carl was wrong, at least about the dishes. After Arleen blew out the candles, her mother put a piece of cake on each plate—it was snow white and the pink ice cream had flecks of strawberries in it. It looked so good I forgot my homesickness for awhile and ate most of it but then I remembered my present of oatmeal rocks, tied with plain cord instead of pretty ribbon. I wished now that Mamma had let me bring a kitten as I was sure that Arleen would like that better.

After the dishes were cleared away, Arleen opened the presents one by one and held them up to be admired. There were games and books and hair-bows, even a little bottle of perfume. Last of all came my gift and Arleen rattled the shoe box saying, "I think it's a game!"

"No, it's something good to eat," her mother said. "A little bird told me."

Then Arleen opened the package for all to see and no one said a word. Now, instead of looking like good tasting cookies fresh from the oven, they looked like blobs of cold oatmeal left over from breakfast. And the oatmeal was not the finely slivered, anemic "Quick" oats of today but strong, upstanding, thickly rolled kernels which let you know in no uncertain terms that they weren't party fare.

"Are these something to eat?" Arleen finally asked with a funny look on her face and then all the girls laughed.

"They're oatmeal rocks," I managed to say. "But they taste real good."

"Indeed, they do," Arleen's mother said, coming to my rescue, as she took a bite out of one. "And they have black walnuts in them, too. Just try them and you'll see." But no one took any, not even Arleen, and I felt my face getting hot and prickly with shame.

Arleen's mother put the open box back on the sideboard but it must have been too near the edge as when Arleen tried to pull something from under it, the box tumbled off, the cookies crumbling and scattering as they hit the floor. Mandy was called from the kitchen with a broom and dustpan and as Arleen's mother shooed us into the big living room, the black lady was sweeping up the mess.

"I'm so sorry," Arleen's mother said as she led me through the archway, patting my shoulder. And then to get my mind off the cookies, she announced, "Our first game will be *Pin the Tail on the Donkey* and since we have a little girl here who knows all about farm animals, we'll blindfold her first."

But in my haste to make good on her kind words about me, I pinned the tail on the wrong end of the donkey which brought forth another peal of laughter.

A peanut hunt was next and the first place I looked was on the sill of one of the front windows, hoping and praying that my brother would be there by now. For once my prayer was answered as there he was, nonchalantly kicking a stone along the side of the street.

"My brother's here to get me," I told Arleen's mother as I hurried toward the door.

"Tell him to come in, there's plenty of cake and lemonade left."

"Oh no," I told her. "He doesn't like parties, he won't come in."

"Well, he can have a piece of cake there on the porch and wait 'til Arleen's father gets back, then he'll drive you both home."

"But Mamma said to start as soon as he got here so we get home before dark," I fibbed.

It was only mid-afternoon but I think she understood my determination to get away as soon as possible. "Here, take these peanuts, there are enough for both of you," she said.

I grabbed the sack and was out the door without a look back or a goodbye to anybody. I was afraid something would happen to keep me at the party.

"Where's the Stearns?" Carl wanted to know as I dashed by him.

"The what?" I asked without stopping.

"You know, their car, the Stearns-Knight!" "Whatch your hurry anyway?"

"Arleen's father went somewhere with it," I told him when he caught up with me. I didn't add that there had been an offer to drive us home.

"Oh, shoot!" Carl exclaimed, plainly disappointed. "I was countin' on gettin' a good look at it, maybe even a ride. Resorters got nothin' else to do but drive around."

"Here, you kin have all these peanuts," I said, hoping to take his mind off the Stearns-Knight.

He was somewhat mollified by the peanuts and I was willing to let him have them all as I felt a little guilty about his walking so far to get me but not getting to ride in the Stearns-Knight. He usually outpaced me but this time I kept ahead of him while he was shucking and eating the peanuts. When they were gone and he came abreast, he asked me, flat out, "Howja like the rich kids?"

"Oh, they were quite nice," I told him. I wasn't about to say that he'd been right about the party and that rich kids were different from us, a lot different. And I certainly wasn't going to tell him about the oatmeal rocks as he might blab it to Mamma.

"Whaja have to eat besides peanuts?" he wanted to know.

"Pink ice cream and cake with real purty flowers on top, candy flowers."

"Girl stuff!" he sniffed disparagingly, beginning to kick a stone again. "Didn't you get a chance to see the Stearns-Knight at all?"

"Just when Arleen's father brought her home, then he went somewhere."

"Some day I'm gonna have a car like that, jist wait an' see. Or maybe I'll have the kind with a top that goes down," he boasted.

But I wasn't interested in car talk, I was anxious to get over the big hill overlooking our farm to see if everything was still there. A farm house had burned to the ground a few weeks before and it seemed such a long time since I had left that morning—something bad could have happened.

It was a steep hill and I found myself panting for breath when I reached the summit. But there it was, our farm spread before me, the wheat field on the hillside beginning to get yellow and there was our red and white barn, standing big and strong, the finest barn in the whole neighborhood and oh, how proud of it I was! And there was the house, nestled among the trees, a beautiful house even if it didn't have any porches.

Already the hurt of the afternoon was fading and I was anxious to tell Mamma about the fancy cake covered with rosebuds. But how could I tell her that nobody but Arleen's mother would taste her oatmeal rocks and how they fell on the floor and were swept up on a dustpan. And worst of all, that I was ashamed of them, too. . . .

A decade or so later, I had the same feeling about a dress which Mamma made for me. I was a sophomore in high school by then and had become clothes conscious. As a surprise for me, she had resurrected from her keep-sake trunk her wedding gown, a floor length, full-skirted, be-ruffled dress made of delicately flowered batiste. She took the treasured garment apart at the seams and made a dress in a younger version for me, replete with vertical ruffles on the bosom and around the full, knee-length skirt.

"It will be cool and pretty for spring," she told me as I tried it on so that she could pin up the hem. It wasn't at all like what the other girls were wearing as it was in the mid 20's when flat chests, low waists and straight skirts were the style. I knew I would be ashamed of its old-fashioned look but I didn't know how to tell her as she had already cut up her wedding gown. Wear it, I did, a few times but I hid some of the ruffles under a hip length sweater even though it was in May. Although I never told her that I was ashamed of the dress, I think she somehow sensed my feelings and after that she no longer "made over" clothes for me. Instead, she saved some of her vegetable and egg money so that I could have an occasional inexpensive store-bought dress.

Nor did I tell her how I felt about my present for Arleen and how I didn't like the party. "I guess you must be hungry after walking such a long way for a little girl," she said after I had given her a big, hard hug. I didn't have to fib about being hungry. "Are there any of those good oatmeal rocks left," I asked, wanting to make it up to her that I had been so ashamed of her cookies.

And, as I munched them and drank a glass of cool milk, I told her the nice things about the party, the fancy cake with rosebuds on the frosting, the pink ice cream and the nice lady who was black all over. I did worry for several weeks that Arleen's mother would tell her what happened to the oatmeal rocks but if she did, I never knew.

Like a Diamond in the Sky

MUCH has been written about one-room country schools. Some of them are still standing in Northern Michigan; paint peeling, roofs sagging, out-houses toppling, the big bell in the belfry rusting or missing. Most of those who pulled the ropes to "call school" are now gone, although memories of the best teachers—and the worst—live on. It may be said that teachers are made not born, but perhaps the best ones have a bit of both "makings."

Cousin Celia loved children; instinctively she knew how to win their hearts and minds. As a girl she had little formal schooling—her mother had taught her how to read and write at home and it was not until after her mother's death when she was ten that she attended grade school and then not regularly, since there were younger brothers and sisters to be cared for while her father worked from 6:00 A.M. until 6:00 P.M. in a local grocery.

When she was sixteen she decided on a career. On the upper floor of a downtown brick building in Petoskey there was a "Normal School" for teacher training. With fear and trembling, but much determination, she climbed the stairs and knocked on the door marked "Office," which she later learned also served as classroom and library. A kindly voice, that of a Professor Graves, told her to enter and enter she did into the world of a higher education.

With a brashness of youth she came to the point at once. "I want to be a teacher. What do you have to do to be one?"

In her case the usual requirement, that of a high school

diploma, was waived, apparently because of her pluck and the fact that she had been reading everything she could get her hands on, from recipe clippings to a book about astronomy. Within a year she was teaching in a country school for thirty dollars a month and out of this she had to pay for room and board, the going rate being two dollars a week.

It was shortly after the turn of the century and before anyone in Emmet County had a horseless carriage. In rural areas there was always the problem of finding a suitable home where the teacher could get lodging and meals if her home was not within walking distance of her school. There were no furnaces in farmhouses in those days and often the teacher's room was unheated except for a grill in the floor of her upstairs living quarters or perhaps a stove pipe leading to the chimney from the stove on the floor below. Since the room was usually chilly and uninviting, Cousin Celia preferred to spend most of the after-school hours with the family if its members were at all congenial. She liked to read quietly near the kitchen stove or by a sunny window; also, being an outgoing young person, she liked to discuss current issues with anyone who was interested, which was usually the man of the house since farm women were not supposed to understand the affairs of state in those days. She was fond of playing games and always kept a deck of cards on hand as well as a checker board and checkers.

On Friday afternoon it was her custom to leave for Petoskey where she was making her home with a married sister at the time, returning early on Monday morning so as to get the fire started and the classroom warm for her pupils. When the weather was really bad she would return to her boarding house on Sunday evening so that she wouldn't be obliged to make the long trip before daylight the next morning. This she did one Sunday, she told me years later, arriving at her boarding house about dusk. Finding her landlady busy with the supper dishes and her eighth grader, a shy lad who was beginning to take an interest in book learning, unoccupied, she suggested playing checkers. Shortly after the game had gotten underway, the farmer came in from the barn, apparently much annoyed because his son hadn't shown up to help with the evening chores.

When he found the boy and the young teacher hard at play, there was an unexpected explosion.

"The very idea, playing sinful games on a Sunday yet, breaking the Sabbath, giving satisfaction to the devil, calling down the wrath of God, etc., etc."

Cousin Celia had known it was a Methodist household but she hadn't realized it was quite *that* Methodist. She tried to explain that it was only an innocent game, there was no gambling involved, and that good church people everywhere amused themselves with cards and checkers. However, the man was not to be mollified. He was certain that his son was being led down the primrose path, that the Lord's Day had been desecrated, that there would be a curse on his family forever after. Not even the boy's embarrassed mother could calm her irate husband who, although he wasn't known to attend services regularly, nevertheless believed in keeping the Sabbath holy. Checkers game in hand, Celia went off to her room and an early bedtime as it was the only way to keep warm. There and then she made up her mind to start looking for other lodgings and it wouldn't be a blue-law home if she could help it. She was fond of the boy's mother who was a good woman and an excellent cook but red flannel hash and sourdough bread were not worth bringing down the wrath of a Northern Michigan Cotton Mather on her unsuspecting head. Also, it might be possible to find a room which had a chimney hole so that she could have a stove of her very own.

She had to be diplomatic, however, or risk further offending the bewhiskered farmer as he was one of the school trustees in control of the hiring and the firing. It was therefore necessary to move slowly and with discretion so as not to get set up for a witchcraft type trial in Wabmeme, the little town near where she was teaching.

Several days later when she returned from school late in the afternoon, she found only the man of the house at home, the eighth grader having taken his mother by horse and cutter to a neighbor's to help deliver a baby. The farmer was seated at the kitchen table, poring over a seed catalogue and Cousin Celia, noticing a letter addressed to her from a down-state beau, leaned over to claim her personal mail. The "grizzled old goat" (her words) grabbed her, pulled her onto his lap and began kissing her, apparently expecting her to reciprocate. Fortunately for her, and for him also, she was able to extricate herself from his cowbarn-smelling embrace and get herself safely locked behind her bedroom door before the lady of the house returned. The God-fearing Christian who had been so deeply shocked by the checkers game on Sunday evening was seemingly not so strait-laced on a weekday afternoon. Even though the billygoat trustee might prevent her from being rehired for the following year or even get her fired in the middle of the current term, she made her exit from the blue-law household the very next day.

Sometimes it was the wife who created the problem. Cousin Celia was young, unattached, high-spirited and very attractive, judging from a picture taken in her twenties. She had a great sense of humor and liked to exchange pleasantries with all and sundry; her interest in politics and world affairs made her suspect among some of the housewives; there were even a few who seemed to think that she had designs on their husbands. "As if I were that hard up for a man," she exclaimed many years later.

One time, she told me, she was not able to leave for Petoskey on Friday afternoon because of a blinding snowstorm so she asked the man of the house if she could ride with him on his regular Saturday morning trip to town to take in the sour cream to be shipped to the Blue Valley Creamery in Grand Rapids. When his wife learned about the arrangement, made behind her back she claimed, the offended woman decided at the last minute to go along. As Cousin Celia told the story, she and the farmer were kept waiting in the one horse cutter built for two while the Missus put on her Sunday-go-to-meeting clothes. Breathless and glowering, the voluminous lady came flouncing out of the house and deposited herself between and on top of both of them. The ride to town was spent in silence to say nothing of the agony of being positioned under a very large woman. Three booted sets of feet and a cream can wedged between the cutter seat and the dashboard added to the discomfort.

It so happened that Cousin Celia was hired to teach at our district school several months before I was five years old. At our house a small stove was placed in her upstairs room where there was a chimney hole so she could start a fire there on winter mornings to wash and dress by. But she spent most of her free time downstairs with the family, chatting with my mother (they were first cousins and good friends); often she read stories or played games with us children and sometimes, while Mamma was getting supper, she would rock the baby and sing lullabies.

Although I hadn't quite turned five, I was desperately eager to prove that I was a big girl so my mother agreed to let me start school, thinking I would soon tire of it and be content to remain at home. So off to primer class I went, hand in hand with Teacher, who was wearing a beautiful candy-stripped shirt waist and a long black skirt. When, some fifty years later, I recalled my childhood fascination with that elegant pink and green and white finery, she smiled musingly, admitting that the shirt waist had been one of her favorites, too. Although her budget allowed little for fashion, she did her own dressmaking and her few outfits were always stylish and form-fitting. She saved every cent she could for the life certificate and the degrees that she dreamed of, and which she eventually acquired. She was determined to be beholden to no "billygoat" trustee for a job and to be in no hurry to get a husband. And long before progressive ideas were accepted by the teaching profession, she believed that a child's natural curiosity, imagination and inventiveness should be channeled and directed, not circumvented and destroyed.

Ours was a down-to-earth, no nonsense, work-oriented German neighborhood and there was no attempted billygoating around with young school teachers. Also there was no provision for any teaching aids—things like globes and educational games. It was straight reading, writing and arithmetic with a minimum of geography and history— anything else was a waste of time and taxes. Although very careful with her slim earnings, Cousin Celia could not resist buying a few items to make the learning process more interesting—crayons, anagrams, tracing cards and best of all, a few story books.

Cousin Celia's classes were both a challenge and a joy.

Even the big boys, who at first cared only for playing ball at recess and being in, or egging on fist fights in the schoolyard, began to take an interest in book-learning. Also, they seemed to be combing their hair more regularly, fetching water from the nearby farm pump voluntarily, and replenishing firewood for the big pot-bellied stove. Teacher arranged spelling bees and "times table" contests for the upper grades; she put on the blackboard arithmetic problems that were not out of a textbook but straight out of the fields and the barns and the gardens in the neighborhood—the selling price of a potato crop, the cost of a cement floor in a cowbarn, the yield of two and three-quarters acres of navy beans. There were opportunities to talk about what was going on in the world, the presidential race between Woodrow Wilson and Charles Evan Hughes, the war that was already raging across the ocean. Teacher had been in faraway places like Big Rapids and Detroit, whereas none of her pupils and few of their parents had ever been out of the county.

For those of us in the lower grades, there were pasteboard letters to be formed into words, pictures to trace, and decorations to make. Never were there so many fat turkey gobblers strutting around the ledge on the wainscoting, never were there so many gaily-festooned Christmas trees stuck to the window panes, never were there such bright colored flowers and vegetables (from seed catalogues) pasted to hearts cut out of lacy-looking ceiling wallpaper. And every Friday afternoon, instead of penmanship according to the Palmer Method, Teacher read a chapter from a big thick book, *The Adventures of Tom Sawyer*. That was our reward for having worked hard all week and everyone listened intently, from those of us in primer class to the teen-age boys.

For every good recitation, we received a token and for every ten tokens we got a certificate of merit and for every five certificates of merit, we got a prize—that is, we got to select something from a drawer in teacher's desk; lovely, long painted pencils with pristine-fresh erasers, delicious waxy smelling crayons, picture postcards of distant places. Teacher's philosophy was that of the carrot and the stick but the sticks in her arsenal were newly sharpened pencils and pointed red and green and yellow chalk.

To supplement her normal school training, Cousin Celia had taken courses during the summer at Ferris Institute where she had come to know and admire Woodbridge N. Ferris, who had taught in a country school himself and knew the problems young teachers would encounter. He became governor of the state and later U.S. Senator and was always her idol.

I could not bear missing a single day of school, not even when I had a sore throat, which I purposely would not report to my mother. Once, when the snow was deep and the quarter-mile walk to and from school very tiring, I fell asleep on my parents' bed after the noonday meal so Teacher went off to the afternoon session without me. When I awoke an hour or so later and found Teacher and my brother gone, I was so upset that my mother agreed to let me walk back to school by myself if I would keep to their tracks; no doubt she followed my progress through the snowdrifts from the frontroom window with her young baby in her arms. Cousin Celia, many years later, described my noisy entrance into the classroom that day—stomping the snow off my feet, jabbing my coat over a low hook, unbuckling my arctics, marching to my seat, taking out my reader, glaring all the while. When she asked what was troubling me, I told her in much aggrieved tones, "I'll just never catch up!"

The baby my mother was caring for at the time, had been born in December, on my fifth birthday as it happened, and I remember thinking of the infant as another present. My father did not altogether fit into the neighborhood mold; he believed in productive labor but he also shared my mother's concern that ours be a happy childhood. For that birthday he had made a small-sized cooking range out of a rectangular block of wood with an attached warming oven fashioned out of an open-ended cigar box, all nicely painted black. My mother had made a coat for my doll with a real fur collar, cut down from some worn out grown-up apparel and teacher had given me a lovely story book with glossy colored pictures. I was not sure which of my presents I liked best but I certainly considered it my prerogative to make the announcements at school the next morning.

Teacher went off before the December dawn to light the

fire and make sure it was burning properly since it took a lot of stoking to heat the uninsulated frame building grown cold during the night. An hour or so later my brother and I set out, following the tracks that Teacher had made. He carried the heavy dinner bucket and I brought up the rear; it was a four quart Karo syrup pail filled with sandwiches, cookies and apples, packed for our lunch that day since Mamma would not be cooking a hot meal for us that noontime.

There had been a storm and the cut on the road was drifted full so we took the more sheltered route across a neighbor's field. I was bursting with pride, looking forward to making a regal entrance and proudly announcing the arrival of my birthday baby, as well as describing my other acquisitions. But first, we had to get over a gate that separated the field from a cow pasture.

"I'll climb over while you hold the pail," my brother told me. "Then I'll hold it while you climb over."

I was in an obliging state of mind, already enjoying the envious "oh's and ah's" my announcements would call forth. But, once over the gate, Brother Carl took off as fast as he could through the foot-deep snow. I was left squalling in frustration on the opposite side of the gate, which I somehow managed to clamber over, syrup pail and all. My entrance on stage, however, must have been far from regal—sniffing and tear-smudged and furious as I was with that eight-year-old brother of mine. Every one of my presents had already been described, but Teacher, sensing my raging disappointment, suggested that I report on the name given my little sister, which my brother had forgotten. But the name was merely greeted with "huh's"; my mother's selection of a name, in this case, "Colette," did not generate German enthusiasm—why not Emma or Anna or Hilda or Ada? Mamma had agreed to just plain "Carl" for her firstborn son as a concession to Papa who promised that she could name all the rest—which she did.

Cousin Celia lasted only one term in our district. The hardworking frank-spoken trustees did not quite trust her; they were suspicious of her manner of teaching. They seemed to think that some of her ideas were frivolous and possibly corrupting. They tended to think of schooling as a barn chore, something to get over with so that they could get on to the important work in the fields, plowing, cultivating and harvesting. Since their sons and daughters were beginning to like school too well, they wanted to head off future problems in keeping them at home to pick up potatoes, husk corn and stack firewood. Nowhere was the "Protestant ethic" more pronounced than among those German Catholics. In fairness to them and to most eighty-acre farmers in those days, the only way they could make a decent living and set aside something for their old age was through the unpaid labor of their wives and children. To actually like school and not insist on quitting was considered unnatural for a teenager. Cousin Celia was changing all that so it was not surprising that she was not asked to teach another year.

Although Teacher knew that she would not be rehired, she put on a gala program the last day of school. Every pupil was coached to take part in the event—reciting a poem, reading a story or taking part in a skit. Teacher's desk was moved aside and the raised platform was made ready for the first theatrical performance ever to take place in our neighborhood. My part in the program was to recite a little poem about a seed which was planted in the rich brown earth, awaiting the warmth of the sun to make it grow. After every pupil had a chance to bask in the limelight—even the teen-age boys, who had been reluctant at first, recited things like "Casey at the Bat"—there were "choral numbers" with the words of some of the songs we had learned written on the blackboard. There were *Twinkle, Twinkle Little Star, Michigan, My Michigan* and *My Country Tis of Thee* as I recall.

Fathers and mothers were invited but only some of the mothers came, urged on by their children. It was potato planting time and who ever heard of taking off work on a week day? Mamma wanted Papa to attend but he wasn't about to be the only man among all those women and besides what would the neighbors think? However, every pupil brought food whether a parent came or not—food was something they could all understand and the potluck picnic became a tradition that lasted long after the theatrical foolishness had been forgotten.

The mothers left with their empty baskets, the pupils with their books and "passing" report cards; no one was ever known to fail in Cousin Celia's classes even if it meant hours of catch-up work for teacher and pupil during the last weeks of the term. But I stayed on to "help" with the cleaning up; teacher erased the words of the songs from the blackboard—among them, ". . . like a diamond in the sky," which I thought the most beautiful phrase I had ever heard, and I dusted the erasers and emptied the lilac blossoms from the fruit-jar vases. She swept the floor, burned the trash and packed up her few remaining belongings. When she came to our school there had been only a few discarded textbooks on the shelf above the water pail but she had added several story books and these she left as her one concrete legacy.

It had been a wonderfully exciting day and the picnic had been a great success; every last crumb had been eaten and every serving dish scraped clean. But after it was all over and the doors had been locked, I knew that that school would never be the same again since Teacher was leaving. What was there to say? As we walked slowly homeward, she must have sensed my sadness and feeling of loss although I was determined not to cry, and she tried to cheer me up by talking about the poem I had learned by heart for the program.

"Teachers plant seeds, too, and hope they will grow like garden seeds warmed by the sun," she told me. But I was not much comforted because Teacher was the sun and the moon and the stars of our school and she was going to a far, far away place called Big Rapids.

In Fletchers Fields

DURING World War I, my brother and I would hear Mamma reading the newspaper to Papa while he finished his noon-day meal. The price of pigs and potatoes did not interest us but when she read the war news, she would tell us to go and play. Especially after young men in our own neighborhood began to be drafted, we would strain our ears to hear about what was happening overseas. The words and phrases which seemed to be repeated most often were "digging trenches," "gas masks," "President Wilson," "the Kaiser," and "to make the world safe for democracy."

"Digging trenches" I could understand since Carl and I dug them in the snow and as for "gas masks," he had made one out of a stocking cap, a piece of rubber hose and a couple of clothes pins. President Wilson was the good guy and the Kaiser was the bad guy but "making the world safe for democracy" was too much for a six-year-old to comprehend. I had to depend on my ten-year-old brother to explain the concept since Mamma seemed to think that war talk was not suitable for our young ears.

"What's democracy?" I asked Carl.

"Well, it's something we got and the Kaiser wants to get it away from us," he informed me.

"But what is it, what does it look like?" I wanted to know.

"It's a lot of things—our gov'ment, our farm, our horses, cows and pigs too, things like that."

"And he's comin' all the way across the ocean to get them?" I asked.

"Yeah, he's gonna try to get 'em, that's why we gotta keep him from comin' over, that's why we gotta fight him!"

In our country school we sang Civil War songs and to me the two wars were one and the same. "Just before the battle, Mother" was the cry of a soldier about to fight it out with the Kaiser. And "If I'm numbered with the slain" could well be Papa if he had to go to war like some of the neighborhood men. I lived in fear that when I came downstairs some morning, I would find him gone, sent across the ocean to fight and maybe die.

Cousin Celia, my first teacher, who had boarded with us, no longer taught at our school but I remembered some of the poetry which I had heard her quoting. She was fond of reciting some of her favorite poems aloud and sometimes I learned parts of them by heart if I liked them especially. There was one which still haunted me, a poem about the war which had been sent to her from a friend overseas:

> *"In Flanders fields, the poppies blow*
> *Between the crosses, row on row*
> *That mark our place, and in the sky*
> *The larks, still bravely singing, fly,*
> *Scarce heard among the guns below.*
>
> *We are the dead . . . and now we lie*
> *In Flanders fields . . . .*

The farm next to ours, down below the Big Hill, belonged to the Fletcher family and when I substituted "Fletchers" for "Flanders" the picture in my mind of the soldiers' graveyard became very vivid. There were no poppies in the corn field but there were milkweeds which had a kind of purplish blossom. I sounded out the lines:

> *In Fletchers fields, the milkweeds blow*
> *Between the crosses row on row . . . .*

My version had a sad and beautiful ring to it and I wondered how a child could find the grave of her father if the crosses looked all the same like the rows of corn stalks.

I decided that there must be some way to stop the war and since it was all the Kaiser's fault, I figured that getting rid of him would be the best and quickest solution to the problem.

Nothing personal of course, just a simple natural death like being kicked in the head by a horse or gored to death by a gentleman cow. (The word "bull" was not considered a nice word in our house so Mamma used the term she had heard in the Methodist household where she had lived while going to high school. Papa, however, usually called our stomping, dirt-pawing barnyard terror "the Major.")

I had overheard Mamma and Cousin Celia talking about some ladies who had sailed across the ocean in a Peace Ship to try to stop the war but they didn't get it stopped. If only they had somehow coaxed the Kaiser on board and then taken out to sea when he wasn't looking, he might have jumped off and tried to swim back to Germany and drowned. That would have been one way to get rid of him.

Somehow, some way, the Kaiser had to go! And after he was dead, I didn't necessarily want him to go to hell, bad as he was, going around starting wars. Purgatory for awhile would probably be enough to teach him a lesson.

Clearly, somebody had to take the lead in ending the killing and it seemed that no one had yet hit on getting rid of the Kaiser himself. I decided to ask Carl's opinion of my idea—he was almost four years older than I was and was full of all kinds of notions and inventions. The day we heard about one of Mamma's cousins being sent off to war seemed a good time to broach the subject.

I didn't say "Somebody ought to kill the Kaiser." All I said was "I wish the Kaiser would die." Carl often pooh-poohed my ideas but I wasn't prepared for his vehement reaction to what I thought was a modest proposal.

"Don't you know it's against the law to talk like that," he bellowed. "And it's a mortal sin, too!"

I wasn't to be brushed off that easily. "But the Kaiser's the one who started the war. If he was dead, the war would be over, that's what I mean."

"That's bein' against the war," he claimed. You can't go around wantin' people to get killed, just 'cause you don't like 'em."

"But that's what they do in war, they kill people," I insisted, thinking I had the best of the argument.

"That's diff'rent, 'cause it's the guv'ment. If the guv'ment tells you to go to war, you gotta go. And if the Army tells you to shoot, you gotta shoot!"

"But why don't they jist shoot the Kaiser?" I wanted to know.

"They're goin to, but they gotta catch him!"

"But why do they hafto kill other people first?" I asked.

"Cause that's the way wars work. Wars have gotta be big and lots of people hafta get killed and you've gotta have traitors and spies and like that. You've gotta salute the flag and buy Liberty Bonds, too"

"But we didn't buy any," I reminded him. "Mamma said we couldn't afford to, on accounta sugar for canning costing so much. And what about Papa not selling our walnut trees?" (Papa had refused to sell them because he didn't want them to be used for gunstocks for the war.)

"Don't talk so loud 'bout things like that," Carl warned. There's spies all over, hiding around in barns and cellars."

"What d'you mean, spies?" I knew about Northern Spies which we kept in our cellar for eating in the winter time.

Carl was glad to supply me with an explanation. "There's

good spies and bad spies, you gotta have the good ones to catch the bad ones, the ones that are against the war, and the good ones tell the guv'ment."

"Then what does the gov'ment do?" I asked. By this time I knew it would be something bad but I felt I should know the worst.

"The guv'ment puts you in jail, that's what. Anybody who's against the war an' wants the Germans to win is breaking the law, that's why they gotta get caught. Some got put in jail already, prob'ly hanging up by their thumbs by now but that's what they get for talkin' against the war."

By now I was thoroughly confused about what had seemed a simple, straightforward solution to the problem. Wishing the Kaiser would die was wrong but killing other people was all right. Talking against the war was bad but tattling to the government was good. And if not buying Liberty Bonds and not selling walnut trees for gun stocks were wrong, too, then there were three in our family at risk, Papa and Mamma and I.

"People gotta keep their mouths shut, that's the main thing," Carl went on. "Seeing you're my sister, I won't tell on you, not this time anyway. But you gotta be careful and you've gotta do what I say. I'd hate to see you put in jail 'cause all they give you to eat is bread and water."

"That's all they give you?" I inquired weakly.

"Yeah, and it's dry bread, too! And if you try to break outa jail, they hang you up by your thumbs and pull out your toe-nails."

I would certainly never try to break out, just sitting all alone in jail was bad enough, especially on a diet of dry bread and water. I thought of the Civil War song we sang in school:

> *In the prison cell I sit, thinking Mother dear of you*
> *And our bright and happy home so far away*
> *And the tears they fill my eyes, 'spite of all that I can do. . . .*

It was enough to bring tears to my own eyes and reluctantly I decided to abandon my plan for bringing peace to the world and let somebody else figure out how to do it.

But my brother wasn't about to forget my traitorous ideas—for several weeks I was at his beck and call, doing some of the chores he was supposed to do like taking the cows to pasture, going after the mail, feeding the chickens—all while he worked on his inventions. During his free time he was always dreaming up contrivances for me and my sister to try out, some of which worked and some didn't.

I didn't mind doing most of these chores, especially if the alternative was jail but there came a time when Carl took things too far. It so happened that old Mrs. Burrmeister had borrowed a pail of barn salt from us the previous summer and had not returned an equal amount. Papa thought that she had forgotten about it but Mamma wasn't so sure he was right about that. Among its uses, salt was needed to sprinkle on freshly stored hay to keep it from "heating" and bursting into flame. A barn had burned down in our neighborhood because of spontaneous combustion as it was called. Papa was always very liberal with salt after that as our barn was his pride and joy, the only one for miles around which was painted, red with white battens. Since our salt barrel was empty, Papa was considering making a trip to town that day to replenish his stock.

"But it looks like rain," Mamma reminded him. "If you want to get that last field of alfalfa hauled in before it gets wet again, you'd better not take the time—the salt Mrs. Burrmeister owes us will be enough—or else we can just do without."

Alfalfa and sweet clover were the varieties most likely to cause problems and the safety of his barn won out over concern for Mrs. Burrmeister. He always felt sorry for her, she was old, she was a widow, she was having a hard time making ends meet even if she did have a sharp tongue and tended to forget to return things. So it was that Carl was told to go after the salt while Papa was harnessing the horses and getting ready to haul in hay.

"Be polite," Papa cautioned. "Just say we need a pail of salt and she'll remember about borrowing some last summer—I'm sure she forgot."

I noticed that Carl looked rather queasy when given this errand to do but I did not know until later why he was so upset. Earlier that spring two church ladies had come out from town to solicit for the upcoming St. Patrick's Day supper. The farmers of the parish were expected to donate things like roasting chickens and smoked hams while the townspeople contributed cakes and pies. Apparently when Mrs. Burrmeister saw the ladies coming, she decided to go into hiding rather than give up one of her good-laying hens.

That day Carl happened to be digging snow trenches with one of her grandsons and he took note of the old lady's getaway so when the solicitors came to our house later that afternoon, he was able to report on Mrs. Burrmeister's whereabouts while they were trying to get her to answer her door.

"When she saw you coming, she took off for her outhouse—didn't even take time to put her coat on!" he informed them.

Words like "outhouse" or "backhouse" or "privy" were somehow considered a matter for tittering amongst townspeople. They could hear "going to the bathroom" without lifting an eyebrow but country folks were left without a term acceptable in polite conversation.

Relishing their laughter, Carl ad-libbed a little more in order to make his story even better, now that he had center stage. "She was running like a witch out of hell!" He had a fertile imagination.

Poor old lady, she had really taken refuge in her barn which provided a little more coverage. Her outhouse, like most others, had a door which did not extend to the floor—this for ventilation and also to indicate when it was occupied. Carl had a habit of embellishing the facts which won him laughs at the time but often got him into trouble later.

Of course it didn't occur to him that the story would travel over much of the parish and eventually get back to Mrs. Burrmeister and as it traveled the "w" in witch got changed to "b" and she was hopping mad about the whole business, and let it be known among some of his friends that she was just waiting to get her hands on him.

In defense of my brother, his version of the old woman's flight from the St. Patrick's Supper solicitors was probably not the only reason for her fury. Along with some of her German neighbors she may have thought that the Irish parishioners ought to provide the makings for their own saint's fund-raiser.

Carl wasn't about to tell Papa about his predicament and to admit that he had somewhat falsified the widow's destination as he knew that Papa would insist that he make an apology in person to the maligned lady. Instead, he commandeered his sister, me, to accompany him on the quarter mile trip to get the salt. Although I had some misgivings about the whole thing, I was unaware of his intentions until we were within a stone's throw of her house. He then handed me the pail and informed me that I was to go on alone while he proceeded to lie down flat in the tall grass by the side of the road.

"But why do I have to go by myself—I thought you just wanted me to help carry the salt home."

"It's got something to do with the Kaiser," he hinted darkly.

By now I was certain that there was a mysterious danger lurking somewhere but I had no choice. Papa had told us to hurry back as he needed Carl to spread the hay around on the load while he pitched it on and mention of the Kaiser had gotten me worried.

Inwardly quaking, I knocked on Mrs. Burrmeister's kitchen door. Even in broad daylight she looked very much like a witch—she had a small bony frame, she was sort of humpbacked, she pulled back her sparse graying hair tightly from her thin wrinkled face and she was almost toothless. Her kitchen was as dark as a cave as she opened the door and glared out at me, cowering on her doorstep. I nearly fell off backward as I mumbled weakly. "I came to get the salt you forgot you owe us."

"I'll give you your salt," she snarled. "But where's that good fer nothin' brother of yours, he knows I wanta see him!" By now I realized that Carl's life was in mortal danger and despite our differences from time to time, I felt that I had to tell a lie to protect him.

"He's home," I fibbed. "Papa sent me to get the salt, he said you'd remember you didn't pay us back."

"Home" she humphed. "How's a little pimple like you gonna carry a big pail of salt?" Her anger at my brother was plainly spilling over on me.

"Oh I carry heavy pails all the time," I told her.

Ignoring my assurances, she told me to go straight back home and let that scaredy-calf Carl come after the salt himself.

"He can't, he's helping Papa haul in the hay before it rains." One fib had called for another but this one seemed to make sense to the widow who was trying to keep her farm in operation with the help of several grandsons.

"Well, you tell him," and here she wagged a bony finger in my face, "That if he ever spreads around any more lies about me, I'll skin him alive." And with that she grabbed the pail and ordered me to follow her to the barn. I did, not being given an opportunity to do anything else as she kept looking over her shoulder to make sure I was right behind her. And all the while she was emitting a stream of invectives, mostly words I'd never heard before but I could tell by the way she said them that they were black, black cuss words.

The basement of her barn was even darker than her kitchen and I became fearful that I was being lured to an early death while Carl was safe and sound in the grass by the side of the road. He had told me stories about how witches tricked people and as the old lady led me through a narrow passageway, my imagination ran wild—perhaps there was a trap door under the thin layer of straw and as I walked across it, the door would give way and I would be dumped into a dungeon below where government spies were lying in wait.

I began saying "Our Fathers" and Hail Marys" as fast as I could since I didn't want to die with lies on my soul—even if I hadn't reached the "Age of Reason" yet. That was when you got to be seven years old but I didn't want to take any chances. And I'd only told the lies for Carl's sake, darn him anyway.

However, no trap door was sprung as I crept gingerly along the dark passageway and we finally arrived at the salt barrel beneath a small window. In the dim light I could make out the shadowy figure of the old lady scooping up the salt and with every scoopful it seemed like she called Carl another name, mostly in German now as she had probably run out of English profanity. She kept it up until the salt was heaped up over the rim and I began to wonder if I could carry it after all.

Still stuttering with rage, she insisted on carrying the pail for me not only out of the barn but out onto the road. This caused me another worry, suppose she kept right on with it and saw Carl lying in the grass, making me a liar, too. She'd skin us both alive.

I grabbed the pail from her to show her I could carry it by myself although it took every ounce of strength I had, and I kept on with it while she called after me, "Now don't forget what I told you to tell that good for nothing . . . . . ." but I wasn't listening any more, I was just trying to get away. By the time I reached Carl's hideaway, I was breathless, exhausted and boiling mad.

"What'd she say about me?" was his first whispered question.

"She's gonna get you and skin you alive for all the lies you told on her."

"Don't you tell Pa," he warned.

"Maybe I will and maybe I won't," I snapped at him, confident now that I could counter his threats.

The opportunity to try out my new found power came a few days later. It was Carl's job to clean out the chicken coop which meant scraping out the hen droppings from under the night roosts and hauling the foul-smelling liquidy mess to the manure pile by the barn, all of which would later be spread on our fields for fertilizer.

"You clean out the chicken coop," he told me.

"Clean it out yourself," I shot back, secure in the knowledge that I was on an equal footing with him threat-wise.

It took him a few moments to recover from the shock. "Well, you can kinda help me clean it out—I'll let you wear my gas mask."

"It doesn't work and I'm not going to help neither!"

I had suddenly gotten uppity and he was at something of a loss as to how to proceed. "Guess I'll have to tell on you then, 'bout the Kaiser I mean."

"Go ahead, I got something to tell on you, too." I fired back.

A neighbor, Andy Messner, was coming down the road

with his team of horses and Carl made one last try, "I know for a fact that Andy's got spies hiding in his barn, they sleep in his straw mow every night. If I tell him 'bout you and the Kaiser he'll tell them and you'll get put in jail for sure."

"Then I'll tell Papa 'bout you and Mrs. Burrmeister," I threatened.

It worked. He opened his mouth as if he was going to yell out something as Andy went by but all Carl did was sort of wave his hand and Andy waved back.

I had struck a blow for the equality of the sexes but my crusade for world peace had suffered a setback—but a temporary one. I had made a secret pledge that when I grew up I would never break faith with those who lie beneath the crosses, row on row.

Choirs of Angels

HEAVEN and Christmas were almost interchangeable terms in my childhood back in the first quarter of the century. God was a long-bearded, white-robed, all-wise, all-knowing figure who dwelt high above the sky. Santa Claus was a long-bearded, red-coated, all-wise, all-knowing figure who lived far to the north—not as far as the North Pole which defied common sense in our family, but more like Good Hart or Cross Village. Both didn't like it when we were bad and both gave us rewards when we were good.

Not that the rewards we got at Christmas-time were very lavish, certainly not when compared to today's standards. On an eighty acre farm—with most of the back-forty too hilly for cropping—which had a big $700 mortage, there was not very much cash left over after the interest and the taxes were paid. But Mamma was not one to grumble about having so little to spend. Her way was to "make do" with whatever there was and stretch that as far as possible. With Christmas in mind she made it a point to buy and store away much of what was absolutely needed like shoes, long underwear, stockings, arctics (overshoes with buckles)—things which could not be cut down or made over from outgrown or cast-off clothing from our better-heeled relatives.

The new and recycled articles would be wrapped in the holly-figured paper and tied with the red cord dispensed in the weeks preceding the 25th of December by the one department store in Petoskey—Fochtman's. Even the paper, if not too badly crumpled was saved from year to year. After

Papa and we older children had set off for Midnight Mass, Mamma would gather up the wrappings, smooth them out, trim off the ragged edges, erase the penciled names and, no doubt, start making plans for the following Christmas.

There was one hitch in this form of economy. Sometimes the name of the previous recipient was inadvertently overlooked and when one of us girls got something bearing last year's name on the uppermost side of the package and in that package there was a fleece-lined union suit clearly not intended for one of our gender, there was bound to be some puzzlement. However Mamma was quick to set things straight by explaining that Santa was very busy and sometimes made mistakes.

Since we were a large family, there would be quite a number of bags and boxes of various shapes and sizes. Every child from the youngest to the oldest opened each gift in turn while the onlookers "oh'd and ah'd" in admiration—all except Brother Carl who was busy squeezing, shaking and pinching off corners of the wrapping to determine the contents of his packages.

The first year I helped with Santa work I persuaded Mamma to let me enlarge on the idea of making the gift-opening last a long time by wrapping each shoe or mitten of a pair separately, thus making twice as many packages. This took some doing as it was before the day of scotch tape and later caused considerable confusion in matching up pairs but it helped to make a magnificent number of presents.

Not everything we got was utilitarian. Somehow Mamma always managed to provide each of us with at least one gift which wasn't the least bit necessary in a practical way. After the fall work in the fields was done and before logging and wood-cutting were underway, she would get Papa busy with saw and hammer. Under her direction, dolls' cradles and dolls' cutters, miniature trunks and tables and kitchen cabinets would emerge from packing boxes and scraps of lumber. These she would sand and paint and hide away in an inaccessible part of the straw mow in the barn. Also she would spend hours sewing at her foot treadle machine after we children had gone to bed; while dozing off to sleep I would hear the whirr of it, a sound which was somehow associated with good things to come.

One year I remember getting a fur bonnet and muff for myself and a matching set for my doll. Another time I got a small bassinet made out of a large grape basket with a dotted swiss hood and a beribboned ruffle below, all made out of remnants. Our dolls, although they had chipped faces and sagging bodies never lacked for pretty clothes and accessories. The first time I was ever away from home, staying in town with an aunt while taking instructions for First Communion, Mamma came in with the horse and buggy, bringing me a dress and one just like it for my doll to comfort me in my home-sickness. Through a blur of tears I can see those dresses still, both made of navy blue serge with bright red yokes. But when I got back from Catechism Class I wept bitterly, not because I didn't like what she had brought me but because she had already left for home.

The four weeks before Christmas were Advent which Papa believed should be set aside for penitence and fasting as prescribed in Church teaching. That, I think, was the chief reason for his putting off getting our tree until the last possible moment—there was a time to be penitent and a time to be joyful and the two were not to be mixed! A moderate amount of prayer and fasting was all right with Mamma but she didn't favor overdoing it. After all, she reasoned, how in the world could a hard-working farmer find the time or the opportunity to commit mortal sins in a quiet place like Emmet County, surely no den of iniquity! And how could such a person spend long hours in the woods without three good meals a day. Sins and fasting were for the rich and idle city folk.

Mamma was always anxious to get the Christmas season underway early and make it last as long as possible whereas Papa considered it a time bounded on the one side by Advent and on the other by Lent. Always he made sure that the tree was taken down by Ash Wednesday while Mamma, I think, would have preferred to keep it up until Easter. The spot where it stood, across the room from the wood stove and in the corner between two windows which rattled in the wind, was ideal for keeping it fresh and green—no water pan was ever needed.

One year on a Sunday several weeks before Christmas when it was unusually cold and blustery, Mamma decided that it was too wintry for my sister, Madeline, and me to go to church and we heartily agreed. Papa didn't approve of the idea of our missing Mass because of the weather but he finally consented to let us stay at home provided that we say the rosary together on our knees, both knees. As soon as he and Carl had set off for the 10 o'clock service and were safely out of sight, we began to coax Mamma to let us go fetch a little tree which, we assured her, was only a short way from the house and right near the road. We promised we would say the rosary, maybe two rosaries, when we got back and then we could all enjoy the little tree until Papa got around to get our big one. At first she was hesitant, probably torn between parental wisdom and the pleasant prospect of getting holiday decorations underway, but finally she agreed to let us go and helped us get bundled up with extra sweaters and neck scarfs. And so it was that we set off down the road with small saw in hand and great expectations in our hearts.

In truth there was a little tree by the side of the road not far from our house but it was lopsided and scraggly and we really had in mind something much grander even though it was a lot farther away. There were logging sleigh tracks to follow and since we were a little nervous about our deception and the length of time it would take to carry it out, we ran as fast as we could until we were out of breath, rested briefly, then ran some more. The Heinrich Grosskoph swamp had Christmas trees of all sizes in abundance but it was almost three miles distant.

Finally we arrived at our destination and with the wind blowing harder and the snow swirling around us, we knew we had no time to lose. We settled on the first acceptable tree we found and as the saw wasn't very sharp, it seemed to take forever to zig-zag through the gummy trunk. Just as I managed to get it cut through, Madeline spied a much prettier one—more symmetrical and thickly branched as well as being somewhat bigger. After a hasty consultation we propped up our first selection in the snow to make it appear uncut. It was about then that we remembered that we hadn't asked permission of the bachelor who owned the swamp nor did we have any money to pay for what we were taking, something which Papa always did religiously. Perhaps, after all, we should have been satisfied with the scraggly little tree on our own farm!

"You go ask him," I told my sister. "Or he'll think we're trying to steal some of his timber"—a crime punishable by a jail sentence as we knew from overheard adult conversation.

She wanted me to ask him but I was able to prevail, being older and all—also I was in possession of the saw.

The owner's cabin was about twenty rods away and although it was barely visible because of the storm, I considered it the better part of wisdom to keep my sawing operation shielded from view; this meant hunching over as if I were merely closely inspecting the tree of our choosing.

My sister still remembers her encounter with the crusty old bachelor who finally came to the door after his huge hound set up a howl.

"Can we have a tree, just a little one?" she shouted, trying to make herself heard above the wind and the wildly barking dog which had to be restrained.

"My God, you're not here by yourself in this blizzard," he bellowed.

"No, my sister's out there sawing down . . . I mean she wants to saw down a Christmas tree but not a big one 'cause they cost money," she tried to explain. "She made me come ask you 'cause we don't want to steal one."

"You're the Schmitt kids," he roared as if that somehow meant being totally deranged.

"Yeah, but you always let Papa have a tree."

"Your Pa must be daft—does he know where you are?"

"He's gone to church so Mamma sent us to get a tree."

"That's a hell of a note! Take any goddam tree you want but come in and get warm first."

The idea of getting warm was very tempting but she was afraid of his snarling dog, also she was aghast at his language—at our house no profanity was ever used. When Papa's patience was exhausted as when one of our cows switched her tail across his mouth for the second or third

time while he was milking, he was known to let go with a strictly non-sacrilegious expletive, "You bastard, you!" Occasionally, too, he railed against a recalcitrant horse in like manner. Usually though, he was harder on cows.

"No, I'm not cold," she chattered as she backed away.

"Wait 'til I get my boots on and I'll help you," he yelled after her.

But she was in no mood to let him accompany her. I think we were well out of sight by the time he got his mackinaw on and his boots buckled. If he ever found our first selection or tried to follow us, we never knew.

Back on the road we took turns dragging our dear-bought Christmas tree which had somehow lost most of its appeal. Our noses were running, our feet were freezing, the wind was swirling the snow around us and I had lost one of my good mittens.

There was a bend in the road where a path could be taken through the woods, a path which we knew well in the summer time when we went wild-raspberry picking. As I remember, the main reason we took the short-cut was to throw Heinrich off our trail in case he tried to pursue us. The snow on the path was deep, there were no tracks to follow and it looked the same in every direction—black snow-fringed branches above and a white snow-blanketed expanse below. But on we plodded, hoping and praying that we were still headed in the right direction. Maybe we were lost and God was punishing us for not going to church and then not saying the rosary as we had promised. And on top of that we had cut down one of Heinrich's trees which we didn't tell him about and then tried to cover up our crime.

By now my sister was blaming me for the whole predicament. I was the one who had the idea in the first place, I was the one who should have known better, I was the one who had told Mamma we weren't going far—but she was being equally punished! It did no good to remind her that she was the one who had wanted the prettier tree and she was the one who hadn't told Heinrich about spoiling the first tree, she was the one who wanted to take the shortcut path. But that was the trouble with sisters; if things turned out well, they expected to get much of the credit and if they didn't turn out well, they didn't want any of the blame.

In the meantime, Papa and Carl had gotten home from church but instead of being able to sit down to a hot Sunday dinner, they were commandeered for a search and rescue mission by our distraught mother who hadn't been able to leave the house herself because one of our younger sisters was coming down with the croup. The menfolks took off hurriedly, thinking to find us somewhere on the road. Fortunately Carl spotted the faint traces of boot and branch marks where the footpath entered the woods so he was sent to follow our tracks while Papa took the horse home as there was no way he could get the cutter through the trees on the narrow path.

When Carl caught up with us, we were both sitting on a log, completely exhausted and half-way resigned to freezing to death for our sins—or my sins as my sister kept insisting between sobs.

But we got no sympathy from our brother. "Dummies," he upbraided us and added a few choice words he had learned from the neighbors. But he took over dragging the tree and since he seemed to know the way, we followed him as best we could, wholly subdued by now and quite willing to overlook his verbal onslaughts.

When we glimpsed Papa coming toward us with a hand sleigh, loaded with blankets, we would have welcomed a good scolding and the assignment of half a dozen rosaries for penance but all he did was to shake his head in bewilderment. However, as he wrapped us up in the blankets, he was undoubtedly thinking—if it was too cold and stormy for us to go to Mass why in Heaven's name had Mamma permitted us to go out looking for a Christmas tree.

Mamma didn't say anything either as we came clumping into the kitchen, our feet like blocks of wood and our faces crusted with snow and frozen tears. She pulled off our footgear and began gently massaging our legs and feet which were numb and white. Papa helped, too, and although he didn't say anything to Mamma, I think he was trying to tell her something. However, I think she was trying to tell him something about the folly of being too penitential in the matter of going after the family Christmas tree. As for Carl, he was busy gulping down home-made chicken noodle soup.

On the morning of the day before Christmas, even though Advent wasn't quite over officially, Papa couldn't put off going after our big tree any longer. So away we went on the logging sleighs, the work horses kicking up their heels in delight over getting out of the barn in the crisp December air. It seemed the appropriate time for singing "Jingle Bells" which we had learned at school but as a concession to Papa, we hummed "Stille Nachte, Heilige Nacht" while he sang it in German. After all, now that we were on the way to the swamp, we were joyful and triumphant and Christmas was Christmas in any language. Later, we sat patiently silent while Papa and Heinrich exchanged comments in German and had the usual discussion about the price of the tree. Papa thought that fifty cents was about right but as usual, Heinrich insisted on giving back a quarter.

Papa always picked a tree tall enough to spare some lower branches which he would use to adorn the large holy pictures which graced the walls of our house. The first thing he would do when we got home after putting the horses in the barn, was to hack off the bottom branches and saw off the lower section of the trunk. Then, at last, all was ready for the grand entrance to the house, Papa ahead and we children all trying to help guide the tree through the kitchen, the unheated dining room, and into the living room where it would stand ceiling-tall. Even the toddler was part of the parade at the risk of being toppled by the spreading branches. Then came the task of whittling the trunk to a size to fit the tree holder which was made of two crossed pieces of planking with a hole bored in the middle.

The whittlings and needle sweepings were put in the stove, a few at a time, and as we heard the snapping and crackling and breathed in deeply of the lovely resinous fragrance, we children set about hanging the ornaments on the tree, even Mamma's treasured little red and blue glass birds which looked ready to sing. Papa reserved for himself the job of clipping on the twisted colored candles which were saved from year to year, so infrequent were the burnings because of the danger of fire. And it was he who always hung the tinsel-edged Star of Bethlehem on the tree-top, reminding us pointedly that *it* was what Christmas was all about.

After a quick lunch, usually a bowl of bean soup, it was time to get ready for our trip to town to go to Confession— not Mamma who had our younger sisters to care for and the wood stoves to tend. I think that Papa would have preferred that the whole family make the pilgrimage but apparently Mamma had long since convinced him that her first duty was to stay at home with the most recent little ones he had fathered.

Although loathe to leave the newly trimmed tree and the wonderful whiffs from the kitchen where sweet rolls for breakfast were baking, we would set off for church, there to examine our consciences and confess our sins. Carl who, it seemed to me, had the most transgressions to report always made short work of his penitential obligations and hurried off to look at store window displays while my sister and I, being girls and younger, had to stay with Papa. For some reason it seemed to take him a very long time to prepare to confess what must have been a very short list of sins. Mamma said it was because he was over-considerate of other people— he would let everybody get ahead of him, old ladies, young ladies, old men, children, those who were infirm, those who were in a hurry—everybody! It was sheer torture for us, watching the early dusk of winter darken the church windows and all the while fearing that Santa Claus might already be on his way. But there was nothing we could do but kneel it out and pray that Papa would soon get the confession-business over with so that we could head for home.

At long last we would be on our way and I would be peeping out from under the buffalo robe, watching intently for a glimpse of that white-bearded, red-coated figure who must be on his appointed rounds by now, considering how much ground he had to cover. And once, I swear, in the semi-darkness I did catch sight of him in a heavily loaded sleigh drawn by prancing reindeer, approaching Mitchell Road from the North. But as I stared in breathless wonder, the apparition disappeared—Santa, sleigh, reindeer and all. But so real was the experience that I was left with the comforting knowledge that my school friends were wrong, totally wrong, in questioning the existence of Santa Claus.

Mamma would have a hot supper ready for us when we got home, with the oven door of the kitchen range open to provide some extra warmth. But food and warmth were secondary, what we were interested in was watching from the front window for the elusive figure on his gift-laden sleigh.

After supper the menfolks had to milk the cows and bed them down with fresh straw and complete the other evening chores. With our faces pressed to the cold window panes, we girls would wait and hope and pray. At our house Santa never came down the single-flue chimney in the dead of night; he was a common sense sort of fellow who brought our presents in grain sacks which he dropped off in a snow bank, usually near the barn, and then hurried off to make his other deliveries.

It was Carl's job to make the rounds and sound the alert. "He's come, he's come" were the magic words and we would dash to meet him at the door, dragging the well-filled sacks through the snow. With squeals of delight and no concern for the snow trail which we were leaving on the floor, we would dump the presents into a beautiful pile in the middle of the living room. Mamma would be standing by, beaming with plasure over the happiness she had wrought and Papa would be smiling too, now that Advent was over and the joyous season begun.

Before the opening of our gifts, the candles on the tree would be lighted briefly and the kerosene lamp turned down while we sat there in what Papa said was to be a few moments of silent prayer. I don't know about the others but I had done enough praying that afternoon and I was mesmerized by the scent of new-cut spruce, entranced by the majesty of our tree strong-limbed and tall, bedazzled by the ornaments shimmering in the flickering light of the candles, and enraptured by the pile of presents so mysteriously magnificent in the dimly-lit room.

It was usually Carl who broke the spell with his, "Hey, isn't it about time we start opening our stuff?"

Interspersed with our gifts were boxes and bags of all manner of sweets—home-made fudge and peanut brittle, molasses taffy and caramel popcorn, also something which Mamma considered essential for hanging on the tree—store-bought ribbon candy and peppermint sticks. For these and the makings for our Christmas goodies, she had bartered black walnuts at Fochtman's Department Store. If ever there was a labor of love, it was shucking those green-husked walnuts by hand. Through holes in a board, the nuts had to be pounded to separate them from the moist and messy outer shuck—her hands would be stained for days.

The edibles would be dumped into several large dishpans and mixed, later to be put into small red-net stockings, each one containing enough for a family go-around. These Mamma would tie on the tree branches near the trunk, one for every day until the supply was gone.

There were repeated warnings from Papa that those of us who were going to Communion at Midnight Mass must observe total fasting from suppertime onward. I tried to keep a sharp eye on Carl so there would be no snitching in the dim light of the kerosene lamp—not that I was overly concerned about his soul, but because he wasn't entitled to more than his share.

Presents opened, admired and tried on for size, it was time to get ready for church again. Mamma would have some bricks heated and these she would slip into old woolen socks and put them at our feet when we were tucked in under the buffalo robe on the floor of the cutter between the dash and the seat where Papa and Carl would sit. It was somewhat cramped as we had to contend with the menfolks' booted feet but no matter, the night was silent and holy and the stars were brightly shining. For this very special occasion Papa would attach to the horse's harness some sleigh bells left over from his courtship days and we would set off a-jingle. Now and then we would hear Topsy snort as if she resented being forced out of the warm barn on a cold winter night, especially after having made the eight mile round-trip to town that very afternoon. We would then hear Papa trying to soothe her injured feelings, "Never mind, Old Girl, it's just once a year that we have to do this to you and you'll get some extra oats in the morning to make up for it."

But mostly we dozed and the hour that it took to get to Petoskey seemed only a matter of minutes. The church bells would be ringing out through the frosty air as we drove through town and we could sometimes catch a glimpse of the glistening steeple rising heavenward above the lighted stained glass windows.

Then we would find ourselves stumbling out of the cutter, our legs cramped and prickly, while Papa tied up Topsy in the drive-through shed at the Gruler Feed Store. The blanket, all nice and warm where we had been sitting with our bricks, would be used to cover up the horse and Papa would tell her not to worry as we were going to Midnight Mass and would soon be back. Then it was off to church with Carl leading the way, his brand new arctics squeaking in the snow.

The afternoon confessions had taken place in the basement chapel but now we mounted the long flight of steps to the main floor and it was like ascending to the Gates of Heaven. As Papa opened the massive oak doors for us, the words of the choir singing "Oh, Come All Ye Faithful" came floating out as if it were meant especially for us, a devout young father with three children in tow. The great pillars, like two rows of mighty tree-trunks with over-arching branches, led to the altar resplendent in celestial light.

Before taking us to the family pew, as the service had not yet started, Papa would guide us to the area which had been magically transformed into an almost life-size nativity scene flanked by spruce and pine trees.

Surely it must be what the real heaven was like—a midnight clear, choirs of angels singing Christmas carols, the fragrance of the fresh-cut trees mingled with that of incense and burning candles, the Babe in the Manger extending his arms to us in loving welcome—and all the while my hand clasped firmly in Papa's and in my mind the delicious knowledge that Mamma was at home, humming to herself as she stuffed the red net stockings with goodies and hung them on our tree. No greater joy than this could the real Heaven offer.

Turn, Stand, March

MY second teacher was a good and dutiful woman. From the district trustees she had undoubtedly gotten the message: Stick to the three R's as much as possible, no fancies, no feathers. She had kinfolk in the neighborhood and even if she had been inclined to follow in Cousin Celia's footsteps, it is unlikely that she could have withstood the pressure from all sides.

In addition to the moral scruples against frivolous extras, there was the all important matter of school taxes to consider. The income from farm produce was seldom in balance with the operational expenses, something which seems to plague farmers to this day. And, then as now, holding down school costs was the chief way property-owners could express their opposition to paying high property taxes.

Furthermore, children were not being sent to school to get notions about the "world away." They were being sent to learn to read and write and figure, especially to figure so as to be able to keep from being "skunked" by local tradesmen and peddlers. It was getting so "a person couldn't trust anybody no more," one woman said.

And as for a higher education—higher being anything beyond the eighth grade—who needed that anyway? Given too much book learning, girls especially were apt to rebel against growing up "to be a plain woman like Ma," and settling down to raising a big family; they were apt to get high-faluting notions and go off to the cities, leaving the countryside low on women power. Boys were less likely to kick over the traces but they needed wives and children to help with the work. Whoever heard of a successful farmer who didn't have a woman behind him to do some of the chores?

Teacher II had not only come back from "away" to take over Cousin Celia's job, but she took care of her aging mother, cooked and washed and cleaned for her bachelor brother, even helped him with some of the farm tasks—she was indeed a dutiful and hard-working woman. Living as she did a stone's throw from the school, she could dash home at noon-time to check on things there, put food on the table for her mother and brother, and get back in time to ring the bell for afternoon classes.

Carl and I almost always went home for a hot meal in the middle of the day—only when the weather was really bad did we take lunch for both of us in a Karo Syrup pail. One such time when the schoolhouse with its four exposed, uninsulated walls seemed to creak and shudder in the hard cold, two of the big boys who came to school only when there was no work to do at home, turned up before Teacher got back to ring the afternoon bell. Chilled from working in the woods all morning, they built up the fire, opened the lower draft and the stovepipe damper, tilted back their chairs (they were too big to sit in the regular seats), took off their boots and put their feet on the fenders.

The big stove—it had to be big to heat the building—was getting hotter and hotter, the stovepipe was glowing red almost up to the ceiling and Carl and I were plainly worried. The fire safety rules which we had learned at home were being violated and Teacher wasn't there.

Finally Carl, unable to contain his concern any longer, burst out, "You wanta burn the place down? You better shut that damper and close that draft!"

The bigger of the two boys glanced at his ten-year-old critic and scornfully exclaimed, "Why it's little Schmitt Schitt! Thinks he knows more'n we do jist 'cause his pa's got a gas'line engine!"

"I was jist sayen. . . . " Carl began.

"You was jist sayen we gonna burn the place down. Well, mebbe we will but we're gonna burn you up first!"

While one of them opened the stove door, the other one grabbed Carl and held the head of the wildly kicking boy close to the shooting flames.

"Singe the hair off his head!" one of them shouted.

I was terrified. My brother and maybe all of us younger kids would be burned to death before Teacher got back. "Stop, stop, please!" I begged.

"Nother Schmitt Schitt heard from," the biggest boy joked. By now Carl's face was fiery red from the heat and to keep him from struggling, each bully was holding a hand and a foot while Carl's head dangled downward. They were swinging him back and forth, first toward the flames then toward me and since my brother was either too brave or too frightened to beg for mercy, I had to do it for him between bursts of sobbing.

One of the other pupils had the good sense to rush to the door and cry out, "Teacher's coming, Teacher's coming!" She really hadn't been coming at all but the warning had the desired effect. By the time she did arrive some ten minutes later, the fire had calmed down, the damper and the draft were closed, the big boys were casually slicing off pieces of apples with their jack-knives, Carl had smoothed back his tousled hair and I had dried my tears. We knew better than to tattle on our tormentors as they might try to "get us" at some future time when Teacher wasn't around to keep order.

Yes, Teacher believed in law and order and she kept order according to the letter of the law as she understood it. She took her job seriously, she was seldom if ever late, she never called off classes, not even during the first weeks of the terrible flu epidemic which swept through the country in the fall of 1918. Not until the few schools still open were closed by the County Commissioner was the bell in our belfry silent.

Since the octagonal clock on the side wall had long since ceased running, Teacher II kept a Little Ben wind-up clock on her desk and she called school at exactly the prescribed time by pulling the rope over her desk which rang the big iron bell that could be heard all over the district. And she dismissed school just as promptly, tailoring the length of the last recitations to fit the time schedule. According to her lights there were only two ways to do things, the right way and the wrong way. Each day's routine was like that of every other day, the only variations being the lesson assignments which must always move forward, whether or not the pupils had mastered the previous material.

Cousin Celia's innovations did not survive, learning was not supposed to be so interesting and inspiring that a child wanted more and more of it. It was dull, hard work like digging potatoes or husking corn. There were to be no special holiday activities—at Christmas time no bells and reindeer, at Thanksgiving time no pilgrims and turkeys were colored and pasted on the windows. There was no gaily decorated tree, no programs and skits; however as we left the building the last day before Christmas vacation, Teacher handed each of us a bag of store-bought candy and a neatly wrapped gift such as a pencil box or a dinner pail. These were paid for out of her meager earnings and must have taken most of a month's salary.

During early February Cousin Celia had reserved time for making Valentines. From town she brought some large sheets of construction paper, red mostly, and a roll of lacy looking ceiling wallpaper and we children were told to bring old magazines and seed catalogues. Under her direction we cut out faces and bright flowers, large red hearts and white pasteboard arrows. With the ceiling paper as lace we were able to make some not altogether original Valentines, and on them we would copy verses like:

> "Roses are red, violets are blue
> Sugar is sweet and so are you."

Or, if there wasn't room for that, we wrote "I love you" on those from girl to girl, or boy to boy. On those from girl to boy, it was usually "Be my Valentine." I don't recall that the boys wrote any such messages to girls.

Teacher II told us that if we wanted to make Valentines we should make them at home, not during school hours. At our house Mamma made some paste with flour and water, cooking it until it was thick and sticky and she found some left-over scraps of wallpaper. After we wore down our red crayons making hearts, we made them with other colors, mostly orange and blue and purple.

The number of Valentines which one received was considered to be a kind of measure of one's popularity and counting and announcing the count was started by one of the girls who seemed to be getting more than she rightfully deserved, many of them signed "From Guess Who."

Not to be outdone the next year Madeline and I proceeded to make a number of extras and sign them "From Guess Who" with the added precaution of varying the handwriting a bit, using ink on some and pencil or crayon on others. Since our supply of faces and flowers in color was limited, we had to resort to vegetables such as red radishes, orange carrots and yellow squash. We did win the numbers game that year but our deception backfired. The girl whose underhandedness we had copied suggested that we were guilty of fraud—without admitting her own misdeeds!

Under the reign of Teacher II, we continued to have a potluck picnic on the last day of school when we went to get our report cards and clean out our desks. But sadly, there was no opportunity for each of us to "strut and fret" for one brief moment on the raised platform with Teacher's desk removed and the program written on the blackboard, listing our names in large letters.

But at least we had lots of good food—that concept was well appreciated in our neighborhood—potato salad, baked beans, hard-boiled eggs, beet and cucumber pickles, apple strudel, cakes and pies and cookies. And Teacher always did herself proud that day, bringing a huge tray of bakery rolls and a big kettle of hot wieners—all bought with her own wages. Accustomed as we were to just plain homemade bread and pork sausage links which Mamma made, Teacher's beneficence was enough or almost enough to make up for our disappointment over not getting a chance to "speak a piece."

Summer vacation was over all too soon and then it was back to the usual routine. After the second bell rang and we were all sitting at attention, Teacher said, "Good morning, children" and we responded with, "Good morning, Teacher." Then she clapped her hands and said, "Turn!"

After we had done so she clapped her hands again and said, "Stand and salute the flag and say these words after me." This we did in a monotone with very little if any understanding of what we were pledging.

The Stars and Stripes, tacked on the wall above the blackboard behind Teacher's desk, was the one touch of color in the whole drab room. The flag had been given to the school, saving the district the expense of buying one since all schools were now expected to have a flag, presumably to have something to salute. And since our neighborhood was largely German, it might have been taken as evidence of a lack of patriotism if there had not been one on display.

Of course, no family relished having its sons drafted to fight kinfolk across the sea, also manpower was needed to plant and harvest the navy beans and potatoes which were very much in demand for feeding the troops. But orders are orders and there was no public protest against the war although there was some private grumbling.

As for the Pledge itself, we children didn't pay much attention to the words—after all, "allegiance" and "republic" and "indivisible" were too abstract for most of us to comprehend. The Pledge was simply a kind of mumbo-jumbo with which we started out the day. Nor did most parents seem to know what it was all about except that it was required, like paying taxes.

Had my paternal grandfather been alive in 1917–18, I think he would have wished a plague on the flags of both the Yankees and the Prussians. According to what I was told, he thought that the cause for most wars was wanting to get bigger or wanting to remain the biggest. He believed that his native Hesse had been about the right size for a country—it was roughly the size of Switzerland, large enough to have a cathedral and a university in the capitol city surrounded by fields and villages where craftsmen and farmers could live in peace and harmony—nobody very rich or very poor.

In his opinion if a country got much larger, its ruler got the "Gros Koph" and wanted a standing army instead of a local militia and first thing you knew it was making war on a neighboring state. If Grandpa had ever worded a maxim, it might have been, "Bigness corrupts, trying to be the biggest corrupts absolutely."

But Grandpa was dead and since Papa had no first-hand experience with the Iron Chancellor, he thought of war in strictly moral terms. As far as he was concerned, nothing could be more explicit than the commandment, "Thou shalt not kill," no matter what flag flew over the land or what words were in the Pledge of Allegiance. As for Carl, he said the Pledge was invented by the "Republicans for which it stands!"

For me, a six-year-old, it made no sense at all but if it would help get rid of the Kaiser, I was willing to say it every day just as I said my prayers. For my husband-to-be, who was then a schoolboy in Ohio, the pledge had a precise meaning—our nation was "invisible," it was so far ahead of every other nation that it was completely out of sight. Thinking of one's country in such glowing terms is not limited to nine-year-old boys. It is the stuff of which wars are made!

After the Pledge we sang, "O Columbia the gem of the Ocean" which didn't make much sense either as I didn't know that Columbia was another name for the USA and that "gem" was a precious stone, not like the jam which Mamma made with berries—so it was an ocean kind of jam. Then we sang a Civil War song, "In the prison cell I sit" and its meaning I could well understand. My brother had described prison life in imaginative detail and my heart went out to the poor soul who had been unjustly jailed. I didn't know that the person in the song had been taken captive by the Rebel Army—I assumed that he was in jail because he wished the Kaiser would die, just as I had done.

"And the tears they fill my eyes" in the song brought tears to my own eyes, too. To be far from home and mother, to be fed on prison fare which, according to Carl was dry bread and water, was enough to make anybody cry. Lastly we sang *America* and although Teacher wasn't a gifted choir mistress, she helped us belt it out, those who could carry a tune and those who couldn't.

After the morning sing, class by class we turned, stood and marched to the recitation bench for reading, each pupil to read one page. The idea seemed to be to get through one's

stint without stumbling over a single word. Never mind if you didn't get the meaning, never mind if you didn't stop for a comma or a period, never mind if a sentence was broken at the bottom of a page—the correct pronunciation was what was important. Each word was sufficient unto itself and the pupil was to tick them off as quickly and as evenly spaced as possible, no inflection whatsoever.

Usually there were about twenty in attendance on any given day with four or five absent because of illness or because they were needed at home. It was always a race against time to cover each subject for all eight grades, nine counting the primer class. In addition to reading, there was spelling, arithmetic and penmanship for the lower grades, plus geography, history and grammar for the upper grades.

After school was called in the afternoon we all had penmanship. The Palmer Method was then in vogue, the theory being that all movement should be made by the arm, not the fingers. Anyone caught moving the fingers was apt to get rapped on the knuckles with a ruler, not the paddle which was reserved for more heinous offenses. The upper grades worked with pen and ink whereas we younger pupils had to suffer the indignity of using plain lead pencils on rough tablet paper.

I knew that I was capable of using pen and ink so one day when my brother was at home with a sore throat, I quietly transferred the needed equipment from his desk to mine during the morning recess. When it was penmanship time, I casually began to practice the Palmer Method the big-pupil way. I was doing very well, too, the beautiful blue ink making lovely liquidy ovals when Teacher unexpectedly came up behind me, grabbed my shoulders, lifted me from the seat and shook me like a cat shakes a rat. The pen flew out of my hand and the ink bottle tipped over on my handiwork which I was planning to take home to show Mamma. It was the only physical chastisement I ever suffered at her hands and I was forever after careful not to overstep her guidelines for correct behavior.

The segregation of the sexes insofar as possible was still the custom of the day, at least in our district. There were two entrance doors, the one on the left for the boys, the one on the right for the girls; they opened into an unheated, cloakroom, which had firewood piled in the center, fully separating the two sides.

To the rear of the far corners of the one acre plot, were the two outhouses, the one on the left for the boys, the one on the right for the girls. The boys were to play on their side of the building, the girls on the other side. During the spring and fall the boys played mumblety-peg or baseball and during the winter they played fox and geese or made snow forts but they had fist fights during any season. For the most part we played ladylike games like "Drop the Handkerchief," "Ring around the Rosie" and "Farmer in the Dell."

Sometimes before Teacher got back from lunch, the boys deliberately invaded our territory, pretending they came to retrieve a ball and some of the older girls seemed to encourage such invasions. One time, things got so much out of hand that my sister Madeline mounted the front steps and with all the authority a six-year-old could muster shouted, "Girls play with the girls, boys play with the boys!"

Even the seating arrangements were segregated as much as was numerically possible. When I was in my third year at school, there were more girls than there were small seats on the right side of the room so I was obliged to sit in front of a boy who came from the other side of the tracks, rurally speaking. When there is overcrowding, sickness and overwork, cleanliness is not always next to godliness. Be that as it may, I came to blame that seating arrangement for all my social problems that year.

"What's that crawling on your forehead?" Mamma asked me when I pulled off my tasseled cap one afternoon. It turned out to be a louse and there were still others as she soon discovered. With a fine-tooth comb she worked on my hair and as she deposited the little "beasties" on a piece of newspaper, we counted them together, arriving at the grand total of twelve as I remember. It seemed quite a record, a record worth reporting at school the next day.

Accordingly, after I'd been de-loused and had a hair-wash, a tub bath and a complete change of clothing, I announced our findings with innocent pride, perhaps even increasing the number a bit to make the achievement more noteworthy. I had not the gift to see myself as my classmates saw me and I was not at all prepared for their reaction. The two girls whom I considered my best friends set up a great hue and cry, "She's got lice, she's got lice, don't play with her or you'll get lice."

This was in the morning before the second bell and when recess-time came and my classmates went out to play, I remained in my seat, determined that I was not going to give them a chance to taunt me any more. When Teacher asked me why I wasn't outside on such a nice fall day, I told her I wanted to get caught up on my lessons. Studying at recess was permitted, in fact required for those who were behind on their work because of absences.

While Teacher wasn't looking (I was afraid she might not approve of my choice) I selected for my outside reading *Tom the Bootblack*, one of the few works of fiction on our library shelf—mostly they were old school books left behind by long-gone pupils. I found Tom to be a heroic figure in Horatio Alger's rags to riches tale; he paid no attention to the taunts of his peers, he toiled from morning to night, he suffered all kinds of hardships and in the end, he rose high in the world. It was a great book even though I had to skip some of the words.

Some years ago, in recounting the "head lice" story to one of our young grandsons, I told him that I had really wanted to play outdoors at recess time but I thought I wasn't wanted and I didn't care to be rejected. He came up with a simple, ingenious solution to the problem, "Well, why didn't you go out and play with the kid who did have lice?"

In looking back at that troubled year, I can now say that "Sweet are the uses of adversity!" I discovered that I really enjoyed reading things beyond the call of duty and I began to read everything I could get my hands on and I also found that I could survive without the all-encompassing approval of my peers.

Perhaps because I never forgot the violent shaking I had gotten for disregarding the rigid rules of Teacher II, I learned how to evade some of them by being a bit secretive. But not so, my brother, Carl. For one thing, he had started out on the wrong foot with her; he had challenged her way of teaching by frequent remarks about how her predecessor had done this or that; he brought a picture of Cousin Celia to school which by comparison made the attire of Teacher II look positively dowdy—our cousin's outfit being a fashionable dress and an elegantly decorated hat which, however, she didn't wear teaching! And Carl never failed to mention that she was 'lationed to us and how school wasn't fun any more. Just as he was not about to be fitted into the pupil-mold of Teacher II, she was not about to be fitted into his kind of teacher-mold.

She had certain inalienable rights according to her way of thinking and first and foremost was the right to make and enforce the rules. And the first and foremost rule was, "Do not question my authority!" One of her rules was "Do not put your hands in your pockets during school hours" and it was this which got Carl into deep trouble one winter day. Instead of putting his right hand in the correct positon for a salute to the flag, he used his left hand.

"Take you right hand out of your pocket and salute the flag properly," she ordered.

"I kin salute jist as well this way," Carl retorted whereupon Teacher came charging down the aisle, grabbed him by the collar and marched him to the front of the room. "Empty both your pockets on my desk," she commanded.

"Nothing in 'em," he mumbled.

"Turn them inside out!"

Carl said and did nothing. I never did find out whether he was hiding some contraband or whether he was merely testing Teacher's mettle. She then marched him back to his seat, sat him down hard and told him to see her after school, pointing to the paddle on her desk.

We had taken our lunch with us that day and I tearfully urged him to go home before Teacher returned and not come back for afternoon classes. My tearfulness was probably a mistake—otherwise he might have done that very thing. As it was, he sniffed loudly and said, "Think I'm scared of that old hen?"

Much as I had suffered at his hands, I could not bear the thought of his getting a terrible licking. And he did have some redeeming features—he made a lot of contraptions for us girls to play with and he had once gotten a bloody nose while trying to retrieve my tasseled cap which had been snatched off my head by one of the big boys. Teacher had looked mad enough to whack him to pieces if there was no one there to stay her hand.

I decided to remain close by in case of need after the lower grades were dismissed. Both to keep out of sight and to keep moderately warm, I took shelter in the girls' outhouse until it was time to stand vigil at the schoolhouse door. By holding my ear to the crack, I could hear what was going on inside.

"Now tell me why you wouldn't empty your pockets!"

"Cause there was nothing in 'em."

"Why didn't you take out your hand?"

"Cause it was cold."

"Well, take it out now and I'll warm it up for you and I'll warm up something else, too!"

After that there were half a dozen resounding whacks,

then dead silence. Could it be that he was mortally wounded? Should I go for help?

Before I could decide what to do, he came bursting out the boys' door. "Whatcha doin' here?" he wanted to know as he put on his mackinaw.

"Nothin', jist waiting for you to make tracks for me," I said, my teeth chattering. "But did she hurt you?"

"Naw, she couldn't hurt a fly. But it is gettin' to be the limit these days when a person can't even say the rosary in school!" So that was what he was going to tell Papa if there were repercussions at home! I was so relieved that he wasn't bleeding or anything that I let the rosary story go by. Carl was never one to do any extra praying—one time during Lent when we were all supposed to be reciting the rosary as a family, he was off in a corner rolling dice.

It was one thing after another until he quit school before he finished the 8th grade. Teacher couldn't abide anybody who broke her rules and Carl broke any rules he couldn't abide. It was too bad because Cousin Celia always said he had the makings of an Edison.

Of Horses and Men

MY paternal grandfather did not like horses. He may have had an unfortunate experience in his boyhood, but the chances are that his very strong dislike had something to do with Otto Von Bismarck and there certainly was no question as to how he felt about the Iron Chancellor. The Prussian Junker had requisitioned all the able-bodied horses and men in Grandpa's native Hesse for the Cavalry and Transport in his army which was being used as a kind of grapple hook to pull together the German principalities and to build an empire in Europe.

Until his dying day in 1915, when yet another German leader had led his people into war, Grandpa would hold forth on the subject of Bismarck whenever he could find a listener. In his native tongue—the only language he could or would speak—he would describe how drawings of uniformed men astride handsome, sleek-limbed horses were posted in his village for recruiting purposes. And he reported that several of his brothers and cousins had been tricked into joining up because they thought that fighting on horseback would be romantic and patriotic.

But not Grandpa—he had heard the stories of returning soldiers and he still remembered a battle scene painted by one of his artist friends—the horses plunging and rearing, their nostrils flared, their mouths agape and in the foreground a fallen rider pinned to the earth by the hoof of his mount. Horses and war-making and the Iron Chancellor, he lambasted them all!

Grandpa had grown up in the village of Obertifenbach where he was trained in wood-working skills and he had youthful visions of becoming the maker of fine violins. He played duets with his brother, Philip, on an instrument which he had made with his own hands and he served as a substitute organist in the village church while Philip was off studying to become a teacher at Wiesbaden. He was looking forward to a quiet life making music and violins until the Prussian interloper shattered his dreams!

Grandpa had raised no objections to serving in the local militia and this he had done, but becoming a part of a jackbooting, goosestepping army was another matter. Every healthy man not engaged in farming or a military-related occupation was being wheedled or tricked or drafted into the Imperial Army and in the Jacob Schmitt brood, there were seven sons.

For three hundred years family members had farmed the acreage which surrounded Schmitthaus, first as caretakers for the Cistercian Order. But when church property was secularized around 1800, Jacob's father took title to the land with the provison that the estate would not be broken up into small plots as was the custom in the Province of Hesse—a custom which meant that the area was a hodgepodge of strips of land, many of them only an acre or so in size. In Grandpa's time, Schmitthaus was special—his father was one of the largest and most successful landowners in the region because his property, all 30 acres of it, was in one piece! However, there was no land for the younger sons.

Making music and violins was not essential to war-making, and Grandpa decided to remove himself from Bismarck's reach and follow his two younger brothers, Philip and Aegidius, to America where he joined them in Baltimore. All three had left Obertifenbach, not because they were turning their backs on the land of their birth but because they did not wish to be pawns in the war-making games of the imperialist-minded Prussian.

Aegidius found work as a gardener and Philip took a position as a teacher in a German-speaking parish where he also became the church organist. Wilhelm, my grandfather, served as a kind of handy-man in the same parish, repairing pews and school desks, building storage cabinets, making and gilding altar decorations and singing Latin and German in the choir. Also, he was sometimes called upon to witness a marriage along with three-quarters-German Mary Boyer— the Boyer quarter being a French officer who had become stranded on his way back from Russia with Napoleon's retreating army. She had come to America as a child and after both her parents died in an epidemic, was apprenticed to a seamstress. Later she was employed by the Baltimore Parish to make and care for the altar linens and the priestly vestments.

A rather lengthy courtship followed; it seemed that Wilhelm was hesitant about linking his fate with someone who had French blood in her veins, also he was fearful that she might not want to go back to the "old country" when the opportune moment arrived. However, time and nature eventually overcame his reservations and the two celebrated their own marriage ceremony.

After their quiet life in Obertifenbach, the three brothers found it hard to adjust to the rush and roar of a big port city. Aegidius was the first to leave Baltimore for Northern Michigan where the newly laid railroad was bringing in settlers, many of them German immigrants. Land for homesteading had become available and Aedigious was determined to have a piece of it. It was he who alerted Philip to an opening in the St. Francis Parish in Petoskey, a small, lumber-mill town. Needed was someone to become the first teacher in a projected classroom in the rectory, a teacher who knew both German and English and who could serve as the church organist. Philip was qualified and, being a bachelor, he could room and board at the rectory as part of his salary— $20 a month was all the parish could afford in hard cash. He got the job.

Wilhelm was the last to leave Baltimore; by now he was three years married and there was a year old daughter, Rosa. He was hesitant to give up his church-related work which was moderately satisfying. Also he was reluctant to dig into his savings which were meant for returning to his homeland, once Bismarck had departed from the scene.

But his brothers painted such a glowing picture of the new

settlement and of its similiarity to Obertifenbach in climate and topography that he was finally persuaded to follow them despite his misgivings. However, he found no job to his liking awaiting him in the bustling fast-growing town. One offer was to haul logs to the mill on Bear River with a feisty team, the other to drive a rig for the local livery stable, both of which he disdainfully declined.

By the early 1880's most of the desirable land in the immediate area had been homesteaded but Aegidius and Philip had a secret plan. In Four Mile Clearing east of Petoskey and not much more than a stone's throw from the farm the younger brother owned, an eighth section with a frame house and a log barn was for sale. It had been homesteaded in the late 70's by an Edmund Knight and now that the required five year tenure had been fulfilled, he was ready to sell it for $1800, a princely sum in those days, and this figure included the livestock—a team of horses, a couple of cows and several calves and pigs.

The brothers began to promote their plan vigorously and just as vigorously Wilhelm opposed the whole idea. He knew very little about farming; at Schmitthaus his father and oldest brother had taken care of the fields and the animals and he had never so much as milked a cow. And now that he was approaching middle age, he certainly could not be expected to begin a brand new way of life.

Wilhelm was told that it was the chance of a lifetime; Aegidius promised to help with the field work involving horses; Philip agreed to put up half the price and Mary said she would learn to milk the cows. And when all three brothers had made their fortunes, they would go back to Obertifenbach and live out the remainder of their lives in comfort and music-making. By then Bismarck would be in his grave or in exile and they could return to the kind of village life they had known and loved.

Wilhelm could not withstand the mounting pressure from all sides forever. Mary was pregnant for a second time and she was anxious to put her feet down under her own table. Even the priest advised him to accept the proffered help from his brothers and to thank God for the many blessings which had been bestowed upon him. And so it was that the die was cast, the deal was made and the deed was recorded in the Emmet County Courthouse on May 5, 1884.

Most immigrants would have been overjoyed at taking title to 80 contiguous acres, some of which was still in virgin timber but Grandpa was merely overwhelmed. How was he to cope with so monumental a task, so vast an acreage with a hoe, the only farm implement he had learned to use back in Obertifenbach? He was indeed bowed by the weight of the problem which had been thrust upon him and on his back was the burden of a growing family.

It so happened that the homesteader, the English-born Edmund Knight, had felled every tree in sight around the farm buildings, something which deeply offended Grandpa's aesthetic as well as his conservation-minded sensibilities. As the new owner set about to remedy the situation, he must have been thinking that a German could certainly tell an Englishman a thing or two about planting a seedling for every mature tree cut down; from the woods he transplanted saplings where shade was needed and beauty desired. Besides, digging up young trees and hauling them in a wheelbarrow to freshly dug holes was something he could do with his own two hands and a shovel. And it was ever so much more satisfying than grubbing roots out of the fields and picking off stones in preparation for planting corn and potatoes.

Aedigious did the plowing and between the other two brothers they managed to get the crops sown after the school term ended that first spring. But no matter how much he was coaxed and prodded, Wilhelm refused to drive the team. Convinced against his will to buy the farm, he seemed determined to prove that his brothers had been wrong and insofar as the horses were concerned, it was "Nein, nein, un tausand neinen." For the sake of his family he would hoe the potatoes and the corn, he would scythe the hay, he would cradle-cut the grain but he refused to have anything to do with the horses except to feed them. Eventually Aedigious became resigned to Wilhelm's stubbornness and they exchanged labor, hour for hour.

On September 16, 1884 my father was born and shortly thereafter he was baptized "Philip Aloysius" after his schoolmaster uncle. As a present to his godson, the elder Philip gave the child his half-share of the farm.

As the months and years went by, there were added responsibilities—another son, Albert, and a second daughter, Mary put in their appearance—and the dream of returning to Obertifenbach became dim and then dimmer. Furthermore, the letters from the "old country" were not encouraging. Otto Von Bismarck had consolidated his power and the principality of Hesse was firmly under the Prussian's "diktat." The independence of his beloved homeland was apparently to be no more.

Wilhelm was not a happy man nor was his wife altogether satisfied with the state of affairs. The anticipated fortune with so much acreage had not materialized, in fact the cash earnings were largely hers from making fashionable wearing apparel for the fine ladies of the town. If the family was to continue to live in Four Mile Clearing, Wilhelm must learn to farm the "new country" way, otherwise she wanted to move so as to be closer to her clients for fittings.

With no prospective job in town and with a wife who was taking on the overbearing ways of American women, Wilhelm decided on a compromise—he would substitute bovine for man power, rather than attempt to deal with Prinz and Koenig whose names had been Germanized for his benefit.

So it was, that one fine April morning when most of the men in the neighborhood were spring plowing, he managed to harness to the plow one of the cows, a slow-moving cud-chewing creature, but she had neither the strength nor the inclination to turn a furrow. No doubt remembering the yoke of placid oxen in use on the Schmitthaus acreage in Obertifenbach, Grandpa took what seemed to be a reasonable approach to the problem at hand. The bull calf which had come with the farm was now grown to full size and the cow and bull in tandem by his logic should make a well-balanced pair, the one providing the wisdom and stability, the other the strength and forward motion.

With its massive head in a grain pail, the bull was somehow tethered to the cow which was hitched to the plow. But once the grain was all devoured and the pail-blinder shaken aside,

the bull supplied the forward motion without so much as a "giddyap" or a flick of the whip, plunging through the orchard with the dumbfounded cow and driver in tow, the plow bouncing along this way and that but turning no furrow.

Pell-mell they went with Grandpa valiantly trying to dig in his heels, all the while shouting, "Halten, halten," interspersed with German expletives which he rarely used since he was not a profane man. The young fruit trees were trampled and bent, the chickens were scattered with much squawking and fluttering, the herd dog was awakened and took chase with excited barking and Grandpa was eventually brought low.

A neighbor, hearing the hullabaloo left his team standing obediently in his field and came running to head off the mis-matched runaways. Glad to be relieved of the responsibility of trying to stop the stampede, Grandpa managed to pick himself up and head for the house, there to nurse his bruises, both physical and psychological. Poor man, music maker that he was, he had forgotten if he ever knew, that making an ox out of a bull calf requires a bit of transposition.

After this unfortunate experience, Grandpa did not learn to like horses more, he merely enlarged his dislikes to include the genus Taurus and took to his hand tools permanently. No matter what his wife or his brothers said, he would never again try to cope with the brute strength of a draft animal just as he had been unable to cope with the unbridled power of the Prussian Chancellor. But he could hoe and he could pray and he did both without stint.

There then came a series of worse catastrophes. Philip lost his teaching job when the convent nuns came to town. Whether to blame the growing number of Irish parishioners who wanted English and English only taught in the classroom or whether to blame the nuns for taking over what was surely the male prerogative of schoolmastering was the question. Grandpa settled the matter by blaming them all.

The only opening to be found for a German language teacher was at North Dorr near Grand Rapids, two hundred miles away. And there the young Philip was to go also the following winter since Wilhelm did not want his son to attend a non-German school nor to entrust him to the care of female teachers even though they did wear the veil. Wilhelm had become dependent on both Philips and he missed them sorely.

My father, then seven years old, was not told that he was to be left at North Dorr, merely that he would be going to see his Uncle Philip. He had never had a train ride nor been away from home overnight but his mother would be with him and he looked forward to the trip with eagerness. It was mid-January and the coach windows were partly frosted over so he could see little but cut-over woodland, bare-branched young trees and stumps capped with snow.

The lumber kings had come and gone but the towns they spawned remained and now there was little activity to be seen. What he remembered mostly in later years was the great hip-roofed barns on some of the farms, so magnificent in comparison with the small log barns at home. And he remembered looking back at the disappearing rails and wondering whether his father was taking good care of Prinz and Koenig.

Weary from the trip, he slept soundly in the rooming house where his uncle had engaged a room for them. When he awoke he found his mother gone; she had taken an early morning train back to Petoskey and her duties there. She had been afraid that the boy would make a fuss about being left so there had been no explanation, no parting embrace, no "Auf Wiedersehen," but she had been assured by the menfolks in the family that the experience would be good for her shy son, make a man of him!

The schoolmaster uncle was a strict disciplinarian and he would not tolerate any homesickness tears. When his nephew was listless in the classroom and did not respond to questioning, his knuckles were rapped and he was told to act his age. The roughneck boys called him a sissy and challenged him to fist fights, the food in the dining hall tasted like straw, his sleep was broken by nightmares. He thought of running away and following the train tracks north but where would he sleep at night and what would he eat? And what if he froze to death, would anyone find him. And what would happen to Prinz and Koenig, would his father get rid of them as he had sometimes threatened?

After several months the exasperated schoolmaster shipped the boy, now pale and thin, back to his parents. "Dummkopf," he called him. "Let him farm."

And this he was very willing to do in the months and years that followed. The horses were his special charges—he spent hours stroking their noses, curry-combing their backs, braiding their tails and giving them apple and carrot treats. They stood motionless while he cleaned out their stalls and bedded them down with fresh straw and shortly after his return from North Dorr, he set about learning to harness them. According to a neighbor lady's story, she once found him in tears as he tried unsuccessfully to lift up the heavy collar and at the same time buckle it behind the horse's ear. But soon, with something to stand on and much practice, he was able to fully harness the team and hitch it to the stone boat to haul off the boulders so numerous on the hills near Lake Michigan.

Then came a terrible tragedy. Aegidius and his young

daughter were taken violently ill, his wife ran to the nearest farmhouse and the neighbor took off on horseback to get a doctor. But as he was on another call, it was hours before he got to the stricken father and child and by then it was too late to save them. It was later surmised that one of the cows, after breaking out of the rail fence pasture, had eaten some poisonous plants, not enough to kill the cow but enough to poison the milk.

And still another blow was to befall the family. While stooping over to draw up a bucket of water from the hand-dug well pit, Wilhelm slipped on the icy platform and fell head first into the frigid water, some fifteen feet from the surface of the ground. He was somehow able to maneuver himself into an upright position and with water up to his chin, he began to yell for help. "Helfen, helfen" and between his shouts for human aid, he called upon the Lord for rescue, vowing that he would build a chapel in thanksgiving if his life was spared. It was, but the Lord got all the credit even though it took a neighbor, Prinz and Koenig and a pulley and a rope to do it.

And praise be to God, Grandpa emerged from the chilling experience a more contented man. Now, in good conscience, he could put his wood-working skills to excellent use; he could erect something aesthetically and spiritually pleasing on the raw and windswept Four Mile Clearing. He could become a creator and artist of sorts in the bleak cultural wasteland to which he had been consigned by fate and family. He could even resign himself, like the biblical Ruth, to being a permanent exile amid the alien corn and potatoes.

Thenceforth, without any sense of guilt, he could see his young son go off to work in the fields with the team; he could see his wife sewing late into the night on fancy dresses and feathered hats for other women of the parish; he could accept cash from his schoolteacher brother for paying the taxes and buying materials for the chapel. After all, a debt to the Lord must take precedence over all else—earthly considerations, family responsibilities and yes, learning to handle horses.

A heavy burden had been lifted from his shoulders. Hymns of thanksgiving—in German, of course—could be heard above the sawing and hammering as he went about building the edifice which he had promised the Lord. And after its completion, after the altar had been fulsomely decorated with curlicues and gilt paint, after an organ had been acquired, he and his brother Philip, when home on vacation, could resume the satisfying life they had known in the "old country." And now that his obligations to his Savior took priority over dealings with horses and men, Grandpa had taken time to handcraft another violin to replace the one he had left in Obertifenbach.

Both father and son were happy—the father because he was able to at least partially fulfill the dreams of his youth and the son because he had become a man in the fields—he could now steady the plow and turn a deep furrow, the true test of manhood in that time and place.

Untimely Beginning

THE winter of 1911–12 was long and bitterly cold in Northern Michigan. From early December until late March, there was scarcely a day when Mamma could see the snowbanks outside the kitchen window without first scraping off the frost. But although there were no thermo panes, no furnace, and no attic insulation, there was an ample supply of oak and maple firewood.

In the kitchen there was a pitcher pump for drawing soft water from the cistern in the side yard which held the summer rains, piped from the eaves troughs on the house. If the supply was exhausted before spring, snow was melted on the cookstove for wash-tub baths and for laundry and cleaning. Water for drinking was pulled up in a bucket from a shallow well. And to the rear was the "closet," a less countrified term than "outhouse" or "privy," which had neither heat nor light nor plumbing but plenty of ventilation.

A new baby was expected in mid-February and all must go well this time. There had been a premature stillbirth the year before, possibly brought on by overwork—Mamma was young and ambitious and it was hard for her to slow down when there was so much to be done. Both she and Papa wanted a sizeable number of children, maybe not as many as ten or twelve but at least six or eight. By now their first-born was almost four years old and it was high time that they get on with their family-building.

At the first sign of trouble on the morning of December 12, Mamma had taken to her bed in the hope that God and

Nature would await the prescribed nine months and for a time it seemed that the Higher Powers would cooperate. However, by nightfall it became apparent that hope and prayers were not enough and that a doctor should be called. A neighborhood midwife had been on hand the year before and although neither parent blamed her for the stillbirth, they wanted to take no chances this time.

The nearest telephone was a short distance away and was on a party line with a dozen or more other subscribers. One turn of the crank was to get "Central" who would ring the desired number in town; to call anyone on the party line itself, there were longs and shorts while a sustained ring meant fire or some other emergency calling for community action.

Papa's one turn of the crank to get in touch with the doctor did not constitute an emergency signal but within a short time after he got home, there was a stomping on the back porch and a pounding on the door as Hilda, the midwife, put in her appearance.

"Figured you might be needin' me if the doctor can't make it on accounta the storm," she boomed without a trace of embarassment as to how she had come by her information.

"Well, er . . . I mean Gertie's not feeling very good . . . , could be she ate something to upset her stomach," was Papa's way of trying to keep from actually fibbing or from saying too much.

"When's she due?" Hilda wanted to know. "She wasn't showing hardly atall the last time I seen her."

"It could be appendicitis or something like that," Papa said, embarassed by such bluntness and avoiding her question.

"Got the foot of the bed propped up?" Hilda asked as she hung up her coat and pulled off her arctics. "If 'tisn't her time yet that could do the trick—get some good solid chunks of wood. In case it don't, we'll have to be ready," she told him as she washed her hands and filled the tea kettle.

Although Mamma kept saying that she didn't think it was true labor, Papa found himself taking orders from Hilda. "Food don't spoil in cold weather like this and cows aren't eatin' poison weeds in the woods, naw it can't be a plain belly ache."

Papa knew that Hilda, helpful soul that she meant to be, was upsetting Mamma. On the other hand he felt that the midwife was right and that preparations had to be made. It was the consarned party line which was to blame, it had brought Hilda to the house unbidden. Still, if the doctor couldn't make it. . . .

It was before the advent of radio and televison and especially in the wintertime when farm wives had a little respite from gardening and canning and other chores, they often "listened in"—some made no bones about it, even chiming in with bits of additional information. It was the chief way that neighborhood news was disseminated and most conversations were innocent—such as how the mail carrier's rig had tipped over in a snow bank, overturning the wood stove which was used to keep the driver warm and the water for the horse from freezing, and how it was feared that a Blue Valley cream check had been burned up since it was overdue. The chief drawback to "listening in" was the height of the set on the wall—too high for the listener to sit down in comfort.

"You sure you counted right?" Hilda asked Mamma after the bed was propped up to her satisfaction.

"Yes, yes, of course I can count right," was Mamma's answer.

"I been told wrong couple of times, 'specially when they was only married five, six months. And the baby, when it come, was about ready to cut teeth! They couldn't fool me."

The pains were coming quite regularly now and Hilda warned, "Looks like we can't hold it back, no use gettin' your hopes up. It'll jist have to be like last time, but you're young yet, you kin have lots more."

Papa kept trying to shush her as she recounted stories which she had heard from other midwives, but Hilda was not one who was easily shushed. And every time he tried to change the subject by making some remark about the weather, she predicted that because of the worsening storm, the doctor would never be able to make it on time as even the best horse would founder in the big cut on Crooked Hill.

Things had to be readied for what all three were now sure would take place, doctor or no doctor, and Papa was trying to do as directed while managing to rattle a stove lid or bang a door to keep Mamma from hearing the most harrowing details of the midwife's stories.

In later years, when recounting the events of that long three hour wait for the doctor, what Mamma remembered most were Hilda's tales of woe and her unabashed inquisitiveness—she made the whys, whens and wherefores her business, something which Mamma did not appreciate.

I remember one time when Mamma and I were returning home with several crates of strawberries which had been bartered for rhubarb and cottage cheese. As we passed by her house, Hilda flagged us down, "Been buyin' strawberries?" she asked as Mamma reined in her horse. That June our strawberry patch had produced only a few seedy berries and Mamma, as usual, wanted to make some jam for winter. The berries were covered with some unbleached muslin to shield them from the sun but a corner of one of the crates was visible.

"Two whole crates," Mamma said airily, letting Hilda think she had paid hard cash for them.

"Awful expensive, dollar a crate, huh?"

"No matter what they cost, good berries are worth it!" was Mamma's response.

"Don't see how folks kin spend money on stuff they kin raise themselves! Thought you folks had some of your own!"

"Wouldn't be buying them if we did. See, it's like this—Philip doesn't smoke, he doesn't chew, he doesn't drink but he does like strawberries. Giddy-up, Topsy." And with that we drove off, leaving Hilda sampling several of the berries she had helped herself to from our crates. Hilda's husband not only smoked and chewed but he sometimes drank too much.

Between the labor pains during those long hours of waiting, Mamma must have been tempted to consign Hilda to the nether regions but profanity was not permitted under our roof, certainly not when help from the Almighty was needed to keep things from going from bad to worse.

Despite the continuing storm, the doctor managed to get through the drifts and Papa met him with words of gratitude both to God and the horse which he unhitched and took to the barn where he gave the weary animal a rubdown and a mangerful of hay. No doubt he was willing to leave the last part of the procreation process to others.

The doctor agreed with Hilda that Mamma was in true labor and that Nature was not to be restrained. He complimented the midwife on the preparations she had made, he praised Mamma for the way she was coping with the situation and thanked Papa for his concern for the horse. He had no complaints because of being called out on such a blustery night—instead he was glad that he had been able to get to his destination on time.

An hour after midnight on the alarm clock ticking away on the dresser, a tiny squirming mite was born, a baby girl with a head the size of a tea cup and limbs the size of a woman's little finger.

"It'll never live," was Hilda's greeting to the infant. Her own babies had all been hefty ten pounders who had gone full term and beyond.

"Don't be too sure," the doctor cautioned. "She seems to be a feisty little thing."

Hilda had the butter scales ready, apparently to prove to one and all that the baby's weight precluded its survival.

"We won't bother with that," the doctor told her. "But she weighs less than two pounds, I know. What we've got to do is to figure out some way to keep her warm."

"No use tryin'—it'll never make it 'til morning—I been around a long time, never saw one teeny as that live more'n an hour or so."

By now Mamma was ready to take over arrangements for the infant. "Those big ironstone platters in the cupboard, put them in the oven," Mamma told Papa.

"For God's sake, you gonna try to keep it warm in the oven?" was Hilda's excited question.

"No, no, we'll put a pillow on one of the hot platters and keep changing them as they cool off," the doctor told her.

"I can keep the fire going an' change the platters every so often," Papa volunteered.

"Now we'll just pat her with warm olive oil—no bath with water—we won't even dress her, just put her on the warm pillow with a couple of diapers under her and cover her up lightly," the doctor instructed Hilda.

The midwife was still shaking her head and mumbling to herself but she followed the doctor's directions.

To Mamma he said, "She may not be strong enough to nurse very long so you'd better supplement her feeding with as much as she'll swallow, a few drops at a time. I have a breast pump here and an eyedropper but put them in boiling water first," he said, turning to Hilda.

She had probably never heard of such nonsense before but she did as she was told and while Mamma tried out the contraption, Hilda made hot coffee for the menfolks in the kitchen.

It was about then that Hilda remembered that nothing had been done about baptizing the infant. "It oughta be done in case she don't make it," she warned.

It must have given Mamma some satisfaction that Hilda

was now saying "she" instead of "it" and was not ruling out survival completely.

Again, Papa was in something of a bind. Failing to baptize the seven months baby would be taking a terrible chance but agreeing with Hilda would not sit well with Mamma who had made up her mind that the newborn would live.

It was Mamma who settled the matter. "Go ahead, baptize her but make it warm water."

This must have sounded rather flip to Papa but it saved him from having to side with Hilda as his conscience would have dictated—for the sake of the newborn's soul of course.

So it was, that the doctor who had not been inside a church since the funeral of his young wife and who had the reputation of being a non-believer, performed the brief ceremony after asking Mamma, "What name?"

"Just Baby B for now," Mamma told him. The name she had in mind was much too formal for the scrawny mite beside her.

His mission accomplished, the doctor made ready to leave after some last minute instructions and some handshakes all around. "Want to ride to your house with me, it's right on my way?" he asked Hilda.

"Think I'd better stay here, never kin tell when I'll be needed." she answered.

"Oh I think they'll both make it all right. What they need most is to get some sleep so you'd better let me take you home now before the drifts get any deeper," he told her. "And you must need some rest, too—you've been a big help here tonight, I can see you've had plenty of practice and there's no substitute for experience. Get your wraps on while Philip gets the horse."

Coming from a real doctor, it was a great compliment. He had studied books in faraway Ann Arbor but he knew that it was experience that counted and he recognized her skills which by now were not much appreciated by the young folks. "Well, if you say so—and I am kinda tired—can't work like I use to."

The cutter was now at the door, the horse warm and rested for the trip back to town through the swirling snow and the deep drifts. Cheered by the doctor's recognition of her talents, Hilda was in a magnanimous mood. "I'll be back in the morning with some chicken broth—nothin' like broth to make mother's milk. And don't let the fire go out, gotta keep those platters hot," she told Papa.

"That's the spirit!" the doctor said, opening the door for her in gentlemanly fashion, a gesture so unusual for her that she stood half blocking the doorway, letting in a blast of cold air. The doctor took her by the arm and steered her out to the cutter and as he covered her lap with a robe, he turned back and with a wink at Papa said, "Don't forget what Hilda said about keeping up the fire."

"She *was* a big help, even the doctor said that," Papa told Mamma in defense of Hilda. "And she means well!"

"Yes, yes, I know." Mamma answered. She was relaxed now that the ordeal was over and her baby was sleeping peacefully on her warm pillow. "And thank Heaven there are people like that doctor even if they don't go to church, coming all the way out here on a night like this. Church isn't everything!"

That was too much of a philosophical challenge for Papa to take on at 3 o'clock in the morning. Besides, he was hungry and anxious to get a bit of food for himself and for Mamma. Neither of them had eaten any supper.

The baby not only lived through the night but thrived under Mamma's watchful eye and the frequent changing of the platters through the long hard winter with the wind howling around the frame house, rattling the windows and sifting in under the doors.

By April when the trailing arbutus was beginning to bloom around the stumps in the woods on the back forty and the crows were coming out of the swamps to look for the food uncovered by the thaw, Baby B was adjudged strong enough and weighing enough—almost five pounds on the butter scales—to be taken to church for a proper baptism. After all, it was possible that the first one didn't take, administered as it was by a non-believer, or so said Hilda. Nevertheless she was now boasting that "Me and the doctor, we pulled that baby through." Also, she was saying that the birth weight of the infant was "just a little over a pound". It made a better story.

And by now it was time that Baby B become Beatrice officially, a name which Mamma had chosen months before but which had not seemed fitting for a tiny creature which had such an untimely beginning.

The Little White Church on the Farm

IT was during one winter in the mid-1890's that my grandfather lost his footing and fell into a dug well on the family farm. As he struggled to keep his head above the icy water, he promised the Lord that he would build a chapel if he got out alive. It took some doing on the part of both man and horse to make the rescue but it was God who got the chapel. When we were children it was still in good shape, a proud reminder of Grandpa's determination to keep his word even though he had made it under duress. And it was also a reminder of the substantial aid given by his schoolteacher brother from his salary of $20 a month.

The chapel he built wasn't very large, perhaps 25' by 12" but it was every inch a church, with two arched windows on either side and a narrower gabled section at one end for the altar. At the other end over the entrance, there was a steeple, a bell and a cross. It was painted white and had two steps leading up to the doorway; on one side there was a churchyard with lilacs and flowers and on the other, a row of maple tress—all of which Grandpa had lovingly planted and tended.

Grandpa was great on prayer and meditation even when the weeds were high in the cornfields and the pasture fences were in need of repair. It had been his dream that some day, Holy Mass would be celebrated in his chapel but a special blessing by the Bishop was a prerequisite so it never served as a public house of worship. Instead he used it as a kind of private prayer closet, also as a fitting place to teach his children their catechism. And when his brother Philip was on vacation, the two played church liturgies, the teacher on the organ and Grandpa on his violin. Some of their music books, with four rather than five lines to a staff and square notes, were stored in our attic until Mamma threw them out as a fire hazard.

Grandpa rang the steeple bell three times each day for Angelus but no farmers in the neighborhood were ever known to stop their work and bow their heads in prayer. Instead, since few of them had watches in those days, the tolling of the bell meant it was time to eat. Grandpa, however, took the ritual very seriously. As my mother reported, he often kept the family waiting while he rang the bell and recited the prescribed prayers every day, rain or snow. He didn't insist that others join him there—Mamma's explanation for that was "Well, somebody had to put the food on the table!"

Inside, the chapel was as churchlike as space would permit. Grandpa had a talent for tools and a passion for gilt paint so the altar was very ornate. Above the tabernacle there was a sizeable hand-carved figure on a wooden cross, flanked by candlesticks and flower vases in descending order. During his lifetime he kept fresh bouquets on the altar in spring and summer and sprigs of cedar and artificial flowers during the fall and winter. In the churchyard there were two clumps of bridal wreath, red and pink rosebushes, peonies, iris and lilies of the valley. Mamma said it was a pity he didn't plant some sunflowers also as their seeds made good chicken feed.

Inside the tabernacle there was a chalice which we thought was pure gold and which we boasted about at school to counter the bragging by other kids about Model T Fords. On each side of the main altar, there was an elaborately carved, gold-tinted niche which enclosed a statue, the one for the Virgin Mary, the other for St. Joseph. In Grandpa's time, votive candles were burned frequently in thanksgiving for past favors and perhaps also, in the hope that more would be forthcoming.

There was no chimney, hence no heat in winter. I think

that the very thought of a plain old heating stove, and stove-pipe rising to the vaulted ceiling offended Grandpa's sense of decorum but he did not let Northern Michigan winters cool his religious fervor which peaked at Christmas time. All the fuss about Santa Claus and reindeer and presents he considered a lot of hokum.

His nativity scene was set up at the end of Advent and not taken down until Ash Wednesday. As a child I remember seeing the miniature stable with the infant on a bed of real straw; surrounding the creche was a coverlet of white cotton batting and I felt sorry for the new-born baby whose scanty clothes seemed not enough to keep Him warm as I shivered in the chill chapel. When Lent started, the figures were stored away and the altar was draped in black, symbolic of the sin and sorrow in the world.

For sin at least, there was a remedy and our little church had a confessional which for lack of space could accommodate only one sinner at a time. The prescribed number was two, one on each side of the compartment where the father-confessor held forth. Ours had one advantage over the real thing as in the two-sided arrangement, the penitent making his confession might be overheard by the penitent on the other side, especially if the priest was a little hard of hearing and kept saying, "Speak up, speak up!" That happened to a girl cousin who overheard her young brother blaming her for all his misdeeds, "She made me steal cookies, she made me forget my prayers, she made me tell lies"—male excuses which have been used since the time of Adam in the Garden of Eden!

There was a short altar rail and an attached communion cloth which could be flipped over just like the one in our church in town. There was no pulpit but there was a sanctuary light with a red glass globe and there was flowered carpeting in the altar area. There wasn't much room for pews, there were only four but they had kneeling benches (no cushions) and to the rear on one side of the door was a small parlor organ and on the other a large holy water font.

It was not until after Grandpa's death that we began to play church in his chapel. He would have considered it a sacrilege which perhaps it was, but Mamma said that somebody might as well get some good out of it. She had come to the farm as a bride and would have much preferred to find a pump in the kitchen to a church in the dooryard.

Papa wasn't so sure that making a playhouse out of what was meant to be "God's House" was a proper use of the edifice. However, on being reminded that it had never been blessed by the Bishop, he relented on two conditions: we were not to light any candles and we were not to ring the steeple bell which might bring the neighbors running, thinking there was a fire or some emergency.

The windows were not of the stained glass variety and this, we thought, was an oversight. A real church should have pictures in color on its windows so we set to work with our crayons. The glass didn't take the color very well but our figures, inspired by pictures in the Bible History, were very imaginative. When Papa noticed them, he made us wash them off as he said it looked like we were making fun of holy people.

Mostly however, Papa did not bother us very much. He didn't spend time in the chapel the way Grandpa had done but he seemed to feel that tending the land and the animals was also in the service of the Lord, a feeling wholeheartedly shared by Mamma who was anxious to get the farm free of debt. She thought the playhouse idea a good one, especially on rainy days when she was trying to get the baby to sleep. And as she often said, "Children grow up soon enough to a world of toil and trouble, let them have their fun and playtime while they can!"

To give a realistic rendition of the Mass was rather difficult as we lacked the vestments. Carl, of course, was usually the priest—no thought was ever given to the proposition that a female could ascend to so high a rank. But this policy presented a problem since any outfit we girls could rig up made him look like a girl he said. Vainly we tried to get him to wear a flowing garment which we found in an old trunk, but he finally consented to use a fringed shawl with his overall legs showing. There was also the problem of providing an altar boy to serve the priest and ring the offertory bell.

When our cousin, Albert, came to visit, we considered him a godsend both because he was of the right gender and he knew Latin since he was an altar boy in the parish church. He could intone the Mass with genuine artistry, the phrases rolling off his tongue in splendid Gregorian Chant fashion. "Dominus Vobiscum" called for a response from the choir but since we had no choir, he performed that function also in a higher tone of voice, "Et cum spiritus tuo."

What was more, he had a wonderful theatrical sense and he didn't mind wearing the fancy outfit which Carl scorned. And not only was his chanting superior to Carl's whose phrases were "Shu-be-gosh, shu-be-gosh, shu-be-gosh" sounding more like Chippewa profanity than church liturgy, but Albert's sermon topics were more diversified. He could discourse on anything from Angels to Zachariah whereas Carl preached almost exclusively about hell in the hereafter. Our cousin's experience as an altar boy gave him a big advantage and Carl resigned himself to providing the props including a sauer kraut barrel for the pulpit and a gilded salmon can for a censer.

But despite their differences, they were agreed on the basics—in church matters boys were better qualified than girls, also that Catholics had God on their side. I remember a neighborhood fist fight once in which my brother and cousin cheered on one of the boys, yelling, "Lick him, lick him. You can do it 'cause you're baptized and he isn't!" Christening didn't count—it had a distinctly Protestant sound.

As we girls were given to understand, the lost souls were all those from the Bolsheviks to the Chinamen with Protestants and Jews somewhere between. To me it seemed a little unfair that, since our missionaries hadn't gotten to all the Chinese yet, the latter should be lumped together with the Bolsheviks who had the right religion once but now were godless heathens. Calling somebody a Bolshevik, of course, was the worst possible insult just as "Communist" is often considered today.

In addition to the Masses and the sermons, the administering of the sacraments were frequently scheduled. Since there was no Latin involved, Carl was just as good as Albert or maybe better in this department. Insofar as baptism was concerned, it was merely a matter of pouring water on the head of the infant and pronouncing the prescribed words. Since Mamma wouldn't allow us to practice on the baby, a doll could be substituted.

However, I would never permit my doll, Marjorie, to be subjected to the ordeal as she had real hair and I was afraid that water, even holy water, would take out the curl. My sisters' dolls were less vulnerable as they were wigless and when wrapped in a blanket, their deficiencies, like missing limbs, were not noticeable.

I didn't know what Methodists did in regard to Original Sin but whatever it was, I was sure it was incorrect and I was worried about the soul of my doll's namesake. The live Marjorie was one of the daughters in a Protestant family where Mamma had been a mother's helper before her marriage. She was six or seven years older than I was, and she had all the attributes of an angel—beautiful long auburn curls, heavenly blue eyes and she read us stories in a lively lilting voice. I couldn't bear the thought of her going to hell so when a marvelous opportunity presented itself one day when she was visiting us, I took advantage of it.

We had a rain-water cistern whereas in town there was only hard water from the tap as I heard the grown-ups say. I therefore suggested, with well-intentioned aforethought, that Marjorie wash her hair in our nice soft water. With the wash-bowl on a stump in our back yard, she lathered her hair with Ivory soap and when it came time for the rinse, I got a dipperful of warm water from the reservoir in the kitchen range and poured it slowly over her head. Unbeknownst to the young Methodist, I pronounced the saving words under my breath. It made me feel very accomplished to have provided for the salvation of my idol with so little effort. Earlier I'd had some misgivings about good Protestants going to hell but Carl had convinced me that it happened all the time.

Baptism required little in the way of priestly expertise but when it came to the Sacrament of Penance, Carl was very inventive. Being older, he had already had some experience, so we girls assumed that he was well versed in this particular ritual. According to him, the regulations called for a stick to be thrust through the grill which separated the priest from the sinner and if the sin being confessed was a minor one, only a light poke was called for; however, if it was a mortal sin, a really powerful jab had to be administered, all in the interest of being absolved from serious sin. As I recall, he pronounced most of our misdeeds "mortal."

In addition to the jab with his stick, the sinner was given a penance—the lightest one being three Our Fathers and three Hail Marys. Often it was a rosary or the Stations of the Cross, but the worst penalty was to be locked under the altar, crowded in with the Lenten shrouds, the paper flowers and some mouse traps. Once, I remember, Carl carried a younger sister kicking and screaming and pushed her headlong into the cubby hole, not as a penance but because she had gotten into the communion wafers and eaten them all. That got back to Papa who said he'd padlock the chapel door if it ever happened again. It didn't.

In the celebration of the Catholic Mass, the priest drinks a little wine but alcoholic drinks were never permitted in our household—Mamma had been thoroughly indoctrinated against the Demon Rum during her stay with the Methodist family. It was probably the church ritual which Carl had in mind when the Blue Law lady was visiting Mamma one day. The subject under discussion was Prohibition, the most controversial issue of the time.

After listening to the adult conversation for a few minutes, Carl who was then about eight years old interrupted the visitor with a loud-spoken challenge, "I'll bet I can drink more wine-beer than you can!" Apparently he thought that by linking beer with wine, the challenge would be doubly shocking. It was, and after an awkward silence, the good lady made a stiff departure. Mamma never scolded us when guests were present but I have a clear recollection that Carl was reprimanded severely later.

During the chapel service Carl made it a point to drink liberally of the altar wine which was sometimes cider but usually just plain sugar water; however we girls were given only communion wafers. In place of unleavened bread he used apples, radishes, turnips or raw potatoes sliced thin on a sauer kraut board. From the golden chalice he lifted the small white discs and placed them on our tongues after making sure that our eyes were closed and our hands folded in prayer on the communion cloth. Once he served us rounds of horse radish and then upbraided us for spitting out Jesus!

Then there was the Sacrament of Confirmation which required the good offices of a Bishop. Carl had not yet been confirmed when he first tried it out on us but, as always, he had heard enough about it to come up with an imaginative performance. The "swat" from the bishop seemed to be the high point of the ceremony as far as Carl was concerned. As officially administered, the swat was only a light tap but Carl always gave a resounding enactment of "the laying on of hands." Also he got to wear a tall, stiff hat which we made out of cardboard and colored red. Carl didn't care for flowing robes but the mitre was impressive and couldn't be construed as being feminine.

The thing we liked best about this sacrament was that the person being confirmed got to choose another name, that of a saint who would be one's spiritual guardian forever after. I don't think we gave much thought to the guardianship angle but it was great fun to be able to select one's own name, almost like being another person and being able to live a more eventful life. Even my brother was not happy with the "Carl Gervase" which was on his baptismal record. Papa had wanted to name the first-born in the family and promised Mamma that she could name all the rest which she did. However, she tacked Gervase onto the Karl and substituted a "C" for the German "K". Carl would never admit that he had a middle name!

Carl confirmed himself and I don't remember his replacement for "Gervase" but I well recall my choice for a more pleasing name—Mary Magdalen, altogether different in spelling and sound from that of my sister. It had a lovely roll to it but Papa said it wasn't a nice name and he didn't think the Mary Magdalen of the Bible History was a saint.

The sacrament of Matrimony required something special in the way of costuming, at least for the bride. Mamma used a large piece of mosquito netting to drape over the baby carriage during outdoor naps so we could borrow that for the veil. We tried to schedule our weddings for June as that

was when the bridal wreath was in bloom and it was a simple matter to make a crown of the delicate white blossoms to hold the veil in place.

A long dress plus some high-topped, high-heeled shoes completed the bride's attire. Lacking a male to be the groom as Carl was needed to perform the ceremony, we had to "make do" with a girl in overalls. And as for the wedding band we used a ring left behind by Aunt Rose with its set turned inward. Instead of rice there was always wheat in our granary—rice cost money at the store.

We never got around to Holy Orders which has to do with the ordination of priests. For one thing it called for an all male cast and in a family with only one boy old enough to qualify, it wouldn't have been very practical. Also, Carl figured that it would probably take a pope to handle an ordination and although he was brash, I don't think he ever saw himself that high up in the hierarchy. We had a picture of Pope Benedict on the wall in our living room and since popes were supposed to have extraordinary powers, I think Carl was content to leave well enough alone.

Extreme Unction, the rite for the dying, was another matter. The terminally ill patient simply lay down on one of the pews and the priest anointed her with oil—olive oil as Mamma always kept a bottle of it on hand, not for gourmet cooking but for diaper rash. Once, I recall, while Carl was reading the prayers for the dying and vigorously applying the oil, the supposedly comatose patient let out a shriek and a lively, "Get your finger out of my eye!"

Usually, however, the terminal case was content to pass away quickly so that we could get on with the funeral which provided a little more action. For the casket Carl made an oblong box out of some old packing crates and although it was far from air-proof, he made some augured holes in the sides just in case more air was necessary when the lid was made secure with shingle nails. Nailing down the top he considered important so that the corpse would stay put until the service was over.

Fortunately for me, I wouldn't fit into the coffin without doubling up my legs which meant the cover wouldn't fit on. Thus a younger sister always had to play the role of the deceased and be covered over with the black shroud from under the altar. If there were no fresh flowers to lay on the casket, some paper flowers were used and the holy water which Carl sprinkled on the finished product made something of a mess.

We never had enough mourners for pallbearers so when the blessings and the sprinklings were over, there was nothing to do but pull out the shingle nails and help the occupant to her feet, a little like raising someone from the dead. One time we considered doing a re-enactment of the Lazarus story in our Bible History but playing Jesus, like playing the pope, might be taking things too far. Carl had heard about people being struck dead by lightning for "making like God" and he didn't want to take any chances.

We children spent many creative hours in the chapel before it came to a sad end. On the recommendation of the Parish priest it was moved to the Cemetery near Petoskey where it was to be used for graveside services when the weather was foul. However, before it could be moored to its new foundation it was burned to the ground. The Pere Marquette Railroad was just to the north of the graveyard and it was surmised that someone who was riding the rails had taken refuge under the structure and fallen asleep while smoking.

I hope the hobo made it to Heaven and that for his carelessness, he apologized to Grandpa who surely must be there—after all, Grandpa had faithfully kept his promise when he fell head first into the farmhouse well.

Babies from Heaven

IN our family there was no nonsense about storks delivering babies in a blanket with its corners tucked in their beaks, or about parents finding babies in a cabbage patch. Babies were sent directly by God on the wings of angels and children didn't ask God impertinent questions about the why, when and wherefore.

When the Almighty was pleased, He bestowed babies and other blessings on His creatures here below but when He was displeased, He sent the thunder and the lightning which was His way of telling people to behave. And when God was really mad, He sent tornadoes and earthquakes and even plagues like the terrible flu epidemic in 1918 to punish people for fighting and killing each other in war.

It was Papa who emphasized the celestial origin of various happenings, including the babies which came our way regularly. Mamma was not as imaginative on such matters—she was more concerned about the practical aspects of Heavenly blessings like getting a bolt of outing flannel on hand for clothes to keep the newcomer warm and dry. And as for possible curses from the Creator, it was she who insisted on lightning rods for our house and barn.

She needed no child care and psychology books to teach her what she had learned by early experience. As the eldest daughter in a family of eight, she had mothered babies and young children from the time she was a child herself. And as a teen-ager she worked as a nursemaid in the home of a

well-to-do couple in town in order to be within walking distance of the high school.

During her sophomore year she was left with the full responsibility of caring for her two young charges while their parents went south for several weeks, apparently having no misgivings about leaving their toddlers with a fifteen year-old girl in the dead of winter. For Mamma it meant staying out of school which happened to be at the time that *The Merchant of Venice* was being studied in her English Class and I remember her quoting passages from the play from memory. When her employers returned they showered her with high praises and small souvenirs.

When Mamma expressed concern about making up the lessons she had missed, they did not encourage her to go back to school; instead, they offered her $2.00 a week for her full time services and thereafter they were able to take unencumbered trips frequently. Not that Mamma ever showed any resentment over the interruption of her education—I got the story from Cousin Celia many years later when she happened to notice a small, glass, cherry-decorated hatchet which had belonged to Mamma.

"They chopped off her schooling with that!" Cousin Celia said.

But Mamma didn't seem to think she had been exploited. She often spoke of having been treated like a member of the family and she had enjoyed taking care of the two curly-headed tots and strolling around town with them as if they were her own.

However, she had no intention of mothering other women's children forever and at the age of nineteen she became a farmer's wife. By now her young charges were in school and had outgrown the need for a nursemaid so there were no obstructions put in the way of her leaving her place of employment—besides she had agreed to care for the girls at the farm occasionally. As a wedding present she was given some hand-painted moustache cups and a slightly used Morris chair. Papa didn't have a moustache but the cups looked very pretty on the top shelf of our sideboard and the chair was used for many years.

Two years later Mamma became a mother herself and in the course of the next fifteen years there were seven more pregnancies. She welcomed each newcomer not as a duty but as a blessing from Heaven and I remember taking for granted that babies came mysteriously from the skies just as gifts from Santa Claus came from the North.

Some farm-reared children learn about the birds and the bees very young but such was not the case with us girls. We were always shielded from sights like a pig's throat being slit on butchering day or what took place in the barn when a neighbor brought a cow to be bred. And although Carl was probably younger when he learned about the calves and the colts, he did not attempt to impart such information to his sisters. Perhaps he thought it was a male prerogative to be well informed as to the facts of life and to keep them closely guarded. Instead, he sought to keep us in the dark on the subject. Once when I suggested the possibility that the doctor brought the baby in his satchel, rather than its being brought down from heaven by an angel, he scoffed at that idea, "Naw, a baby couldn't breathe in a satchel, it needs lots of air!"

As a nursemaid in a moderately wealthy family, Mamma had become accustomed to the creature comforts of the day such as running water in the kitchen, a stationary bathtub and an indoor toilet, gas lights in every room, grocery delivery at the door and washer-woman service once a week. It must have been hard for her to revert to rural type living especially insofar as child care was concerned.

In our farmhouse the baby's lower limbs had to be restrained in a pinning blanket to keep them warm in winter and a child of creeping age had to spend most of its waking hours buckled into a high chair because the floors were cold and drafty. Diapers had to be scrubbed clean on a washboard in water heated on the kitchen range, then clothes-pinned to the line in the back yard; in summer that was no problem but in winter, baby garments had to be left for hours to "freeze dry", then transferred to the clothes bars to complete the drying process beside the wood stove.

I don't recall that there was ever any sibling rivalry regarding a newborn—that came later. I remember very little about Madeline's arrival when I was almost two, except that I was allowed to pat her soft skin with olive oil after she was given a bath on Mamma's lap by the open oven door for extra warmth. And when the next little sister was born on my fifth birthday, I assumed that she was my very own present from Heaven, probably first in the order of gift preference. Babies were very lovable except when they cried whereas, when they got older they were often a nuisance.

Whether by design or otherwise, we were all born during the months when Mamma would be free of the garden work and therefore able to give more time to the newcomer. Babies were meant to be loved and fondled and rocked and those who considered them a burden were missing a great deal of pleasure.

There was one neighborhood mother, a dissenter sect-wise, who announced at the annual school picnic that she was not going to have a "big litter", it was too much work and she preferred to put all the brains in one head. However, when her Stevie reached primer-book age, he was at the foot of his class of three and I remarked one evening at the supper table that he didn't even know his ABC's yet. In response Mamma couldn't resist a not so gentle barb, "And he was supposed to have the brains of a whole litter!"

"Sh-sh", Papa interrupted, murmuring something about kids telling tales from home. He didn't like to hurt people's feelings even when they deserved it.

The same mother came to see Mamma after my sister Eileen was born. "How will you ever get any housework done with another baby underfoot?" she asked.

Mamma was never one to worry about a few finger prints on the wallpaper or some dust mice under the beds. Her answer to the question was, "Oh, I can always tie the children to the trees!" We had dozens of trees around our house—maples, poplars and the black walnut variety to say nothing of a large orchard.

"But what if you run out of trees?" was the woman's next question.

"Then we'll just set out some more!" was Mamma's light-hearted response. She always managed to give back as good as she got, if not better.

While there was no thought of interrogating God as to the when, and wherefore of babies, there came a time when God was put on probation. Carl was told to go to the barn and finish up the chores and I was sent upstairs with my sisters several hours before bedtime. A call to the doctor had been made on a neighbor's telephone and we sat huddled in our bed quilts by the window awaiting developments.

The baby had not been expected until after Christmas, as I learned years later, but in late October Mamma began to hemorhage. The doctor came in an "enclosed" car which we could see in the moonlight from our upstairs observation post and he was carrying a satchel.

We could hear doors opening and closing downstairs, we could hear the kitchen pump go into action, we could hear muffled voices and what sounded like moans and we exchanged guesses as to what was taking place. We kept hoping that the doctor would leave so that we could go down to see if there really was a baby—doctors never came to our house at any other time. But still the doctor stayed and stayed.

A couple of hours into our vigil, Papa came upstairs and asked us to kneel down with him and pray that God would let Mamma get well. By now I knew that she must be very sick and maybe she might even die. I knew what death was as when I was four, Papa had lifted me up to see Grandpa for the last time, white and still in his coffin with a rosary in his folded hands. Even my sisters who had not seen death were numbed and silent as Papa tucked us in our beds and told us to go to sleep.

I woke up several times during the night and went to the window, always to find the doctor's car still there. Early in the morning Papa awakened me, saying that he was going to Grandma's house to bring her back to take care of us. I was to get up and get my sisters dressed and give them some breakfast but I was not to let them go into the bedroom where Mamma was.

I tiptoed down the stairs and found the kitchen strangely silent without Mamma bustling about, getting our food on the table and reminding us to get washed and to get our hair combed. By now Papa had left with the horse and buggy for the other side of town and Carl was in the barn trying to do the milking by himself.

My sisters were still asleep so before I called them I went quietly to the door of our parents' room where I could see Mamma in bed, her face white and drawn, her hands folded on the coverlet clasping Papa's black rosary. God had let her die after all our prayers—how could He do that to a person like Mamma and what would we do without her?

And then, although I hadn't made a sound or uttered a word, she opened her eyes. "Don't worry," she murmured weakly. "Just take good care of the children. . . ."

I thought she was leaving us forever and I wanted to cry out "No, no," but I couldn't speak, my chest felt so tight I could hardly breathe.

"I'll be all right." she said, trying to comfort me. "It's just that the doctor wants me to be very quiet, not let anyone sit on the bed. . . ." Her knees were propped up on pillows and she lay perfectly still. "Now you better check the stove, be sure the draft isn't open too much. . . ." And with that she closed her eyes again.

I put some wood in the stove and checked the damper. I put some oatmeal on to cook and set the table. I got my sisters up and helped them wash and dress and all the while they kept asking about Mamma, and wanting to know why they couldn't see her. They complained that the oatmeal was lumpy and that the bread was cut too thick.

Carl came in from the barn and got himself a dish of the cereal I had cooked, poured some milk on it, then left it untouched saying he wasn't hungry and he had to get back to finish the milking. I had never seen him look so scared and I knew how he felt, I wasn't hungry either.

I did the dishes, I scraped the uneaten food into the dog's dish and fed him on the back step, I swept the kitchen floor, I filled the reservoir in the range with water from the soft water pump, I washed the lamp chimneys and I didn't ask Madeline to help with the work—anyway she was busy taking the knots out of Colette's shoe laces. I had to keep explaining that Mamma was very sick and mustn't be disturbed.

I tried to tell them stories but my voice would trail off and I couldn't remember what came next. I got out my cherished box of crayons, not a single one of them broken and let my sisters use them to color pictures. While they were busy I tiptoed to the bedroom door again where I could see that Mamma's eyes were still closed—asleep or dead I didn't know which. If God would let her live I'd never be bad again but if He let her die—well, He'd never get another prayer out of me.

It seemed like hours before Papa got back with Grandma who came bustling into the house as if nothing was wrong. In her arms she had a big sack of oranges and she said, "There's one for each of you and the rest are for your mother."

That sounded hopeful but when Papa came in after putting the horse in the barn, he went straight to the bedroom and when he came out he looked as if he'd been crying and I was not reassured.

Grandma busied herself making coffee and fixing a tray for a sick-room. She peeled an orange and divided it into sections, encouraging us to do the same with ours. Oranges were an almost unknown delicacy in our household as we had canned and dried fruits from our orchard—apples, cherries, plums and pears. When the tray came back empty I forgot my quarrel with God and suddenly got very hungry.

"She's going to be fine," Grandma announced as if her breakfast tray had effected the cure. I then proceeded to enjoy the delicious fragrance and taste of my beautiful California orange.

The next morning Papa led us to the spare bedroom where our dead baby sister lay, a tiny mite almost lost in a long white dress. Again we knelt and prayed with him, this time for the soul of the baby and also to thank God for saving Mamma's life (I privately apologized to God for doubting his good intentions). By now the color was coming back to her cheeks and we were allowed to see and talk to her but not to give her a big hard hug which I wanted so much to do.

That afternoon Papa sawed up some clean pine boards and made a box for a coffin. Then he and Grandma went into the bedroom where our dead baby sister was and we heard him nailing on the cover. He carried it gently to the buggy and we watched him drive off with the little coffin on the seat beside him with a flower on the lid. We knew from our catechism that babies who were born dead and not baptized went to Limbo, not the real nice Heaven, a concern which Madeline voiced when she went in to see Mamma. I overheard what she was saying and rushed in to try to keep her from making Mamma feel bad but Mamma had an answer ready, "Our baby's already in heaven and when we get there, she'll be at the door to meet us."

This wasn't strictly according to doctrine but Mamma was never a stickler on the letter of the law if it didn't make common sense. Her words comforted us, easing the pain of thinking of our little dead sister all alone in the graveyard.

By now I was pretty sure that neither an angel nor the doctor was the intermediary in the baby business and Mamma's part in the arrangement was not at all to my liking. And while I still thought that babies were nice after they got here, I wanted God to keep the rest of them for Himself.

Several years went by and it seemed that God was complying with my prayers but then one day, in great excitement, Madeline announced that we were going to have another baby and that she had the proof.

I pooh-poohed her assumption even after she showed me her "proof"—a dresser drawer full of baby clothes in the spare bedroom. "They're prob'ly for Aunt Rose's baby," I told her. Another cousin had been born in Grand Rapids three or four months before.

"Then how come Mamma didn't send the things yet?" Madeline wanted to know.

My sister had a point which I didn't know how to counter and I was worried. We finally agreed to keep an eye on the drawer and see if any new items were added.

Shortly thereafter my secret fear was confirmed when Mamma confided in me that, indeed, there was to be another baby, a boy this time she hoped. She cautioned me not to say anything about it to the younger children as they weren't old enough to understand about such things.

I was flattered that she felt that I was competent to handle this information but I still didn't want to believe it—I preferred to think that it was all a mistake. Mamma was obviously happy about what she had told me so how could I tell her that I didn't want it to be true?

"There's more stuff in that drawer!" Madeline informed me several weeks later. "See, I told you but you wouldn't b'leeve me!"

Now I had still another worry. Mamma would think that I had betrayed her confidence if Madeline let it be known that she was in on the secret and it would be just like her to try to act big! "Naw, I don't believe it," was all I could think of to say.

"C'mon I'll show you," she called, sprinting toward the spare bedroom while I tried vainly to head her off. By the time I reached the dresser, she had pulled the drawer open and I proceeded to slam it shut, smack on a couple of her fingers.

Of course she set up a howl and I was afraid that Mamma

would come running in from the garden so I had to do something quick. I pulled the ring off my little finger, something she'd been wanting, and gave it to her to make her shut up—it was getting too small for me anyway.

"Now don't you dare to say anything to Mamma about this stuff," I cautioned.

"Oh, she knows about it anyway," was Madeline's flip reply after she had the ring securely on her finger.

Mamma did not help with the potato digging that fall. Usually on sunny October days, country school pupils were released from classes at noon-time so they could help with harvesting what was the chief cash crop in our area. That year Papa and Carl did all the digging while we girls picked up the potatoes and carried our pails to the wagon to dump them. It was mid-October, the time that Mamma said the baby was due, and I wrestled with the fear that something would again go wrong.

It was mid-afternoon of our very last day in the field and as we neared the outside cellar entrance with a full load of freshly dug potatoes, Mamma beckoned to Papa from the back step. After a few words with her, he directed Carl to unhitch the team and take them to the barn and then to harness the buggy horse, Topsy, while he went to a neighbor's house to use the phone.

I was standing on the rear of the wagon and the horses, apparently sensing the change of command, pulled forward abruptly under the wire clothesline which caught me under the chin and toppled me to the ground. I thought my neck was broken but I knew it was no time to make a fuss—the signal was what I had feared so I pretended my neck didn't hurt. Papa told me that Carl would be taking us girls to the house of one of Mamma's friends where her teen-age daughter would be looking after us—it being too early to send us to bed he must have figured.

I was humiliated. While I was being brave about my neck, I was being treated like a child. Here I was, eleven years old, I knew about babies and where they came from and I was to be "looked after!"

"Let me stay," I begged. "I'm old enough to help."

Papa seemed shocked. "No, no, it's no place for a girl your age."

Mamma, who had been spreading a layer of newspapers on the mattress of her bed, settled the matter. "Of course you're old enough to help, but the way you can help the most is to go with the children. They'll be upset being away from home and it'll make me feel better if you're with them."

Carl drove us to the house of Mamma's friend and took her back to the farm as Mamma had arranged beforehand. Poor old Hilda couldn't see very well any more and wasn't able to take care of neighborhood birthings, not even to assist the doctor.

As Mamma had foreseen, my sisters were not happy with the turn of events. The teen-ager's idea of amusing us was to do some popular dance steps and sing some silly songs. Who in the world cared about "Yes, we have no Bananas" and "Sleepy Time Gal" when a mother might be dying? To make matters worse, she didn't offer us anything to eat and I didn't like to mention the matter. I wasn't hungry myself but the two younger sisters fussed and fretted until they fell asleep, Eileen in my arms and Colette leaning against my knees, while Madeline stood watch at the window.

"Please, God, let Mamma live," I prayed secretly, refraining from making any threats for the time being.

"I think there's a buggy coming down the road an' I bet it's Carl," Madeline yelled as she dashed out of the house. It was already dark but she was right—there was a buggy and it was Carl coming to get us.

It was she who broke the news as she came rushing back "See, I told you, I knew we were having another baby an' you wouldn't b'leeve me. And it's a boy, Carl says it's a boy!"

Indeed, Carl was so cocky about the advent of a brother at last that I knew Mamma must be all right. I could finally relax and think about my neck but by now it had almost stopped hurting so I knew it couldn't be broken.

Giles was the last-born in our family but if there had been more babies, Mamma would have welcomed them just as she welcomed her grandchildren when they began to arrive. Her love of babies was truly a gift from heaven.

Requiescat in Pace Aeterno

PAPA didn't drink, he didn't smoke, he didn't chew, he didn't cuss, nor did he cast a covetous eye upon his neighbor's wife. However, he did waste quite a lot of time going to funerals, even those of people he didn't know very well. Especially if the deceased person had no family and there would likely be few if any mourners, Papa would be sure to be there.

In his opinion every human being, whether saint or sinner, farmer or townsman, rich man or poor man—even a Protestant!—deserved one last hour of respect and a fair hearing at the Seat of God. There were some unfortunates, Papa said, who had been lacking in opportunities to do good in the world and had therefore never been appreciated and these poor souls especially needed some recommendation to carry with them on Judgment Day.

Mamma had a different slant on things. If she had time and energy to spare, she turned toward the living, that is, the *deserving* living. But if opportunities were squandered, if there was cheating or drunkenness or woman-chasing, she said "Good riddance!" And if there was laziness or gossiping or uppityness, she shed no tears.

Only in case of a funeral would Papa deign to go inside a Protestant Church. Perhaps he thought that those who had not embraced the one true faith would need special intercession with Peter at the Gate of Heaven. Or perhaps he hoped that the family and friends of the deceased would be edified by his concern for the dead and eventually come to see the light. At any rate he would make that one exception, he would attend the burial services in a non-Catholic House of Worship.

Mamma didn't think that so much funeralizing was necessary. It was right and fitting to be present at the burial rites of kith and kin or of close friends but it was wasting time and prayers to attend those of every Tom, Dick and Mary within driving distance for a horse. Especially when it looked like rain and the hay was ready to be hauled into the barn, especially when an October freeze was threatening and there were potatoes to be dug and apples to be picked, it was folly for him to neglect his duties at home for what was really none of his business.

But, being a practical person, Mamma apparently decided that wasting time at a funeral was less objectionable than spending time—and money—in a saloon, to say nothing of the principles involved. Accordingly, on the day of the services she would lay out his Sunday suit which was black, make sure he had a freshly ironed shirt, and shave the back of his neck for him. Even though it was only a week-day, Papa believed in showing deference to the dead.

Insofar as the station in life of the deceased was concerned, Mamma didn't see much to choose between banker and bum, neither of which in her opinion had done an honest day's work in his life. It was before there was such a thing as organized public welfare and she was thinking in terms of the tramps who rode the rails into Northern Michigan during warm weather and asked for hand-outs whenever they got hungry. Some there were, who said they felt too weak to split wood or dig fencepost holes until they got something to eat. But then, after being generously fed, they took off down the road at a good clip whistling jauntily as they disappeared.

Even worse were the money lenders who produced nothing but profited mightily on the misfortunes of the farmers and the bluecollar workers. They sat behind their polished desks and twiddled their pencils and swiveled their chairs while deciding to say "yes" or to say "no." And it angered her that these "white-collared bums" were able to rise high in the world. As Cousin Celia, quoting some old-timer, had said,

"Steal a ride on the railroad, six months in jail. Steal a railroad, six years in the Senate!" And to this day, it does seem as though the peccadilloes of the rich are more excusable than the lapses of the poor.

A case in point was that of a grocer turned money-lender who became a pillar of the church. He had started out as a humble storekeeper in a finger-smudged white apron and a pencil behind his ear. In those days the grocer rushed back and forth behind the counter while the customer stood idly by, reading items off a list. From scooping sugar out of a barrel into a paper sack and using a long-handled claw to topple down a package of yeast cakes from the top shelf to adding up the prices on a little pad with a carbon sheet between the pages, the grocer earned his living the hard way.

But one does not climb high on the economic ladder by bagging up groceries. Instead of working to make money, the thing to do was to make his money work for him. So the grocer sold his business and instead of having to get up early in the morning to sweep out the store, he could keep bankers' hours and sit in starched collar splendor and collect interest on his loans—loans which had been needed to buy grass seed for spring planting or to pay for a casket for an aged parent.

The rate which Mr. Money Lender casually mentioned was 7%—a rate which sounded reasonable enough unless the borrower realized that the interest was for three months, not twelve. Apparently Mr. M.L. figured that the applicants were either dumb or desperate—or both and those who complained were Bolsheviks, the old name for Communists, and were therefore poor credit risks.

The farmer who owned a good team of horses and who didn't ask obnoxious questions usually got a loan and if he couldn't pay off his debt in ninety days, he could add the interest to the principal and sign another note. But woe to the farmer who failed to show up at the designated time—his horses which had served as collateral would be "possessed" by the sheriff.

Mamma was not amused when Papa announced that he was planning to attend the funeral of Mr. M.L. and she had more than generalities as a reason for being annoyed. She had always made sure that our debts were paid on time even if it meant going without eggs for breakfast or without chicken for Sunday dinner, but she was not to be tricked into paying the same debt twice.

In those days few if any small farmers or day laborers had checking accounts; they paid their bills with cash or with produce or they worked off their debts. Anyone who was trustful or careless enough to fail to ask Mr. M.L. for a receipt or who misplaced it later, might find himself in default. The money-lender seemed to have a special faculty for picking out the losers.

However, his antennae did not alert him to Mamma's vigilance and when she confronted him with the carefully kept receipt, he scratched his head in great puzzlement and sputtered, "That's my handwriting all right—I don't see how I could have made such a mistake."

To this Mamma could not resist one of her verbal jabs, "I've noticed that the mistakes you make are all in your favor!"

"You shouldn't have talked to him that way," Papa remonstrated when she told him later what she had said. "Anyone can make an honest mistake."

"Honest, fiddlesticks! And to think a man like that passes the collection basket in church." Knowing how strongly Mamma felt about Mr. M.L., it took courage for Papa to announce his plan to attend the funeral. "Do you think you can pray him out of hell?" she wanted to know.

"If he's done wrong, that's between God and him," was Papa's reply.

"Well, I wouldn't put it past him to try to put one over on God," Mamma sniffed.

"Don't forget he helped us out a couple of times when we were short on cash," Papa reminded her.

"Humph, it wasn't out of the goodness of his heart, he had his eye on the interest he would get."

"But he's always been generous to the church!"

"Trying to buy his way into heaven," Mamma retorted. The discussion was spirited and although I thought Mamma had the best of the argument, Papa went to the funeral.

"The church was full," he told Mamma when he got back

but apparently Mamma thought enough time had been wasted so she merely let him know that she had mended his overalls while he was gone.

After the funeral the story went around that when Mr. M.L. arrived at the Gates of Heaven with his money bags in tow he was turned over to the devil who didn't want him in hell either. The matter was finally settled by putting the money-lender under a big iron, hog-butchering kettle to keep him from falsifying the devil's books. Mamma may have had something to do with the tale.

Mr. M.L.'s body had lain in state in a "funeral parlor," a new concept in our area. Ordinarily when there was a death, a spray of flowers tied with a lavender ribbon was hung on the front door of the home of the deceased. The coffin was placed in the parlor, if the best room in the farmhouse could be called that, and it was flanked by candles which were kept burning day and night.

There would be a round-the-clock "watch" which might go on for three or four days if there were kinfolk to come by train.

There was no such thing as "visitation" hours. The women came by day to pay their respects and to bring food for the family, also sandwiches and cookies for the men who came by night.

Papa considered the "watch" to be a time for prayers for the departed soul and as time for contemplation as to the briefness of life on earth and the lengthiness of eternity. If there was conversation it should be hushed and should deal with the good deeds of the deceased and if there was a sparsity along that line, there could be talk of decorous matters such as the weather, the crops, or the low price of farm produce compared with the high price of town-bought necessities. His presence was usually enough to keep the social interchange on an acceptable level but if it began to get out of hand, Papa could always suggest that it was time for another rosary.

Without a kneeling bench and the pew in front to lean against, saying the rosary could be very tiring, especially for anyone who had worked all day in the fields or in the woods. Resting first on one knee, then on the other, then sitting back in a squatting position, some of the wake-watchers tended to try to rush through the Our Fathers and Hail Marys, but when Papa led the prayers, his way was to intone the words with feeling and reverence. "He drags out the prayers just like a Protestant preacher," someone was heard to say behind his back one time.

As the night wore on and the refreshments ran low, the men began to leave as weariness overtook them. But Papa usually stayed on to keep the vigil and to make sure that there were always candles burning until the family was astir and ready to take over the watch. He would then hurry home to help with the barn chores and to get a few hours of sleep before going to the fields to work.

"One ten-hour stretch is enough" Mamma would say as Papa prepared to leave for another night of prayer and contemplation. "You need some rest."

But Papa would only shake his head wearily and say, "Our turn will be coming soon enough and others will be keeping watch for us."

On the morning of the funeral itself, there was no time for a short nap, barely enough to get the chores done, eat a quick breakfast and change clothes. Sometimes Papa was asked to be one of the pall-bearers, an honor which he gladly accepted even though he was tired and groggy. Helping to carry a heavy coffin up and down the long flight of steps at the church was not easy task.

A horse-drawn hearse or a farmer's rig would lead the procession of mourners from the farmhouse into town. This was continued for some time during the bad weather months even after there were motorized "coffin-wagons", as it was before the day of highway maintenance crews on our county roads. Those who had cars put them up on blocks during the winter rather than taking a chance in getting stranded in a snowbank or getting stuck in the mud caused by a spring run-off. The mourners in their good clothes did not relish having to extricate a gasoline-powered vehicle while their horses were in their stalls doing nothing.

As the cortege neared the church, the bells began to toll in slow and measured tones, a sorrow-laden sound which Papa

said was to remind the living that death was the fate of all creatures, none were spared the passage from dust to dust.

As a child I remember wondering why, if Heaven were as wonderful as it was supposed to be, there should be so much sadness about death—that is, if the person who had died had gone to Mass every Sunday, said his prayers and not eaten meat on Friday!

The flowers were usually roses and carnations from the florist even though there were garden varieties at home, but floral offerings were not taken into the church. It was as if to say that the time for earthly considerations is over, it is now time for the reckoning with God. The soul had taken flight from the body and now must stand in the dock alone and undefended facing eternal judgment—a judgment from which there could be no appeal.

The Requiem High Mass was sung in Latin in those days and although the literal meaning of such phrases as "Dies Irae, Dies Illa" may not have been generally known, the Lord's mood was made clear by the somber chords issuing from the great pipe organ in the balcony and the mournful chants. God, although merciful, was not to be trifled with and He had the last say.

There was seldom much of a eulogy, at least not for simple farm folk. After all, what is there to say, unique or different, about a man who had spent his life tending his fields and caring for his livestock, a man who had been faithful to his wife and good to his children? What was there to say about a woman who had borne many babies, been obedient unto her husband (at least fairly obedient) and who had worked long and hard to keep the home fires burning? What was there to say except that they were good, god-fearing men and women and may they rest in peace, Amen.

And as for those who had failed to walk in the path of righteousness, the less said the better. Anyway, it was now in the hands of the Almighty who would call upon Satan if necessary.

The cemetery was on the far edge of town and Papa seemed to feel that the last wrenching moment when the casket was lowered into the ground was better left to the family and close friends—also he should really get home so that he could get in a half day's work at least. But if the turn-out for the church service was sparse and it looked as though there would not be enough people to make a respectable showing at the graveside, Papa would try to make it up to the deceased for the poor attendance.

It troubled him deeply that there were some who had practically no one to mourn their passing and bid them a last goodbye. Mamma was more pragmatic, saying, "They'll be too busy getting squared away in the next world to pay any attention to what's going on down here," she would tell him. She was more concerned about the plight of people while they were still alive, that is, if they deserved help—like taking a pot of soup to someone old and helpless. Papa was all for the soup but he also believed in showing respect for the dead. There was one time, however, when he hadn't reckoned on the result of his solicitude.

It was the day of the funeral of a woman who had occasionally been the butt of jokes through the years. It wasn't that she was overly homely, overly fat, overly stupid—

it seemed to be just that she had been overly anxious to catch a husband.

Apparently Papa, who was a girl-shy teen-ager at the time, had been one of the many for whom she had set her cap. Frequently she came to his parents' house in the evening and stayed until after dark, then claimed she was afraid to walk home alone. Papa usually managed to be out of sight and sound by the time darkness fell except for once when he was trapped in the cellar. He had gone down to get a couple of apples to take with him to the barn where he planned to take refuge until she got tired and went home by herself.

But while he was in the cellar, the determined young woman had moved her chair over the trap door covering the stairway so there was no escape for him. A short time later when he failed to respond to her call, she went down with a lantern, there to find him red-faced and cramp-kneed in an apple barrel. He claimed to have fallen into it, so the story went, but just how a person could fall into a barrel right side up, he was unable to explain. But a bruised knee gave him the excuse he needed for being unable to walk her home.

It may have been to atone for his youthful lack of human kindness, but he always defended her when anyone made jokes about her. "Never make fun of people," he would say. "There's nothing that hurts more—a wound to the heart is worse than a punch in the nose."

There were only a few people at the church for her funeral service. She had taken care of her aged parents until they died and she had no living sisters and brothers, only one young niece. But with never a man to help with the farm work and with never a penny of charity or public welfare, she had managed to get by somehow and had enough money in the bank to pay for her own burial expenses. She was not without ambition or the willingness to work.

There were even fewer to accompany the coffin to the cemetery so Papa, with his usual concern for the friendless, decided to follow the hearse with his horse and buggy.

Since he was alone in his rig, the niece of the deceased woman invited herself to ride with him, saying that she had no other transportation. No doubt this made Papa a little nervous as the girl was not known to be highly principled, also he well remembered the over-forwardness of her aunt. He never liked the appearance of scandal any more than the scandal itself but, under the circumstances, he could not ask his passenger to get out of his buggy and walk. There was nothing that he could do but hope and pray that she was a repented "Mary Magdalen" and that the ride to the cemetery would not attract any unwanted attention.

Papa had quite a reputation for his way with horses. He had "broken in" colts without breaking their spirit; he had soothed twitching mustangs and tamed them to harness; he had sewn up gashes in horses' hides made by barbed wire fences; he had thrown himself in front of another man's runaway, grabbed the bit and hung on until the frightened creature came to a halt. Daisy, the horse he was driving the day of the funeral had once been involved in a bolt off the road and a buggy upset but Papa had never had any trouble with her.

Perhaps on this occasion, Daisy sensed his unease over the uninvited passenger or perhaps she resented having to follow close behind the motorized hearse with its trail of exhaust—at any rate, shortly after leaving the church and while going through the main part of town, she took off "like sixty" charging past the hearse scraping its ornamented side panels with one of the buggy wheels. And there was Papa, standing in his rig, holding onto the reins trying vainly to get his horse to heed his desperate "whoas" and there was the girl hanging onto his coat-tails for dear life.

Poor man, not only was his reputation as a fine horse-handler at stake but also his lifelong practice of avoiding even the appearance of wrongdoing. Not being the kind of person to express his exasperation with the horse in profanity, he was probably reduced to using his one non-blasphemous expletive, "You bastard, you!"

As I recall the story, which Mamma had pieced together from several sources and perhaps added a few details, (all of which she found very amusing although she wisely refrained from relating the tale in his presence), he did not attend the graveside prayers that day. When he finally got Daisy under control, he proceeded to the cemetery gate where his passenger was left to await the coming of the hearse by herself. And not wishing to go back through town where his record of horse savvy and virtue had been put at risk, he hastened homeward by a somewhat circuitous route.

No doubt Mamma hoped that this chastening experience would cure him of his passion for funerals but that was not to be. He merely became more cautious about attending them by himself and thereafter, he usually took along one of us children to lend respectability in any situation which might arise.

Adjoining the cemetery was the Emmet County Poorhouse as it was then called and I well remember some of Papa's homilies as he contemplated the fate of the old and forgotten paupers who were spending their last years in that godforsaken place. Why should it be, he would say, that anyone should have to live as outcasts with no home to call their own? Better to die working in the fields, in the heat of the sun or in the woods in the winter cold, than to be dumped off in the Poorhouse like a bag of shucks after the beans have been shelled. Better to starve in a shack which is his own than to be treated like a stray dog with his tail between his legs, begging for food.

Once as we stood quietly as a distant relative was being lowered into his last resting place, I noticed one of the old Poorhouse men peering through the fence, clasping the pickets with fingers so bony they looked like overlong claws. Papa saw him, too, and as we left the graveyard, he shook his head sadly, saying, "Poor old fellow, he's probably wondering if there'll be anybody to come to his funeral when the time comes."

There was a catch in his voice and I saw a tear or two on his cheek. "Is that because he doesn't have any family?" I asked.

"Maybe," Papa answered. "But sometimes young folks put their old parents in places like that to die and then forget them."

I wanted to tell Papa that we would never do that to him and Mamma but somehow I couldn't find the words so I put my hand over one of his as he held the reins and squeezed it. I think he knew what I meant and we didn't forget him—he died at home on the 16th of September, the very same date of his birth, and in the same room where he had been born seventy one years before. His funeral was well attended.

My paternal grandparents, with children: (l. to r.) Philip (my father), Wilhelm, Rose, Mary and Albert

My maternal grandparents, with children: (l. to r., back row) Walter, Gertrude (my mother), Frank, Bertha and Raymond (l. to r., front row) Flora, Alice, William Coveyou, and Martha

My mother at age 14 (on left) with her sister, Bertha, and aunt, Loretta Devine

My father (on left), logging in preparation for his dream barn

My parents' engagement photograph: Gertrude Coveyou, age 18; Philip Schmitt, age 20

My parents' wedding photograph, June 6, 1906: (l. to r.) Groom Philip, Rose (his sister), Bride Gertrude, and Raymond (her brother)

Wedding photograph after honeymoon, taken in front of the "Little White church on the Farm." (l. to r.) Albert Schmitt, Mary Schmitt ("Sister Philippa"), Grandpa Schmitt, Grandma Schmitt, Papa and Mamma with Aunt Rose between them, and Uncle Philip Schmitt

Beatrice, at age 2½, with Madeline at 10 months, and Carl, age 6

Celia Coveyou ("Cousin Celia," my first teacher). She was Mamma's "double cousin," as her mother and my grandmother, who were sisters, married brothers, Peter and William Coveyou

Unfirm in the Faith

For some unexplainable reason, my sister, Madeline, was different from everybody else in our family. She was always asking questions that were clearly unanswerable which meant they were often sacrilegious. If not sinful, they were merely stupid, like "If one is the first number, what is the last number?" When I ventured to tell her that it was probably a hundred, Carl said I was way off and that it was a million but Mamma said that wasn't right either.

A question like that was bad enough, but when it came to religious doctrine, it was a serious matter, a purgatory or hell matter. Madeline wasn't adopted, according to Mamma, so Carl and I couldn't figure out why she could not get the simplest things through her head, especially about correct Catholic behavior.

Before Mass Papa would give us each a penny to put in the wicker basket with a long handle at collection time, half way through the service.

"Get your money ready to give the man," I whispered to Madeline across Papa's lap one time.

"What's he gonna do with it?" she wanted to know.

"Give it to the priest a-course, dummy," I whispered back.

"What's the priest gonna do with it?" was her next question. By now Papa was motioning to make us both be quiet.

Dutifully I put my penny in the basket but she hung on to hers and the collection man went on to the next pew.

When I tugged at Papa's sleeve to tell him what she'd done, he whispered that she could give her money the next

Sunday but I doubted that she'd do it. She was probably planning to save it for a licorice whip or a stick of gum.

Sometimes, if Papa let me sit next to her, when she'd start to do something sinful like taking off her straw hat in church—girls were supposed to keep their heads covered—I would try to stop her in time. "Keep your hat on," I'd tell her, giving her a nudge.

"The 'lastic hurts—'sides Carl's got his off," she'd say with a sniff.

"That's 'cause he's a boy an' it's not a sin for him, jist for girls," I'd explain.

"How come?" And with that she'd pull off her hat and throw it on the seat and I'd give her a little kick and tell her to put it back on. Then she'd tell Papa to make me stop kicking her even though I was only doing it for her own good.

"But what if a girl was too poor to have a hat?" Madeline wanted to know after church when Papa said it was a matter of showing respect.

"Then she could use a handkerchief," Papa said.

"But what if she needed it to blow her nose?" That's the way Madeline was, always asking dumb questions, even to Papa.

On the hour-long ride to Mass on Sunday morning, Papa didn't talk to us very much. He didn't like to use the buggy whip so mostly he was urging the horse to hurry so we wouldn't be late for church. But on the way home he would tell us stories or give us little sermons about behaving in the House of God. We must kneel when we were supposed to, we must fold our hands and do our praying and if we had to say something we should whisper; we shouldn't look around and of course we shouldn't laugh at anything.

"But what if it's real funny—Mamma says you're a sour puss if you can't laugh," Madeline told him.

"But not in the House of God," Papa said.

"But if God's everywhere, He's in our house, too, so how come we can laugh there?"

"But church is different," Papa tried to explain.

"Why?" That's the way she talked to everybody, me, Papa, even the priest. We had an awful time with her the day she spotted a ten dollar bill under the kneeling bench. "Look what I found, look what I found!" she exclaimed and she didn't just whisper as she waved it around.

"Sh, sh, we'll take it to the priest after Mass," Papa told her real quietlike.

"But I found it, he didn't," Madeline objected.

"But he'll know what to do with it. It isn't ours, somebody lost it and Father Anthony will find out who it was!"

"I'll keep it 'til he does," Madeline said and it would have taken some doing to get the bill out of her fist without disturbing the whole congregation so Papa wisely waited until the service was over and the churchgoers had dispersed. It then took both Papa and me to talk her into releasing what she considered to be rightfully hers, at least until the true owner was found.

Carl didn't help much—in fact, he was certain that the bill had been dropped by a resorter, who else would be so careless with ten dollars? Resorters were so rich they had money hanging out of their pockets and one bill more or less would make little difference to them. He saw no need to try to find the owner.

"It could have been lost by someone with a big family who needed it to buy groceries," Papa told Carl and to Madeline, he said, "If you're honest and do the right thing, God will reward you."

"When?" she asked, real quick.

Papa didn't have any specific time in mind and specifics were what she wanted. "Just knowing you did what was right is one reward," was all he could tell her.

But that was not enough to satisfy Madeline. I was the one who finally came up with a way to solve the problem—the mention of a reward had put a bee in my bonnet. "I'll bet the owner will give you a big reward himself, enough to buy a walking, talking doll!" The Sears Roebuck catalogue was featuring dolls which said "Ma-Ma" when you squeezed them and walked if you took them by the hand and the price was $1.98 as I remember.

Carl didn't think much of the doll idea, no doubt he had something more to his liking in mind, something like the gun which he had been admiring in the hardware store window.

"I betcha no doll can really talk and walk, things never turn out like they say in the catalogue," he warned. He had been stung several months before when he spent good money on a fishing lure which was supposed to attract big fish like pickerel and pike but when he tried it out in Bowl Mill Creek, he hadn't caught a thing, not even a speckled trout.

I had a few misgivings myself about Papa's course of action. The man in the pew behind us had kept his eye on the bill like a cat on a mouse and maybe he would try to claim the money as he surely must have heard about taking it to the priest's house. But Papa was certain that no church-going Catholic would stoop to such behavior.

Madeline finally became reconciled to the idea of exchanging the bill for a walking-talking doll and Papa handed it over to Father Anthony.

"Now where's my reward," she sputtered.

"I'll announce it from the pulpit and if no one claims it, I'll put it in the Poor Box" the priest told Papa, ignoring my sister, and dashing our hopes.

"I want my ten dollars back," Madeline said, sassy-like.

I think Papa was too embarassed to say anything so I tried to explain matters. "She thinks she should get a little reward," I told the priest.

"Well, yes, she should get something for being honest," Father Anthony agreed. And from a panel on the wall, he selected two rosaries, one a pretty pink, the other one plain white. Of course Madeline chose the pink one and for a moment I thought I was going to get the other one. However, the white rosary was placed back on the wall and I was left empty-handed.

"What's a Poor Box?" Carl wanted to know when we got out on the street. "Seems like we're pretty poor, can't even afford a gun that'll shoot straight. That's why I can't shoot the hawks that're after our chickens!"

"Not until you're twelve," Papa told him. Carl did have a BB gun which an uncle had given him, a gift which had only whetted his desire for something more powerful.

After the novelty of wearing the rosary as a pink necklace wore off, Madeline wanted to take it back and collect her reward in cash so she could buy the doll she wanted.

"Long after you're through playing with dolls you'll have your rosary to comfort you," Papa told her but she preferred what they now call instant gratification and forever after she seemed to blame Father Anthony for bilking her out of the rightful share of her find.

That may have been the beginning of her spiritual downfall. I tried to straighten her out myself rather than tell Mamma and Papa, especially Papa, some of the questions she was asking. I certainly didn't want them to think that she had gotten some of her sinful notions from me—notions like "How's anybody sure the Cathlic Church is the one true Church?" That was one thing she asked me when she was taking instructions in Catechism.

"Because the priest says so, the Bishop says so, the Pope says so, everbody says so," I answered, glaring at her as hard as I could.

"But did God come down and say so?" was her next question.

"Well, in a way He did," I told her.

"How d'you mean, in a way?"

"There's diff'rent ways He could do it," I said, trying to gain time.

"Would He come walking in the door an' say it right out?"

"Oh, no, you can't see God," I hastened to tell her. "He's sort of like your conscience, you've got it, you can't see it but you kin hear it."

"Did the priest an' all them bishops hear Him say it, then?"

"What's the matter with you anyhow, you sound jist like a Protestant, they don't b'leeve what's in the Catechism either!" I answered. One time I'd had an argument with a girl who lived next to my aunt's house in town. She said the Bible was God's true word and the catechism was a bunch of baloney. I took a look at Aunt Bertha's bible then—I heard her say she bought it because the girl's mother claimed that Catholics didn't believe in the Bible—and some of what I read sounded worse than baloney, all about smiting and fighting just like the Kaiser!

"I'll betcha Protestants think they've got the true religion," my sister came back at me.

"Well, they haven't, an' if you keep on talking like one,

you'll end up in hell, too," I warned her. Of course I really didn't want anybody in our family to go to hell, not even Carl in spite of his shortcomings. However, a little purgatory might be good for him and Madeline, too, but not hellfire forever and ever. Once when we were playing Blind Man Buff, I burned the whole back of my hand and it hurt so bad I thought I was going to die. Purgatory was terrible, too, but it was only for a little while.

Even the threat of hellfire didn't seem to bother Madeline—maybe she thought she wasn't in any immediate danger as she hadn't reached the Age of Reason yet. According to Church doctrine, a child was not accountable for sins committed before the seventh birthday.

She still had six months to go before the cut-off point so I was hoping that she could skip Confession since her sins weren't supposed to count anyway, Madeline being only six and a half years old. There was no telling what she'd blab, probably some things that would get me in trouble, too.

But, notwithstanding her age, she was with the other kids in her instruction class the Saturday morning of First Confessions. I was in church, too, six or eight pews back with a group of older children where we were supposed to be examining our consciences. I was on pins and needles—I couldn't put my mind to preparing my list of sins. I was afraid she'd go into the Confessional and make a fool of herself and bring shame to our whole family.

Carl had told me that people who talked like Madeline did sometimes were possessed by the devil and the only way to get rid of him was to have him "exercised." This took a priest and some holy water but somehow it didn't seem like a very safe idea. I imagined the devil running around loose with the priest trying to catch him and douse him with holy water. But what if the priest was big and fat—he'd never make it!

I figured that if Madeline wasn't out of the confessional by the time I counted to five hundred real slow-like, there was trouble ahead. But in no time at all she came out looking okay so at last I could relax and attend to my own affairs.

But my peace of mind was short lived. Shortly after Madeline and the others in her class filed out of church, a fat girl by the name of Gracie came bounding back in a state of great agitation. "Sister, Sister," she gasped as she reached the pew where the Sister Superior was kneeling, "Mad'leen did something turrible, just turrible! She'll have to go to confession again won't she?"

There was no other "Mad'leen" in my sister's class so I knew who was the culprit. Gracie was shushed for talking so loud in church so I couldn't hear the details of Madeline's "turrible" sin but knowing the kind of dumb things she'd said to me, I was prepared for the worst and I suffered mental anguish until I could get the facts.

Gracie was really the culprit as I found out later. What Madeline had done was to reveal her penance, one Our Father and one Hail Mary—no big deal!

"Big tattle tale," Madeline snorted. "She asked me what my penance was so I told her. Then she said she was going to tell on me if I didn't give her my Cracker Jack ring."

It was a clear case of entrapment and this time my sympathy was all with my sister but I had to warn her not to "take out her mad" on Gracie by calling her a mortal-sin-name or she couldn't make her First Holy Communion the next day. We had both learned a few cuss words from Carl who had picked them up outside the family. "Damn" was one of them which was a venial sin but if preceded by "God" was a mortal sin. To go to Communion with a black, black sin like that on your soul would mean hellfire for sure if the horse ran away on the way home from church and you got killed.

"But I betcha there's no such place as hell," she said, and right out loud too, only a few hours after she'd gone to Confession.

"If I tell Papa what you said, he won't let you make your First Communion and wear your new white dress," I warned.

That was enough to shut her up for awhile and the next day she got all prettied in her lace-trimmed dress which Mamma had made over from one of Aunt Alice's long white skirts. She walked up the center aisle of the church with a crown of bridal wreath on her brown curly hair and with her hands folded piously, looking like a little angel, according to Grandma. But if Grandma had known about the things she was saying, she would have called her something else. Grandma had no use for infidels and Protestants.

After the big day was over and my sister had gotten her special presents—a prayerbook with gold letters on the white cover, a frame for her First Communion Certificate and a chain necklace with a cross on it, she fell back into her sinful ways again. "How could a person be on fire forever and ever and not get burned up like a chunk of wood in the stove?" she taunted me, knowing it would get my goat.

"Now, lookit," I said. "You're 'sposed to be a genuwine Catholic now and it's a lot worse for you to talk like that than for somebody who never had a chance to b'long to the one true church. Hellfire's a lot diff'rent from a stove fire, it's bigger and hotter!"

"Then it oughta burn up a sinner faster'n ever," she scoffed.

I couldn't do anything with her so Carl tried his hand at the job, using another tack, telling her she would have to spend eternity with Gracie who had been willing to sell her soul for a Cracker Jack ring. And his description of hell was more fiery than mine—"burning snakes coiled around sinners' necks, red-hot coals stuffed under sinners' eyelids, boiling oil poured down sinners' throats." But nothing seemed to work. Carl and I had both tried to save her from the fate of Catholics like Gracie, also from that of heathens and Protestants, but she just wouldn't listen.

Come to think about it, Carl wasn't always consistent about Protestants and hell. He had a Methodist friend from town who sometimes went hunting with him in our woods. Armed with BB guns they stalked over the hills, tracking big game just like Teddy Roosevelt, they said. They were never able to bag anything except a crow or a squirrel now and then but they claimed to have seen the tracks of wolves and bears. Carl didn't seem to think there was anything wrong with Gene or his religion—in fact Gene was his best friend until the family moved to Detroit.

Once, on one of their hunting expeditions, Gene tore his shirt on a barbed wire fence and was worried about what his mother would say—and do—because he had worn his Sunday shirt instead of the one she had laid out for him.

Carl asked me to sew up the tear so that Gene wouldn't get a licking when he got home, also his mother might never let him go hunting in our woods again. Madeline offered to help and I was glad of that as it didn't seem quite decent for me to do it alone. While I did the stitching, she held the shirt out from his bare back so he wouldn't get stuck with the big needle which was the only one I could thread easily.

Gene was very grateful for our help. Over his shoulder he told us that he liked us much better than the town girls he knew. "Spose they'd help a fella when he's in trouble—naw, they'd just run and tattle first thing!" I wondered if he was thinking of Gracie who lived near his house in town.

After Madeline and I went to bed that night we had a big quarrel. Independently, we had each decided that Gene would make a perfect husband—he had blonde wavy hair, he had a nice smooth face, he appreciated things, he liked farm girls better than town girls and he wore knickers instead of overalls.

"I'm going to marry him," Madeline announced.

"No, I am," I told her. "I'm the one who sewed up his shirt and kept him from getting a licking!"

"But I'm the one who kept him from getting stuck with your fat old needle," Madeline shot back.

"You're too young for him," I reasoned.

"That don't matter. Papa's older'n Mamma," she reminded me.

"But not five, six years—that's way too much," I insisted.

"No, it's not. I said I was going to marry him first so I got dibs on him!"

"He wouldn't want you anyhow, little skinny runt!"

"That's better'n being fat like you!"

"But I can do a lot more things than you can," I told her.

"Like what?" she asked real quick.

"Lotsa things, like sewing up his shirt. You never coulda done that, real neat like I did."

"But I can take knots out better'n you," she claimed. It was true that I often asked her to take knots out of my shoe laces but it wasn't because I couldn't do it myself. She was dumb enough to work at it if I told her she was the best knot-taker-out in the world. She was a sucker for praise.

So it went until a very upsetting thought suddenly struck me. Gene wasn't a Catholic and Catholics weren't supposed to marry Protestants. I wasn't about to endanger my soul, not even for Gene. "Oh well, you can have him, he's a Methodist!"

"I'm not afraid of no Methodist," she scoffed. "I'll marry him anyway."

I was sorry then about removing myself from the running. After all, there was such a thing as turning Catholic and I was quite sure that Gene would oblige, considerate as he was, but I hadn't thought of that in time.

"Go ahead and marry him," I told her. "You'll prob'ly go to hell anyway."

"Well, if Gene's going there 'cause he's a Protestant, I'd just as soon go there, too," she snickered. Just being smartalecky, that's what she was doing.

"I'd hate to be you, burning for millions of years," I told her.

"Who's bad enough to burn that long anyhow," she asked, back to her questions again.

"Lotsa people, like the Kaiser, who go around starting wars," I said. But there was no use in going on with the quarrel. She had reached the Age of Reason and she still wasn't thinking right, probably never would. If Sister Philippa knew what Madeline was really like, she wouldn't be so anxious to make a nun out of her.

Sister Philippa was Papa's younger sister who had gone into the convent when she was a girl and had become a music teacher and a church organist. Everybody said that Madeline was "the spitting image of the aunt that took the veil" which may have been why Sister Philippa was so anxious for her look-alike to follow in her footsteps. During summer vacation when she came to visit us, she nearly always singled out Madeline for special attention even though she was two years younger than I was and didn't know half as many big words and couldn't even carry a tune.

The two would saunter around the yard together, they would sit next to each other at the table, they would spend time in the chapel—no doubt Madeline pretending to be praying hard, too. I had a notion to tell Sister Philippa that my sister wasn't fit to be a nun but in our family we didn't tattle on each other very much—tattling was something which could work both ways. However, had Sister Philippa known about Madeline's heathenish turn of mind, she might have transferred her attentions to someone who was more deserving, someone who was firm in the faith.

Papa's sister was short in stature and although a bit stocky in build, her chubbiness wasn't very noticeable because of the voluminous Dominican garments. The summer that Madeline was twelve, the two were almost the same height and when offered the opportunity to try on her aunt's "habit", Madeline jumped at the chance. Hot though it was that July afternoon, she allowed herself to be decked out in the white serge flowing robes, complete with the stiffly starched frame around her face. Even I had to admit that she looked just like a nun as she came downstairs to primp and preen in front of Papa's shaving mirror in the kitchen.

I was helping Mamma pare potatoes for supper while she was sashaying around the room, showing off how nice she looked. "You'd better get your own clothes back on and help us with the work," I told her. There were always a lot of extra things to do when we had company, like setting the table in the dining room.

Of course she didn't pay any attention to me—she was always good at getting out of her share of helping, and especially when there were guests around I didn't like to make a scene. "I want to go out and see if Papa thinks I'm Sister Philippa—can I use your big prayerbook," she asked Mamma.

"Yes," Mamma told her. "But it's dusty out there where he's cultivating, so don't get too close—it would be an awful job trying to wash and iron that outfit!" Mamma was probably thinking of the flatirons which had to be heated on the stove and were always smudging white things.

"Let's watch and see what happens," Mamma said with a twinkle in her eyes. She liked to play little jokes on people sometimes, but not mean jokes.

For a few minutes Madeline strolled back and forth under the lilac trees, just as Sister Philippa did every afternoon, reading her breviary. Papa continued to cultivate the corn and as he came within good viewing distance of the Dominican clad figure, Madeline began to put on a lively rendition

of the Highland Fling, a dance she had learned from a town cousin.

Poor Papa, aghast at the brazen behavior of a Catholic nun and his own sister at that, was so flustered that in trying to get himself and his team turned around and facing away from the scandalous performance taking place before his very eyes, a part of one of the horse's harnesses got tangled up in some low-hanging branches. While Papa gee'd and hawed and jerked the lines, trying to free the hames from the Maiden's Blush apple tree, Madeline continued to cavort and

Mamma continued to laugh until Sister Philippa came rushing downstairs to retrieve her garments and her reputation.

In recounting the story later, although never in Papa's presence, Mamma considered that the name of the apple tree added an extra chuckle to the tale. The fruit of the Maiden's Blush tree, by the way, was aptly named. It ripened in the early fall and had a delicate ivory colored skin, tinged with pale pink on the side touched by the sun. But like many things which were sweet and innocently funny, that variety of apple seems to have vanished from the fruit tree catalogues.

But Papa didn't think the execution of the Highland Fling was the least bit funny. While it must have been some consolation to him that the dance had not been "kicked" by a bona fide nun, it must have been deeply disturbing to him that one of his daughters had so little respect for the faith of her father that she would put on such an unseemly show of limbs. Even aside from the desecration of the convent robes, the high-kicking fling smacked of dancehall debauchery.

But for me it had a salutary effect as it put an end to the favoritism which had been accorded my sister who had been posing as a likely candidate for the Dominican order just so she could get out of work.

The Great Improvisor

WHENEVER my brother, Carl, got wind of an interesting new invention, he gave serious thought to producing his own version of it or, if possible, an improvement thereof. The airplane which was coming into use by the military during World War I intrigued him greatly but I think he realized that it was a bit beyond his capabilities. There were limited resources at his disposal as well as limited know-how but usually that did not deter him from at least trying to put his fantasies into production. And he did come up with a parachute idea and also a sky ride. But more on that later.

If a device promised to be a labor saver, it had an especially great appeal for him. Milking the old-fashioned way, sitting on a three-legged stool, with the pail held between his legs under the cow's milk-dispensing apparatus was awkward, it was too much work and besides, the cows didn't cooperate with him the way they did with Papa—they were always putting a foot into his pail or worse still, kicking him on the shins. Furthermore it was time consuming and he had other things he could do during the hours saved by a mechanical milker like the one advertised in the farm paper. The milking machine was an idea whose time had come and although he had no money to buy one, he figured he could make one somehow. After all, he was sick and tired of being kicked around by cows.

Not having seen a working model except for the picture, he proceeded with some experimentation which involved clamps and wires and rubber hoses. Unfortunately, however, the perverse creatures strenuously objected to his efforts to force them to release their product the modern way. Even when given the bribe of an extra helping of oats, they refused to oblige.

Not only did they kick with special fervor but they bellowed loud enough to bring Papa running and he was scornful of the new-fangled idea. "No self-respecting cow," he said, "would allow herself to be strapped to such a heartless contraption." As with the tractor, the milking machine was the invention of city folks and what did they know about cows and the care of the land, Papa asked?

As it happened, Carl abruptly abandoned the project, not because of Papa's misgivings but because of the contemptible behavior of Molly, chosen because she was our least feisty bovine. After consuming her bribe of ground oats seasoned with a sprinkle of salt, she had the nerve to pin Carl's head down by thrusting her hind leg over his neck as he tried to buckle a clamp to one of her udder extremities. "Darned cow," Carl muttered. "She tried to kill me!"

But a bean thresher would not be dependent on temperamental females and even Papa admitted that it could serve a useful purpose. After all, wheat and oats and barley were threshed by the grain separator which came rattling thru our neighborhood every August, drawn by a steam engine with mighty-chested Bruno at the controls. So why not beans, especially since they were in great demand at the time?

Urged on by Mamma, Papa had planted several acres of navy beans in 1918. She had been assured in a *Michigan Farmer* article that prices would continue high or even go higher as great quantities of these legumes would be needed to keep the troops well-fed. And although Papa had been unwilling to sell our black walnut trees to the government for gun stocks to kill the enemy, apparently he was willing to sell beans to keep the soldiers alive! Also, beans were his favorite noon-time dish.

Before he died in 1915, Papa's father had threshed beans for the family with a flail, the way it had been done in the "old country" for generations. The well-dried stalks would be spread out on the barn floor and Grandpa would whack away with a tool he had made himself—a stout, round, foot-long piece of wood which swung free on a short length of rope tied to a handle. It enabled the user to work from an upright position and to take advantage of leverage. After the pods were cracked open, they and the stalks would be raked off, leaving the shelled beans to be swept up and then winnowed in the wind.

Carl had watched Grandpa's expert way with the flail and at the age of five or six had tried a mighty swing himself which almost succeeded in cracking open his skull instead. Whether because of that painful experience or because he wanted to supplant "old country" tools with up-to-date labor saving equipment, he decided to build a bean thresher.

Carl had inspected Bruno's grain separator to get the hang of it and promptly came up with a plan for the innards of his machine. First he would make a wood, three-sided tunnel-like box, then pound nails through the top and the sides and these would claw open the pods. Since new nails were not available he would have to make-do with old ones, pulled out of discarded boards, so we girls were set to straightening them out as best we could. Most of them were rusty but no matter, Carl said, they wouldn't poison the beans. As for possible flesh punctures, we hadn't heard of tetanus shots but he told us we could wash out any nail wounds with Fels-Naptha soap.

Next, while he built the frame and fitted it with rollers, one fore and one aft the nail-studded tunnel, I was put to sewing together strips of burlap cut from old potato sacks for the conveyor belt. The theory was that the stalks would be moved forward thru the tunnel on the belt where the pods would be ripped open by the nails, allowing the beans to drop thru the coarse burlap into a container on the floor. For the time being Carl would turn the crank on the main roller by hand but eventually the thresher would be powered by a steam engine similar to Bruno's, which he very much envied.

Supposedly the contraption would turn out beans "to beat the band" but alas, there were several problems. For one thing, it was hard to get the belt tight enough to move readily over the rollers; for another, the bean stalks tended to clog up in the tunnel; and for still another, only about half of the beans fell through the burlap. In other words, nothing worked the way it did in theory.

However, when Papa got around to inspect the thresher, he seemed much impressed by his son's ingenuity and he promised to help make some adjustments as soon as the corn was cut and shocked. Part of the problem, Papa said, was that the bean stalks and pods were not yet bone dry so the operation should be postponed for a few weeks.

Elated by Papa's interest, Carl had visions of becoming the official bean thresher in the neighborhood. Like Engineer Bruno he would become the idol of all the boys and even the girls the country around. And like Bruno, he would stroll back and forth chewing on a wisp of bean straw, holding a stick of resin to the engine belt to keep it from slipping, and checking on this and that. While the threshing crew sweated and sneezed in the hot, dusty barn, he would have a nice, easy but important job. And one in fresh air, of course, for the steam engine with its wood-stoked boiler must be kept several rods from the barn to guard against possible fire. And naturally, he would be first at the wash bench and at the dinner table to say nothing of being able to collect—and spend—the money he would earn.

While waiting for the stalks to get drier, we girls were glad for the respite from the bean business which so far, for us, had been mostly standing around in the chill October weather while Carl made endless adjustments on his machine.

As for him, during the interim he began to give thought to winnowing the beans in a more efficient and modern manner. Grandpa's method had been to lift a pailful of beans shoulder high and slowly pour them into a dishpan on the ground, letting the wind blow away the chaff and dust. Usually the procedure had to be repeated several times, something which Carl considered wasted effort. According to his calculations, if the beans were released from a chute high up in the barn, one winnowing would be sufficient.

The problem of hoisting the beans to the barn scaffold in a time and energy efficient way had not been solved when the Armistice was signed, announced in our area by an hour-long ringing of the big bell in the school belfry.

There had been a bumper crop that year and if the wholesale price were to be what the farm paper had predicted, Carl estimated that the threshing share of the proceeds would enable him to buy a .22 and there should be enough left over for us girls to buy a walking-talking doll. But, as it happened, before we could get the beans to the market, the bottom fell out of it. Farmers couldn't sell their potatoes, much less their beans and that was when Carl lost interest in beans as a career.

For my part I was glad that Papa and all the other fathers were safe from having to fight the Kaiser and since there was no money to buy a doll from Sears Roebuck, maybe Santa Claus would bring one. Besides I was sick and tired of the bean business—tired of waiting around while Carl tinkered on his machine, tired of helping Mamma "look over the beans" which meant separating the saleable ones from those which were cracked or discolored which we kept for ourselves. And I was sick of bean soup, boiled beans, baked beans and mashed bean sandwiches, all made with the culls. However I was soon to find out that whole beans tasted just about the same as the rejects.

From steam engine power Carl began to turn his attention to gasoline power which he came to consider the wave of the future. In Petoskey, gas lighting was giving way to electricity and we girls thought that 'lectric lights would be real nice, no lamp and lantern chimneys to wash, no kerosene levels to check. But Carl said, "Naw, we'll never get 'lectric 'cause the company says the farmhouses are too far apart to make it pay." And in truth, it was to be more than twenty years before the REA set its poles along the Northern Michigan country roads.

Although Papa had no intention of giving up his horses for a tractor, he was willing to concede that there could be a limited use for gasoline power. After our shallow well went dry a deep well had to be driven and something more than a pitcher pump was needed to lift the water 168 feet to ground level. For a time he considered a windmill but he finally settled on a 10 hp gasoline engine with a tall 20 gallon tank for cooling. This he belted to a shaft which had half a dozen pulleys.

Eventually with the lush profits from farm produce during the war years Papa was able to set up other labor saving gadgets in a section of the long woodshed—a grindstone, a rip saw, a corn sheller, a grist mill and "Glory Be" for Mamma's sake, a washing machine, all powered from the shaft while water was being pumped. The arrangement was the talk of the neighborhood and Carl did most of the talking.

A big family had been Papa's reason for the washing machine and when Carl heard that one of the fancy restaurants in Bay View had installed a mechanical dishwasher, he confided in us girls that he had a plan to cut down on kitchen drudgery—pressure, he said, would do the job the modern way.

Papa was very "patickler" about his machinery and wanted his son to learn all the ins and outs concerning its care. Eleven-year old Carl followed him around and was especially intrigued by the engine which had to be cranked by hand to get it started. Cranking it, Carl was told, was something only a man could do. For a boy there might be a kick-back and a broken arm.

On a summer morning when both our parents had gone to town, Carl informed us that the time had come to revolutionize women's work and that as a special favor to us, he would start with dishwashing since we were always complaining about it and arguing as to whose turn it was to wash and whose turn to dry.

As usual there was to be a trade-off. He would do the dishes for us and we were not to tell Papa that he had started the engine. He instructed us to carry the breakfast dishes into the back yard and spread them out on the slightly slanted horizontal doors which covered the outside stairway to the cellar.

"Bring the dishes from the cupboard," he shouted. "They can probably stand a good washing, too." He was always one for doing things in a big way.

When they were arranged to suit him the matter of the water supply came next. The engine pulled it up from the deep well and pumped it through what was about a two inch pipe into the cistern. By attaching a garden hose, which was smaller in girth, to the pipe with a reducing gadget, Carl reasoned that he would have enough pressure to do the job at hand.

After stringing the hose through the open window of the woodshed, he ordered us girls to stand back to give him elbow room to crank the engine. Faster and faster he turned the crank, there were a few reluctant chugs, then presto, the engine took off with the usual earsplitting explosions. Carl was jubilant, he had started the ten-horse power machine all by himself and there hadn't been a kick-back or a broken arm. Next he set the shaft in motion and lowered the belt from the pulley which powered the pump. The pressure was on and the water was spurting out of the hose with considerable force.

We all rushed out to watch the next step of the operation. Carl grabbed the hose and directed the stream of water at the dishes, whereupon some of them began to roll down the slanting cellar doors. Three-year old Colette began to scream that her cat-cup would get broken—there was a picture of a kitten drinking milk on it and she treasured that cup above all her possessions. After the cat-cup was rescued, Carl resumed the spraying—the plates wouldn't roll, he said, just the cups and some of them had missing handles anyway.

The water from the deep, deep well was very cold and there was no way to introduce soap into the stream but Carl claimed that the pressure would dislodge any particles of food from the dishes. Every few minutes he would turn the hose over to me while he dashed back to the shed to check on the engine—the spark, the timing or whatever.

Finally, even though the egg yolk splotches couldn't be pressured off, Carl pronounced the job finished and told us to pour the remaining water off the dishes so the sun could do the drying. "It'll save you all that work," he said.

It had taken well over an hour to do the dishes the modern way and we still had to scrape the egg yolk off the plates and the forks, but Carl seemed to be extremely well satisfied with the operation—the engine had performed for him as well as it did for Papa, nothing had blown up, nothing had gone wrong except for a couple of cup handles. If there were questions about the mud in the back yard and the tracks on the kitchen floor, we could say that it had been so hot in the house that we had done the dishes outdoors and dumped the water on the ground to make the grass grow better.

We girls couldn't see that Carl had done us such a big favor—all he'd really done was make a muddy mess for us to worry about—he just wanted an excuse to start the engine. But maybe that was the way it was in the world, menfolks were more interested in the doing than in the outcome!

Carl continued to have pressure on his mind and was determined to have a try at painting with a sprayer instead of a brush. "Think of the time it took Grandpa to paint the barn, pert near a whole summer," he exclaimed. It was a big, hip-roofed barn but Carl made it sound as though it could have been painted in half a day with pressure.

Papa had a gadget which he used to spray a poison mixture on the potato vines to kill the bugs; several teaspoons of a powder called "paris green" were put in the tank, water was added and the pressure was pumped up by hand. With the tank strapped to his back, he walked between the rows, spraying the vines on either side.

By Carl's logic, if it worked for paris green it ought to work for the red paint which was left over from the barn job. The opportune time for the undertaking came when both parents were attending the funeral of one of Mamma's uncles. Fortunately it wasn't raining although there was quite a wind but no matter, the paint would dry more quickly.

The inducement Carl offered us girls to get our cooperation was his promise to build a sky ride, an idea which had been incubating in his fertile mind ever since he'd seen a Ferris wheel in operation as we drove by a roadside carnival. And he would paint the sky ride red but first he wanted to test the sprayer to see how it worked. The chimney on the house was a kind of dirty gray and a coat of red paint would brighten up the bricks and make them look brand new.

We helped him lug the wooden ladder in place and with the sprayer strapped to his back he clambered up on the roof and straddled the ridge pole.

"Paint's too thick to go through the nozzle," he yelled. "Bring me the turpentine."

So up the ladder I climbed with the turpentine bottle under my arm, praying hard that I wouldn't get dizzy and fall off the roof and break my neck, something I very nearly did when he took the cap off the tank and the pressurized mixture spurted upward and then came raining down. Fortunately the wind blew most of the paint to the side of the roof least likely to catch a parental eye.

Nothing daunted, Carl was determined to finish the job; he dumped most of the turpentine into the tank, shook it and pumped up the pressure again. "Diggety-dogs, she works," he yelled. And so it did—however, instead of turning out to be a bright red, the chimney came out a sickly pink but at least he had proved his point, spraying was quicker than using a brush. We used the rest of the turpentine to clean up our hands and cover our tracks as best we could.

It wasn't until several weeks later when Papa wanted to

"paris green" potatoes that the truth was out. It was too late to do anything about the dried paint splotches on the shingles and the odd-looking chimney but he did make Carl pick potato bugs until a new nozzle could be purchased. And for endangering his life and mine, Carl had to say a rosary every night for the rest of the month.

My brother was never one to let one incomplete success discourage him from tackling another project and his next venture was a great triumph. For its construction he had been hunting materials in various junk piles and when he found a large wooden roller with an iron shaft extending through its center lengthwise, he had everything he needed. On each end of the roller which was supported by posts imbedded in the ground, he attached a 2" by 4" and joined the ends with iron rods. On each rod a seat was suspended which swung free so when the roller was turned with a crank, both riders were head side up.

It really worked beautifully, we had our own carnival, and Carl thrived on our compliments. "Our brother invented a sky ride," we would boast and the neighborhood kids came to see, to admire and to ride. It must have taken considerable energy to turn that crank with both seats occupied by well-fed youngsters. But praise was music to Carl's ears, especially when there were girls aboard, and he huffed and puffed to keep the miniature ferris wheel turning at an exhilarating speed. Eventually he would charge a rider's fee or so he planned but when the novelty wore off the sky ride lost some of its appeal.

Basking in his success in the amusement field, Carl bethought himself of another recreational idea, this time a swimming pool. Crooked Lake was only several miles away and although it had a nice beach, we girls could only dream about cavorting in the water and lolling on the sand. Without saying exactly why, Papa had let us know that he did not approve of public bathing. "You can take your baths right here at home," he said. "No need to go three miles!"

"It wasn't fair," Carl told us, that we girls were denied the pleasure of frolicking in the lake and he proposed to remedy the situation by providing private facilities for us. He would build us a swimming pool if we would do some unspecified chores for him—that usually meant his most distasteful job—but the lure of a private pool was great.

Now that we had a deep well, we had running water in the barnyard area which was lower than the cistern and Carl had helped Papa build a drinking trough for the cows. "There's a couple of bags of cement left an' I betcha I can make a pool just like nothin'" he claimed.

"I don't think Papa'll like it," I warned.

"If it's all right for boys to go swimmin' in the lake, it's gotta be all right for youse girls to go here at home," he reasoned. But just to be on the safe side, he decided to build first and explain later.

There was a large patch of burdocks across the fence from the water trough and this seemed to offer adequate cover for the construction job. The hens sometimes made nests and laid eggs under the broad-leafed burdocks and Carl said that if he were questioned as to what he was doing there, he would have a good excuse, "Lookin' fer eggs!"

When the excavation was about eighteen inches deep, a yard or so wide and about nine feet long, Carl calculated that he would run out of cement if he made it any bigger—besides he was tired digging. Anyhow it was large enough he said, for us to swim the length of the pool and turn around without having to stand up to do so.

He knew how to measure the cement and mix it with the right amount of sand and water and when it was of the proper consistency, he troweled it on the sides and bottom of the hole. This accomplished, and he really did a nice professional job of it, he could hardly wait, nor could we, for the mortar to dry so we could take our first plunge.

We had no store-bought bathing suits but we had sateen bloomers and some old middy blouses in readiness for our long awaited swirl in his man-made lake. While Papa was eating his supper several days later, Carl slipped out to fill the pool with a hose from the cow trough. He could barely conceal his elation after he checked as to how things were going. "It's holdin' real good, not leakin' a drop!" he whispered.

After the barn chores were done and Papa was busy sharpening some tools on his grindstone, we girls told

Mamma that we were going to chase fireflies for awhile. It was late June, it was vacation time and we often played outdoors until it was pitch dark on the warm summer evenings. We had our bathing gear on under our dresses as we had agreed not to say anything about the pool until later. Mamma would be afraid that a child or a chicken might get drowned and we wanted to spare her that worry. As for Papa, Carl said he would handle that problem in due time.

Taking turns, my sisters and I immersed ourselves in the frigid water from our 168' well while Carl looked on, obviously very proud of his handiwork. "How'd you like it?" he wanted to know, always fishing for compliments.

"It's wonderful," I told him, my teeth chattering. "But it's kinda cold."

"It'll be a snap to fix that," he promised and as soon as he got a chance the next day, he scooped out the ground from under the middle section of the pool and started a small fire. "Bet not even resorters have a heated pool!" he boasted.

Papa was working in a field on the back forty so he didn't notice the smoke curling up from the burdock patch and Carl informed us that the water was getting warm fast—although it may have been the sun which was responsible.

We were all set for a lengthy swim that evening but as I stepped into the comfortably warm pool, the bottom caved in, the water ran out and Carl blamed me for putting all my weight in the center. He said I'd ruined everything for the summer as there was no more cement for a patch-up job. Not until Papa started to chop down the burdocks after the haying was done did he discover what had happened to the cement he had been saving for another purpose.

Fortunately for Carl, no traces of the fire were still visible—otherwise he might have received a stiffer punishment than being made to fill up the hole he had so laboriously dug. Being careless with fire near Papa's beloved barn of all places, was an unpardonable sin in our family.

From labor-saving and leisure-time projects, Carl began to shift his focus to money making ideas. For a way to raise funds for his growing list of wants he tried catching frogs near a creek below our farm for a fancy Bay View Dining Room which featured frog legs on its menu (resorters had funny tastes!) but he was paid only 75¢ for a tubful, about a penny apiece. Disillusioned about frog prices, he tried trapping, as pelts were much in demand in those days for neck-pieces and fur coats but he didn't catch a single fox or even a raccoon. Then he hit on a more practical scheme, one which would involve a roadside table.

When Grandpa came to Northern Michigan via Baltimore from his native Hesse, he found that all the trees around the buildings on the farm he bought had been slashed down in typical, unthinking New World fashion. Straightaway he began transplanting sugar maples, also poplar and black walnut trees. Even after the maples had reached maturity, he would not permit them to be tapped as it might spoil their beautiful foliage. But now he was dead and Carl decided that it was time for a maple syrup cash crop.

We girls could tend the roadside table and get a percentage of the profits. Travelers often stopped to ask directions as road signs were few and far between in those days, and resorters out for a joy ride frequently pulled off the road to look at the "quaint little chapel" and they, too, would be syrup-buying prospects. Resorters were suckers for anything home-made, they would even pay good money for gooseberry jam and if they'd buy gooseberries, prickles and all. they'd go for maple syrup like hot cakes.

"Maple syrup wouldn't cost us a penny," Carl commented at the breakfast table one morning. "And we could have it on our pancakes all winter."

"But cooking it down makes so much steam in the house," was Mamma's response.

"Let's try just a quart or two," was Carl's way of getting his foot in the door.

And so began the sap gathering. With some home-made spouts and some four quart pails, Carl began tapping trees right and left and filling up the rain-water barrels around the buildings. Mamma warned him that the boiling down of so much sap would loosen up all the wallpaper in the house but Carl kept mum about his plans.

Near the chapel there was a pile of stones, most of them tinted or sparkly which Grandpa had been collecting for the beautification of the chapel grounds. If properly arranged they would have some practical value as a fire pit, Carl told us, and a shallow rectangular pan which Papa used for hauling the cows' silo feed would serve as a cooking vessel.

Mamma's appointment with a dentist to have some teeth pulled came at just the right time for Carl's purposes—when the sap pails and water barrels were full to overflowing. As soon as our parents were out of sight, the sugar camp operations began, the stones were stacked to form a cooking pit, a fire was built and the pan was hoisted into place and filled with sap.

"Didja wash out the pan?" I asked Carl who was in a sweat to get the syrup-making underway.

"Yep." he answered. "I wiped her out real good."

In a short time the fire was burning briskly, the sap was bubbling and the scum which was coming to the surface had to be skimmed off so that the finished product would be golden clear and bring the top price. When Eileen, the baby at the time, who had been bundled up and stuffed into her high chair so she could watch us, got fussy we put some warm sap in her bottle and she fell asleep.

Carl was in his glory, his work crew was following his orders, fetching pails of sap and replenishing the wood for the fire. He was busy stirring and skimming, the fragrance of the steaming liquid filled the air and our prospects for profits were excellent, he said.

"Papa won't like this big fire," Madeline piped up as she watched the flames leaping up around the cooking pan. She was always one to throw a wet blanket on things.

"Oh, we'll be all done before he gets home," Carl assured her. But the sap didn't thicken into syrup as fast as Carl had expected and the dental appointment didn't take as long as he had hoped.

The moment Papa came over the hill a quarter mile away and saw the smoke billowing up from the house-chapel area amid the still leafless trees, he roused Mamma from a light sleep. "Looks like the house is on fire!"

"Or maybe it's the chapel," was Mamma's response. Please God, she prayed under her breath, if it's got to be one or the other, make it the chapel, not the house with the children in it.

Urging on the horse, lickety-split, over the half frozen, half muddy road, they made it home in record time, Papa even using the buggy whip which he was loathe to do. No doubt they were relieved that no one had burned to death and no one was missing, but there was a second reaction.

Along with our prayers we had all been taught fire prevention rules. A farm building fire in those days was usually terminal—once the flames had a good start, there was little hope. Never play with matches, never put kerosene on a sluggish fire, never open a draft and leave the room, never leave a lighted lamp or lantern where it might get tipped over, and so on.

"But you never said not to make a fire pit for cooking sap," was Carl's lame excuse, "Sides the grass couldn't catch fire 'cause there's even some snow left on it."

Carl's logic didn't impress Papa; not only were a number of rosaries prescribed as penance but Carl's meager savings were impounded. But that wasn't all.

"Chickens have been roosting on the sides of that pan, I've seen their droppings in it and mice turds, too," Mamma told Carl.

"I wiped it out real well," he protested.

"There's still chaff and gudge floating around on your syrup, it's got to be thrown out," Mamma said, her voice rising, something not usual for her.

"I could strain it," Carl countered.

"Strain it, nothing," Mamma shot back. She was really cross.

"But boiling kills germs and it's been boiled real good," Carl insisted, unwilling to give up after all his work. "And we wouldn't have to eat it ourselves, we could sell it to resorters, they wouldn't know the difference."

Although his arguments proved futile, the syrup wasn't a complete loss as Papa fed it to the pigs and they really licked their chops and looked for more.

It was a big disappointment to us girls as well as to Carl as we had been looking forward to tending the roadside stand. Our Sears Roebuck lists had been growing and besides it would be fun making change for people.

While Carl's projects did not always take off according to

expectations, he never lacked in enthusiasm for trying another tack, also he never lacked in resourcefulness in adapting whatever materials he had at hand to whatever purpose he had in mind. And he was usually able to bribe or bully us girls into serving as handmaidens for his undertakings.

Perhaps it was fortunate for us that space travel had not yet entered into the realm of the possible or he might have tried to improvise a thinga-ma-jig to send us on a mission to the moon!

Mary and Martha

WE didn't have a Bible, just my brother's copy of *A Child's Bible History* which had a few pages missing, but there was one in Aunt Bertha's house in town on the table right by her front door. It looked brand new so I don't think she read it very much. Her reason for buying it, I overheard her say, was that one of her Protestant neighbors was always finding fault with Catholics because they didn't put much stock in the Bible and that all their kids were ever taught was "Catechism, catechism, catechism." I hoped that Aunt Bertha had told the Protestant that she was mistaken as we had Bible History every day at the time of our First Communion instructions.

Once while Mamma was chatting with my aunt, I took a look at the big thick book with gold letters on the front, partly for want of something to do and partly because it seemed to be meant for grown-ups with all that fine print and no pictures. I started at the beginning but that whole page of "begots" puzzled me—it said that people lived hundreds of years, Adam nine hundred and something and Methuselah even longer than that. When I asked Carl about it he told me that it wasn't a mistake in the printing, it was just that men lived longer in the old days but hardly any women made it to a hundred.

A Child's Bible History made more sense and it had pictures on almost every page. I can see some of them still—Adam taking a big bite out of an apple while Eve stood there watching him, Jacob at the foot of a ladder which reached up through the clouds to Heaven, Noah leading the animals, two by two, into the Ark, Jonah looking scared in the mouth of a snaggly-toothed whale, Abraham ready to set fire to the brush pile where Isaac was kneeling with his hands tied behind his back. That picture really bothered me and when my sister, Madeline, raised a question about the good judgment of both God and Abraham, I had to stick up for God even though I had some question about Him myself. God had to check up on people sometimes, I told her, and as soon as He was sure that Abraham was willing to sacrifice his son, He sent an angel to blow out the match. That showed how good God was, didn't it?

The New Testament stories made more sense. They were realistic in the eyes of a farm child—the baby born in the manger in a cow stable, the shepherds watching their flocks of sheep on a hillside near Bethlehem, the Wise Men bringing gifts to the stable like Santa Claus dropping off our gifts near the barn, the flight of the Holy Family into Egypt with Joseph leading a donkey with Mary and the Child on its back.

And the miracle of the loaves and fishes I could understand. It took a lot of time to soak the yeast cakes in potato water, knead the dough and let it rise and then fire up the kitchen range to bake the bread. Feeding five thousand people would take a lot of food, even fourteen men at a threshing dinner could eat about a half dozen loaves. And as for fish, there were days when the fish just weren't biting or so Carl told us when he came home without a single one.

But then there was the story about Jesus changing water into wine at the wedding feast and by the number of jugs in the picture, there would be a lot of drinking going on at the wedding. It was setting a bad example, that's all there was to it, and especially now when wine was against the law that story ought to be taken out of the Bible History. If Jesus was going to perform a miracle with the water, let Him change it into lemonade or apple cider.

However, the picture which irked me the most was the one with Mary, the younger sister of Martha, kneeling smugly at the feet of Jesus, pretending to be all taken up with what He was saying, while Martha was carrying a big tray to the kitchen, a tray which looked like it was piled with dirty dishes. There was Martha, trying to get the work done with company in the house and all, and there was her sister lazing around, acting so pious and sweet like she couldn't bear to miss a word that He said!

The worst of it was that Jesus didn't seem to see through Mary's put-on prayerfulness. And not only that but apparently He was annoyed by Martha's tending to business in the kitchen. After all, Jesus should know that food didn't get cooked by itself and doing dishes took a lot of time. Besides, if it was so easy to perform miracles, He could have performed one for Martha and saved her a lot of work. Or at least He could have praised her for doing what had to be done and told Mary to get up from her knees and get busy. Fair is fair!

Of course I saw myself as Martha, the dutiful one, and Madeline as Mary, the laggard. But I was not about to accept meekly my sister's indolence—just as I was willing to do my half of the work, I was determined that she should do her share. She claimed that there were more important things in the world, like poetry for instance. She had found Edgar Allen Poe's "The Bells" in an upper grade reader and learned it by heart but the way she kept reciting it over and over again, you'd think she had made it up herself.

Then she took a fancy to "The Raven" and that was worse yet because it was so long and what sense did it make anyway? I looked up "raven" in the school dictionary which said it was a big crow and although Carl insisted that a crow could talk if it had its tongue slit, he was never able to prove it. He had me hold a young one by the feet one time while he tried to get at its tiny narrow tongue but the crow got away—I had really let it go on purpose but of course, I didn't tell him that.

Well, anyway, all Poe's raven could croak was the one word "Nevermore" and I don't think Madeline got any more out of the poem that I did, she just liked the sound of it and the way the lines rolled along. And I knew she didn't have the slightest idea of what some of the words meant like "surcease" and "beguiling" and she didn't bother to look up words like I did, either!

I liked certain kinds of poems myself—poems that had some point to them and I read a lot more poetry than she ever did but I didn't think that it should interfere with

getting the work done. There was a time for poetry and there was a time for pots and pans.

My devotion to the work ethic began, I think, when I was four years old. It was mid-October and we were in the field on top of the hill behind our barn, trying to get the potatoes harvested before freezing weather and snow set in. Carl was pulling the vines, Mamma and Papa were doing the digging and two-year old Madeline was fast asleep, snug and warm in an improvised tent. I was given a small pail and Mamma suggested that I pick up potatoes so that I would have enough to eat during the long, cold winter which was on the way. I liked potatoes—baked, boiled, scalloped, pan-fried but best of all mashed potatoes with chicken gravy.

I set to work in earnest and with every pail I filled, I was praised, even by Carl—of course the more I picked up, the fewer were left for him after he finished the vines. And that night at the supper table, I remember my mother saying proudly, "She's a dandy little worker, she must have picked up at least ten bushels altogether."

Carl said, "Yes, but I had to take time off my work to empty them in the wagon."

"You were a big help, too, but she's only four years old," Papa told him.

I was so tired and sleepy that I could hardly stay awake but I knew I'd made a big mark in the world. Every year thereafter I bettered my record and when Madeline reached working age, I tried to get her to follow in my footsteps. But she was balky, even Mamma couldn't get her interested in getting the cellar stocked for winter. Interested or not, in my opinion she owed it to the family to make herself useful.

After she had filled up one pail and Carl had dumped it for her, she overturned the pail, sat on it, and called out for all of us to hear, "There, I picked up all I'm going to eat this winter!"

I was so annoyed by her "me only" attitude that I threw an egg-sized potato at her and got scolded for it, unfairly I thought since it didn't even hit her. Carl promised he'd fix up an old tricycle for her, one that he'd found in a dump, but that didn't get her going either. She was just plain pig-headed lazy when it came to work.

During World War I, Northern Michigan farmers could sell whatever they were able to produce for a good price. The army needed lots of beans and potatoes to fill the stomachs of the doughboys and although Papa didn't approve of that war or any war for that matter, he didn't object to keeping the soldiers and sailors well fed—after all the war wasn't of their making. Potatoes were bringing around $3.00 a bushel and navy beans about $18.00 a hundred weight. It had taken a war to give small farmers a break.

But after the Armistice in November, 1918, there was a

glut on the market, prices fell below the pre-war level while property taxes and other expenses remained stationary. Farmers had fallen on hard times and Mamma decided that she would have to supplement the family income by retailing garden produce and dressed poultry, whereas earlier she had been able to do enough wholesaling at Fochtman's to take care of her special needs, like outing flannel for baby clothes and ingredients for Christmas baking.

There was a demand for choice vegetables and freshly dressed fryers in Bay View, the resort colony adjacent to Petoskey and here she found customers who were happy to pay for quality products. To us children, resorters were super-rich people who could sit on their porches whenever they felt like it, who could enjoy chicken dinners in the middle of the week, and could even afford to sleep in beds on the trains which brought them North.

So it was that every Tuesday, Thursday and Saturday during the summer months, Mamma drove our best-behaved horse to Bay View with a spring wagon loaded with vegetables in season—radishes, lettuce, spinach, swiss chard, green onions, carrots, peas, string beans, new potatoes, sweet corn, cucumbers and tomatoes, also half a dozen or more "dressed" chickens. The vehicle was a light-weight, one-horse wagon with buggy wheels and springs and it had a canvas umbrella to shield the driver from the rain and the sun.

The vegetables would be gathered during the late afternoon of the previous day, washed, bunched and kept crisp in cold water through the night. The chickens which had been mother-hen hatched in April would be killed in the early evening, drenched with boiling water and plucked. Madeline had the easy job of pulling out the big feathers in handfuls whereas I was usually stuck with removing the remaining pin feathers one by one. Mamma did the drenching with boiling water and she always took out the innards and slit open and emptied the gizzards, something which the butcher shops in town did not do in those days until after the fowl was weighed. This increased the selling weight and it left a slight odor, thus giving Mamma an excellent sales advantage.

Mamma would get up before dawn, help with the milking,

prepare and eat a hurried breakfast, then set off with her load of produce so that she could dispose of it before it wilted and dried out in the mid-day heat. There was no refrigeration on the wagon except for a chunk of ice to keep the fryers cold.

After delivering her wares in Bay View, she would drive on to Petoskey, there to pay something on as many bills as possible, perhaps $10.00 on the grass-seed purchased in early spring, $10.00 on the loan for taxes, and $5.00 on the fire insurance. With what was left, she would buy a bag of grocery staples—sugar, salt, yeast cakes, oatmeal and Swift's cottosuet (a blend of cotton seed oil and suet which seems to be no longer available). Also, almost always she bought a nickel's worth of candy such as cinnamon drops or chocolate covered peanuts for us children.

It never would have occurred to Mamma to go to a restaurant for lunch—that would have meant parting with hard cash and besides she was anxious to get home as soon as possible. She trusted us girls to take good care of the baby but still it must have been a worry for her. Even without stopping for lunch it would be mid-afternoon before our slow-paced buggy horse completed the round trip on peddling days.

Everything was always in a state of chaos when Mamma left in the morning—dishes and the oatmeal kettle unwashed, the ashes in the kitchen range unemptied, the floors unswept, the vegetable cooling water unemptied or uncarried to the garden if we needed rain—all manner of things undone. But Mamma's instructions as she hurried off were always the same, "Take good care of the baby," as though that was all that had to be done.

Madeline preferred to take Mamma's parting words literally. She would have been quite willing to wheel the baby buggy around all day, reciting poetry as she wheeled. But I, being the Martha-type, felt duty-bound to clean up the house and have everything in apple pie order by the time Mamma got home from her long, hard day on the road—by then she was usually so tired that she didn't even feel like eating although it had been hours since breakfast. All she wanted to do was to lie down and rest for a little while.

Oh, Madeline was willing to do a few things, like washing

the dishes so we'd have some clean ones for lunch and maybe a few fun jobs like feeding the dog, but if I tried to get her to help with anything else she balked. "What's a little dust?" she'd say. "Just pull down the shades and it won't show. If you wanta do any exter work, go ahead, you're older an' you ought to do more!"

That's the way she was, in spite of all that Mamma did for us children, and how tired she was when she got back from town, Madeline was just plain lazy, I thought. Lazy, selfish and stubborn!

I had designed a system which would have accomplished wonders, if I had gotten the right kind of cooperation. Everything could have been done efficiently and done right, there would have been no waste motion, no time arguing about this and that. My way of doing the work was real simple, I would handle the dish cloth and the broom and she could do the running:

"Feed these scraps to the dog on the back step and bring in some wood when you come back."

"Empty the ashes on the ashpile and bring in the dog's dish so I can wash it."

"Empty this dish water and bring back the dishpan so I can wipe it out."

"Pick up those dirty socks and put them in the wash so I can sweep the floor."

"Shake out those throw rugs and bring them back and put them down."

"Hang these diapers that I've washed on the line, then check to see if the mailman has come."

But no, Madeline wouldn't listen to me, she just did whatever she felt like doing, which wasn't much. And the worst of it was, her misbehavior set a bad example. Colette had been born on my birthday and I wanted her to keep looking up to me as the one who did the right thing. And as for Eileen, although she was still too young to work, she might turn out to be lazy like Madeline if I didn't get her started out doing what she was told.

I wasn't being bossy as Madeline tried to make out. I wasn't sitting back, doing nothing while I snapped my fingers, telling her what to do. I always did the hardest things, like washing the baby's diapers. After all, someone had to go ahead with the work, someone had to do the supervising, someone had to show consideration for Mamma, like having the house thoroughly cleaned when she got home. And not just the house, there were other things which needed doing, too.

For instance, the woodshed and the cellar needed cleaning out once in awhile, or the outhouse needed odor control during the hot weather—if I asked Madeline to sprinkle lime down the holes she'd yell at me, "You're taking things too far. Do it yourself if you want to!" And then she'd go flouncing around, reciting some of that sing-songy poetry of hers which set my teeth on edge.

I could never understand her taste in poems—they didn't have any point to them, just fancy words and rhymes, never any that dealt with worthwhile subjects like ending war and poverty and injustice. One that I liked especially was *The Slave's Dream* by Longfellow and I knew it by heart but I did not go around reciting it all the time. It went something like this:

> "Beside the ungathered rice he lay
> His sickle in his hand
> His chest was bare, his matted hair
> Was buried in the sand
> He saw once more his dark-eyed queen
> Among her children stand
> They clasped his neck, they kissed his cheeks
> They held him by the hand
> A tear burst from the sleeper's lids
> And fell into the sand. . . ."

Poor slave, he had sickled the rice for hours in the blazing sun all by himself with no one to help him. He, who had been a king in his native land lay dying, he had probably been beaten by his master because he had not gathered enough rice. Now, a poem like that would do some good, maybe it even made Lincoln free the slaves.

Everybody in the family should work, I thought, unless too young, too old or too sick. I got that idea from Cousin Celia who quoted this verse to Mamma:

> *Work for all who can work*
> *To each the fruit of his work*
> *Help for those who can't work*
> *Hell for those who won't work.*

Mamma seemed to agree with Cousin Celia, she even laughed about it but if Papa had heard it he wouldn't have thought it was funny. To his way of thinking only God had the right to give anybody "hell". But it applied to Madeline, I thought, when she was acting so balky about doing her share of the work.

The biggest quarrel we ever had took place one day when I wanted her to help clean up the woodshed which was a kind of catch-all for odds and ends as well as a place for storing firewood. It was a mess but with a little organizing, it could be made to look half-way respectable.

"Now it's the woodshed," she snorted. "First it was the kitchen then it was the whole downstairs, then it was the upstairs, then it was the outhouse. First thing ya know it'll be the pigpen!"

"Think you're funny, don'cha, talk about pigpens, that's what this woodshed looks like an' we're having comp'ny tomorrow," I reminded her.

"Comp'ny! I thought it was Mamma you were cleaning up for," she hooted.

"It's for both—and it's your woodshed, too, so you can jist help clean it up," I told her.

"Well, you kin have my share of it," she yelled as she took off in the direction of the toolshed.

"You come right back!" I shouted. "I'll give you exactly ten minutes!"

"Try an' make me," she flung at me as she disappeared.

Here it was, the day before a family potluck, with only half the Saturday cleaning done and Madeline was on the rampage. It was true that Mamma never worried too much about the house being slicked up for company—"we'll just do what we can and let the rest go", she'd say. But I wanted the house to look nice even if we didn't have all kinds of fancy things like they did in town, a bathroom and electric lights and a telephone. To get to the outhouse, a person could see the mess in the woodshed and a little straightening up would make it look a lot better.

Madeline ignored my ultimatum so after ten minutes I went in search of her. The toolshed had only one fly-specked window and if she hadn't sneezed, I wouldn't have known where she was hiding. But there she was, perched above the doorway in a small storage loft crammed with tool parts, strands of hay wire, dusty burlap sacks and I don't know what else.

"Come down this minute," I ordered.

"Hah, come and get me," she laughed.

There were some slats nailed on the studding but that avenue of pursuit didn't look very promising. She had the high ground to defend and any assault up that makeshift ladder would be risky. There was a forge in the corner of the shed which Papa stocked with coal for intense heat when he was shoeing the horses or hand-crafting parts for his farm implements. For want of something better to throw, I grabbed a piece of coal about the size of a walnut and fired it in her direction.

She returned fire, not with the coal which she had deftly caught but with an egg which, apparently, some hen had laid on the sacks a considerable time before. Hens who wanted to "set" often made their nests in out-of-the-way places. It hit the floor and its contents splattered on my bare legs and feet—we always went barefoot around home in summer to save shoe leather—and that egg had definitely been there a long, long time.

This kind of foul play called for a response in kind so I picked up a larger hunk of coal and aimed more carefully. Not knowing how much more of her ammunition she had, I then made my exit hurriedly. I heard a kind of thud but no cry of pain.

Back in the house as I tried to wash off the rotten egg splatters, I began to worry. Had I really hurt her, had I knocked her out, had I hit her in the temple and killed her? She'd made me so mad I had acted without thinking but that chunk of coal, like a stone, could have caused her death. And for murder I could go to jail even if I did have a good excuse for what I did.

I waited awhile, hoping and praying that the hit had not been fatal. The minutes dragged on and I was about to go back to the toolshed to assess the damage when there was a sniffling and snuffling at the door. I was torn between being relieved that she was still alive and being furious that she had caused me so much worry.

"Look what you did," she blubbered accusingly. And there on her temple was a nasty black and blue bruise, half hidden by her damp curly hair. It looked terrible, there was no question about that, and bruises don't disappear quickly. What would Mamma and Papa say and what would our Sunday guests think?

The only thing I could do was to try to bribe her into saying that she had been hit by a baseball or that she had stumbled over the anvil in the toolshed. I tried to think of something of mine she would like but which I didn't really want any more. It was a time for negotiations but she could negotiate from a position of strength—she had the bruise.

"Tell you what, I'll fix my hair so what you did won't show if you'll promise not to try to boss me around ever again," she volunteered in a way which she tried to make sound like sisterly generosity.

But, knowing her, I figured she had something sinister up her sleeve. "You mean you won't do any work at all when Mamma's gone to town?" I asked.

"Oh, I'll do some," she answered airily. We'll divide up the work and I'll do mine my way and you do yours your way but you daresent tell me I'm not doing mine right!"

I should have held out a little longer but I was in a tight spot and she knew it. I was anxious to get the matter settled before Papa came in from the field for the noon meal so I agreed to her terms. I had to raise my right hand and with my left on the Bible History, take an oath that I would abide by my part of the bargain but she didn't have to promise a thing.

First, we were to decide on the truly necessary jobs which had to be done on any given day; then we were to make two lists in writing, dividing the work as equally as possible. One list might read: taking care of the baby, doing the dishes, washing the cream separator and the milk pails, mopping the kitchen floor. The other might read: making the beds, emptying the vegetable tubs, feeding the chickens, taking Papa and Carl some drinking water when they were working in the fields. If I thought there was anything else that needed doing, I could just do it myself. We were to draw sticks as to which list we got.

The biggest flaw in the contract was that she could do her work in her usual slipshod way and I could do nothing about it. However, I didn't have to put up with her back talk any longer and Mamma didn't seem to notice the poor quality of the work she did.

It wasn't until a week or so later that I found out that she had spit on the chunk of coal and smeared a black spot on her temple. I had a notion to go back on the contract but I was tired of trying to make her do the right thing and it was easier to do things myself. I would just get what work I could get out of her and let it go at that.

Even so, she managed to make me look bad insofar as the two-list system was concerned. Offhandedly she would say to any visitor we might have, "My sister is two years older but I have to do as much work as she does—we divide up the work!" Of course she didn't add that it was all her own idea. Oh, she was cunning as a fox, she was sharp as a needle!

There was just no fairness in the world and perhaps not in the hereafter either. After all, if Jesus couldn't see through Mary's trickery and didn't give Martha credit for doing the right thing, how could I be sure that justice would be done in heaven?

Pills, Chills, Spills and Swellings

BACK in the early 1900's health was mostly a matter of hope, home-healing and happenstance, at least in Northern Michigan where the farms were small and the mortgages big. Doctors were not called upon very much except to usher in the young and usher out the old. In fact, never in all our childhood years was I, or were any of my brothers and sisters—once launched into the world—considered to be in dire need of a doctor's attention. I'll take that back, before I was born, my brother Carl had pushed a couple of shelled peas up his nostrils. All efforts to remove them failed so Papa hastily hitched up the horse and he and Mamma set off for town at a gallop, hoping and praying that they would get help in time to save the life of their gasping two-year-old. Whether it was their prayers, the bouncing of the buggy on the rough country roads or Nature at work, the peas became dislodged, the horse was allowed to return home at a leisurely pace and a medical fee was avoided.

Not that the doctors charged very much in those days—an office call was a dollar, a home visit was two dollars and if a family could not come up with the cash, a bushel or two of potatoes or a cord of wood was acceptable. A country doctor was lucky if he could afford a good horse and rig to make his round of house calls.

In our family, prevention was the better part of cure. During the deadly flu epidemic which swept across the nation during the final days of World War I, Mamma decided to take no chances and imposed a quarantine on our house. At the time she had four young children and felt that the only help she could give stricken neighbors was to make pots of bean soup or chicken broth which Papa would leave near their mailboxes. For the time being her brood would live entirely off the land; such things as coffee, tea, sugar, cocoa, and spices were luxuries anyway. Sugar had risen from four to thirty cents a pound so she was already doing without it. The price gouging was just another instance of war profiteering, or so she said. The schools were all closed, ours being one of the last ones to shut its doors, and no neighbors or relatives were permitted entrance to our house nor were we allowed to go to church.

Papa didn't mind most of the restrictions but it must have been very hard on him to stay away from church, especially for funerals. Every day or two it seemed, a horse-drawn hearse came over the State Road to claim yet another victim of the dread disease. Papa was a man who felt it was his bounden duty to attend the last rites of everyone of his acquaintance, there to pray for the soul of the departed, just as he would want others to pray for him.

But Mamma said that delivering broth to the afflicted families was much more to the point and that he could pray for the dead just as well at home. And as for missing Sunday Mass during the epidemic, she said that the good Lord had all He could do checking in the newcomers without taking attendance at Mass. She took it as support for her contention when all public church services were cancelled until after the flu outbreak had run its course.

The killer disease was called Spanish Influenza and it was often followed by chills and pneumonia. It was highly contagious and swept through Emmet County in the fall of 1918, having started, it was said, among the troops in Europe and brought to our area by several Government people selling Liberty Bonds to finance the War. Papa wondered aloud if it could be God punishing His people for killing each other on the battle field whereas Mamma blamed Big Business for everything, the war, the flu and especially the price of canning sugar.

I pondered over the matter myself and concluded that it was all the Kaiser's fault since he had started the big fight in the first place. In my prayers I suggested to God that he remove the Kaiser from the earthly scene so that the rest of us would be spared but my solution to the problem was ignored.

Prevention was, indeed, the family prescription for all ailments and accidents. The few medications which comprised the household pharmacy were kept on the top shelf of the kitchen cupboard, supposedly out of reach of us children. But Carl was never one to let top shelves interfere with his plans—he merely waited for the opportune moment to conduct his explorations.

According to Mamma, when she returned to the house one day after a hasty trip to the garden, she found four year old Carl under the bed, gasping and spitting. "Will I die, will I die, will I die," was all he kept saying.

"Tell me what you did," she asked him as she pulled him out from where he had taken refuge.

By standing on the high-chair, so Mamma told me later, Carl had been able to reach the medicine shelf where there was a packet of Rexall's chocolate-covered physic pills along with such items as Sloan's Liniment, iodine and Epsom Salts. It was the pills which Carl had in mind and, apparently to make the effort worthwhile, he had grabbed a handful and stuffed them all in his mouth at once. The chocolate coating was thin, the laxative was bitter, and the consequences unforeseen.

Carl continued to spit and to beg for assurances that he was not at Death's door while Mamma continued to press for details as to what he had done but he seemed less concerned about the sin than about the wages thereof. Fortunately, he hadn't swallowed much of the bitter chemical as a little mound of sucked-clean pills was found under the bed and there were no long-term ill effects. But Mamma's hope that his terror-fraught experience would teach him a lesson was not to be realized. Her first-born had a strong curiosity bent and once he "took a notion," he couldn't rest until he had achieved either success or failure, quite often the latter.

There was the time that he was sent to the barn to get a

small pail of wheat for the chickens. Fearing the worst since he had been gone longer than necessary, Mamma was about to go in search of him when she heard his screams as he came hobbling toward the house. Hopping on one foot, he kept the other one which was dripping red in mid air and Mamma's first thought was that he had gotten side-tracked to the tool shed and had chopped off a toe or two. She ran for a tourniquet to quench the flow of blood but the red turned out to be barn paint which Carl had spilled on himself while prying the paint can open. The effect was so realistic that he was convinced he was bleeding to death.

Carl seemed to have an inordinate concern about death and the hereafter as was the case when he tried his hand at churning. In the cellar we had a wooden, barrel-type churn which fitted into a frame and had to be turned end over end with a crank, thus agitating the sour cream and separating the globs of butter from the buttermilk. After a number of turns, especially rapid ones, it was wise to remove the outlet cork in order to relieve the pressure which had been built up inside the churn. However, having neither the wisdom nor the experience to deal with this problem, five-year-old Carl proceeded to turn the crank too long and too fast.

Without warning the mixture "blew," the liquid spurting out, hitting him smack in the face as he tried to make his escape. "I'm shot, I'm shot," he bellowed as he headed for safety while the remaining contents streamed unchecked onto the cellar floor. It took considerable time, Mamma said later, to persuade him to give up the idea that there was a malevolent force inside the churn, specifically the devil, intent on killing him.

But for physical ailments which couldn't be prevented or soothed away, we had simple, inexpensive home remedies. For sore throats we could gargle with salt water; for a hacking cough there was honey mixed with vinegar; for pink eye there was a boric acid solution; for congestion in the chest, there was a mustard plaster; for a stomach ache there was peppermint tea; for chapped skin there was wool fat; for cuts there was Rawleigh's Salve; for burns there was flour mixed with lard; for bee stings there was baking soda; and for swellings there was Sloan's Liniment.

These remedies seemed to work or perhaps it was Mamma's comforting words which effected the cures. When I was about three years old, I was given the Arm and Hammer soda treatment which as I remember, was not altogether efficacious. One afternoon Mamma noticed that a contingent of hornets was entering and departing regularly through a knot hole in the siding on the outside kitchen wall. Dislodging the buzzing creatures from their new-found nesting place was a job which Mamma thought was better left to Papa who was working in a field on the back forty. She warned my brother and me to stay away from the point of entry which the hornets had chosen.

Carl waited until Mamma had disappeared from view,

probably to get vegetables from the garden or eggs from the henhouse. He then ordered me to stand watch at the knot-hole while he took corrective measures.

"Be on the look-out, see if anything comes out," he told me.

There I was, in the line of fire, my eyes glued to the knot hole, with the job of reporting to him as to whether his strategy was working! With the door safely closed between us, he began to pound on the inside wall and I was left to face the outrushing and outraged hornets by myself. They came charging out in what seemed like endless numbers and of course, I was their unwitting victim.

By the time Mamma heard the screams of the stricken sentry and came running to the house, Carl had taken off for parts unknown. She had no trouble piecing together the chronology of events which led up to the onslaught because of the telltale hammer, and although she didn't believe in spanking, she must have wondered if her approach to child-rearing was proper.

Furthermore there were more immediate concerns, the baby had been awakened from her nap and both she and I were howling at the top of our lungs. Fortunately the wasp family does not leave stingers in the flesh but my face and neck and hands gave swollen evidence of the attack.

With Papa out of earshot, no telephone in the house, the baby upset by all the commotion, and a seven-year-old son nowhere to be seen, she would have been hard put to summon a doctor anyway, so the baking soda and her soothing words were enough to quiet me somewhat as she rocked me in her arms while she jiggled the baby carriage with her foot.

Apparently the hammer strokes had so taken the hornets by surprise and indignation that they did not return to the nest which they had under construction so, no doubt, Carl felt that he had succeeded in the man-sized job he had undertaken. However, when Papa came in from the field and heard what had taken place, he took his son aside and after giving him a good "talking-to," prescribed what he always did—a number of Our Fathers and Hail Marys as penance—a very mild punishment it still seems to me.

I have only a vague but painful recollection of the hornet episode but I well remember the time I very nearly drowned or was asphyxiated, possibly both, while following my brother's instructions to a game which he had invented. It was called "Maple Board" and I've never known for sure whether its outcome was intended or accidental.

Stretching from the cow door through the barnyard to the manure pile was a plank bridge. It was about eight inches wide and crossed a foot-deep puddle where rain water and brine from the silo collected. Added to this mixture was the drainage from the ditch in the cow barn where droppings, liquid and otherwise were deposited. Over the narrow bridge Papa pushed the wheelbarrow to the manure pile with the solid matter which would later be spread on the fields for fertilizer.

"Maple Board" was a game for two with a home base for each player, one being a maple tree stump in the barnyard and the other a maple tree near the house. The players were to start from home base with the shout "Get Going" from Carl, pass each other on the way, touch the opponent's base and return to the starting point, the winner being the one to yell "Maple Board" first. The route, as decreed by the inventor, passed through the horse section of the barn, thence through the passageway and the cow side, then out the cow door and across the plank bridge—the plank, by the way, was also maple.

There was plenty of room for passing each other except on the narrow bridge and whether by accident or design, that was where we met the second or third time we played the game. Carl kept to the exact middle of the plank, forcing me to fall headlong into the briny deep. He did have the courtesy to pull me out before leading me, blubbering and dripping, to the house and there he claimed to have saved me from drowning while failing to mention the meeting on the bridge.

I was covered with smelly slime from head to foot and it took several wash tubs of water to get the muck swabbed off and a long, long time to forget the indignity I had suffered in that final game of "Maple Board."

During World War I, airplane flying and parachute jumping were beginning to make history and Carl was determined to have a piece of the action, at least vicariously. According to him, if an open umbrella were large enough it would work as well as a parachute, perhaps better since there would be no need to pull a cord. We had a big canvas umbrella, much like the beach and lawn types of today, but ours was for strictly utilitarian purposes rather than for lolling on the beach or sipping cold drinks in the shade. We used ours to shield us from the rain and the sun on our trips to town in the spring wagon.

I was selected to volunteer for the trial jump and at first the parachute adventure sounded exciting—to float like a cloud, to soar like a bird, to glide like a leaf—Carl had a way of making his upcoming experiments seem very thrilling. But as the count-up to ten began, I had second thoughts, and refused to cooperate.

It had taken a lot of huffing and puffing to get the umbrella up the ladder to the scaffold in the barn and he tried to make me feel guilty about backing down on my agreement. His plan was for me to make the trial jump behind the big sliding doors in the barn, the need for secrecy being, he said, that Papa didn't like new things—"That's why I gotta prove it works first!" Ever since then, it has always seemed to me that those who are engaged in dubious activities often use excuses like "national security" as the reason for their secretiveness.

"No, I'm not jumping," I told him as I looked down at his "cushion" of straw on the floor below.

"But you'll like it a lot, just hang onto the handle real tight an' you'll drift down, easy like a feather," he assured me.

"I might get hurt, I might even get killed," I protested.

"Naw, there's nothing to it, they do it all the time in the army. That's the way they're going to catch the Kaiser." He tried everything he could think to make me change my mind, but I would not be moved.

"Try your own parachute jump yourself," I told him. In later years he would never admit that he pushed me but I am absolutely sure that I did not leave that scaffold of my own accord. The cushion of straw was not half as bouncy as Carl had said it was and I landed flat on my stomach after my fall of some fifteen feet. I couldn't breathe, I couldn't move, I couldn't cry out, I thought I was done for.

It didn't take Carl long to come down the ladder to inspect the flop of his make-do parachute—there I was, underneath it, still unable to say a word. Did he ask, "Are you hurt?" Did he say, "Can I help you?" No, he didn't even say he was sorry—the memory I have, as he stood over me, is one of a repeated, "Don't tell Pa, don't tell Pa."

Fortunately for both of us, I recovered quickly from having my breath knocked out, there were no broken bones, and the umbrella wasn't damaged except for some bent ribs which Carl hastened to straighten. As a good will gesture he promised to give me his Belgian Hare buck which he said was more valuable than the doe—even though it was the doe which had the baby rabbits.

"Loop de Loop" was another of his aviation inspired ideas. After threshing, when the right side of the barn was piled high with oat and wheat straw, Carl would burrow a tunnel system, starting at the top of the stack and descending in a zigzag fashion to the bottom of the mow. It wouldn't work with hay but straw was less tangled and rather slippery and it was great fun to dive into the entrance head first and go gliding downward, almost like taking a ride on a bob sled on a steep hill in winter. If we didn't appear at the exit point at the expected time, it meant that we were stuck and it was Carl to the rescue, either by digging us out from below or by making the Loop de Loop himself and pushing us through from above. I shudder even now when I think of choking under an avalanche of dusty straw.

But Carl was not the only one responsible for near calamities. An incident took place one time when I was left in charge of the younger children, an incident which could have required the services of a doctor or even an undertaker. I was about ten and very proud to be given the responsibility to take care of the baby and the house all by myself. Mamma and Papa had gone off to town on some family business and had taken Carl with them to be fitted for a pair of shoes, possibly an arrangement intended to preclude any problems at home.

The baby had been given a bottle and was asleep, the

dishes were done, the beds had been made, the floors were swept, the stove had been stoked and it was too cold to do any extra work so Madeline and I decided to cut out paper dolls. Carl had made a miniature school room for us—small blocks of wood for the seats, higher ones for the desks, a long block for the recitation bench, and a square one for the teacher's desk, all on Mamma's pie-crust rolling board which she let us use. There was even a round block, colored black, for the stove and a smaller one for the water pail. That day we needed fresh cut-outs for the pupils and the Sears Roebuck catalogue was our source of supply.

We got two copies every year, one in the spring and one in the fall and after the new one arrived, the old one was relegated to the outhouse where it served as cost-free toilet tissue. The pictures of school-age children had already been torn from the discarded catalogue so we had no recourse but to turn to the latest copy.

The problem was that Papa was planning to send back a wrong-sized emery wheel and for safe-keeping, he had put it and the new catalogue in the massive, glass-doored cupboard in the living room which was off limits to us children. It sat atop a stout-legged table and in it were kept an assortment of family valuables—wedding present dishes, religious articles, farm tax receipts, mortgage papers, wedding and birth certificates and such like, none of which were of interest to us. However, there was the catalogue, it wasn't where it belonged, and we needed it.

It was excuse enough, I thought, to get into the cupboard so I mounted the table but found the glass doors either stuck or locked. In trying to force them open, I must have jarred the heavy oak cupboard enough to cause it to come crashing down off the table with me pinned underneath it.

From the rubble I somehow managed to extricate myself and although I had a number of bumps and scratches, these were the least of my worries. There was no way we could put together the shards of glass and china and the new emery wheel and although the catalogue had been thrown clear of the wreckage, the idea of cutting paper dolls had lost its allure. There was nothing I could do but nervously await my parents' return and try to think of a more justifiable explanation for trying to get into the cupboard. The baby had awakened and I sat rocking her while Madeline and Colette kept silent watch at the front window.

As Mamma came into the house, her glance darted from one to the other of us as if counting the survivors. Seeing no evidence of irreparable bodily harm, she took the baby from me and calmly asked me what had happened.

I had been planning to say that I was looking for a better nipple for the baby's bottle but the enormity of the damage to the family valuables suddenly hit me and I burst out crying—all those treasured dishes and even Papa's emery wheel which now could not be exchanged. Papa did not scold me either; I think he may have blamed himself for not having anchored the cupboard to the table and at least his most precious relic was safe—a hand-hammered nail in a glass-topped box which, it was said, had touched one of the original crucifixion spikes. Carl, however, was certain that there would have been no wreckage if he had been left in charge or so he told Papa as they carried the cupboard to the cellar where it was used thereafter for storing canned fruit, while resting safely on the cellar floor.

Despite all the near fatalities, the only broken bones ever suffered in our family were from a horse runaway. Madeline and I were on our way to church with Mamma one Sunday with a horse which had been sold to Papa by an out-of-town livestock trader of doubtful character, according to Mamma. Papa was inclined to trust people, even horse traders and moneylenders and Daisy seemed to be tractable enough at the time of purchase but very shortly thereafter she exhibited a wild streak which may have meant that she had been drugged. Papa preferred to think that she had not been properly broken in, and he proceeded to work patiently with Daisy who began to show marked improvement.

After she had been on good behavior for several months, Mamma felt that she could handle our new horse, so we set out for ten o'clock Mass without incident until we met one of our neighbors returning from an earlier service in a recently acquired Model T Ford. Whether Daisy was frightened by the flapping side curtain or whether it was just her general perversity, she took off over a roadside ditch, up a steep bank and into a barbed wire fence, overturning our buggy on the way. I wasn't hurt but Madeline got a bloody nose and Mamma had broken bones in several of her fingers. The neighbor came to our rescue and took us to a doctor, while his son stayed with the twitching, high-strung horse whose neck was bleeding profusely.

Before that day, I had never been in a doctor's office, this one in the wing of his home in Petoskey. I was frightened for Mamma and ashamed of my sister's squalling which seemed to have less to do with her bloodied dress than with the loss of her most cherished possession. "I lost my pocketbook, I lost my pocketbook," she kept wailing.

I still remember the blessed relief I felt on seeing Mamma come out of the inner room of the doctor's office with her hand in bandages and splints. The sight of her smiling calmly was even enough to quiet Madeline although she continued to sniff and complain. The neighbor who was very much a no-nonsense sort of man had refrained from any comment on my sister's behavior until, as we drove by the scene of the accident, he stopped his car, climbed up the bank, searched in the trampled grass, then came back to us and threw the purse to Madeline with an explosive, "Here's your damned pocketbook!"

That was the day I had my first automobile ride, something I had been looking forward to with great eagerness. However, because of the runaway, my embarrassment over my sister's cry-babyness and my fear that Daisy was dead, I was not in the mood for a joyful pleasure ride. When last I had seen our horse, her neck was spurting blood and although the damaged buggy was still lying over-turned on the bank, Daisy was gone. Bad as she was at times, like both Madeline and Carl, she was part of our family.

Another reason I couldn't enjoy the car ride was that it was raining and I couldn't see much through the isinglass in the side curtains. Also, when we passed another car, the windshield was spattered with mud from a puddle and the neighbor let out a thunderous oath, even worse than "Damn". It was good to get home and find that Daisy was in our barn, meekly submitting to Papa's doctoring. As it turned out, she not only survived that accident but lived to run away another day.

Sometimes the remedy was not medicinal—such as when Madeline thought she was choking to death on a set of store-bought teeth. After many pregnancies with no prenatal care and no calcium supplements, Mamma had to wear dentures and my sister, who was missing a couple of baby teeth, decided to try them out for looks one day when Mamma was taking a nap and had left them in a glass of soda water. Not satisfied with the upper plate alone, she managed to cram in the lower one also and somehow the two got locked together. She began to gag but could not expel them and rather than arouse Mamma, she headed for the field where Papa was.

Once she reached him she couldn't explain her predicament, she could only point to her bulging cheeks and make gutteral sounds. Knowing her liking for looking-glass preening and her unconventional turn of mind, he was able to size up the situation quickly and remove the extra teeth without damage to either her mouth or the expensive dentures. However, he gave her a lecture about female vanity which, of course, didn't have much effect.

Probably our most useful, multi-purpose, over-the counter stand-by was Sloan's Liniment. It was a fiery, pink liquid which would leave the affected area hot and reddened but it was guaranteed to do wonders for both man and beast. Its many uses were listed on the bottle—sprains, strains, lumbago, charley horse, hoof and mouth disease, rhumatism, arthritis, swellings, you name it.

Despite our frequent quarrels and jealousies and trickeries, we girls did not want to see the break-up of our family. When Carl began to wear long trousers instead of knickers for Sunday good, we girls were upset because it seemed to mean that at the table there would soon be one vacant chair. Nor did we want to leave our comfortable nest ourselves, thus the process of maturation was to be delayed as long as possible.

It was the symptom "swelling" on the liniment bottle which prompted the generous application of the potent liquid for the girlhood affliction we very much dreaded. After all, as with long trousers, the signs of approaching maturity meant that the end was near for all that was familiar especially Christmas togetherness.

However, the user—who shall be nameless—had not reckoned on the long-lasting, red-hot sensation which followed the drastic measure taken to reduce the "swellings." And the worst of it was that the powerful stuff, instead of producing the desired effect, seemed to enlarge the bulges. But at least we learned a memorable lesson—"don't believe everything which appears in print."

Looking back over our childhood years, I wonder how any of us survived. On our bedroom wall there was a large framed picture of a Botticelli-like angel guiding a child over a narrow footbridge. Papa said that it was a guardian angel and that we each had one to watch over us and keep us from harm. Perhaps so, but there were certainly times when those guardian angels of ours let things get a little out of hand.

Hay Power Versus Gasoline Power

AFTER a few months at a German language boarding school near Grand Rapids Papa, then seven years old, was sent back to the farm, homesick and ailing. During troubled nights in the strange place, he had dreams that something had happened to his beloved horses—they had been sold, they had run away, they had been sick, they had died.

The first thing he did when he got home was to rush to the barn to make sure that the dreams had been mere nightmares. He found Prinz and Koenig safe in their stalls but they needed curry-combing and it was hours, his mother said, until he would come to the house for a meal.

Even before he had been sent away, he had been feeding and watering and bedding down the horses with fresh straw, now he set about learning to harness them for work in the fields. A neighbor woman recalled having seen him standing on an overturned tub, crying softly as he lifted the heavy collar again and again so that he could buckle it behind the horse's ears, but again and again it slipped back. If he could not master a boy's lessons at school, he seemed to be determined to master a man's work on the farm.

The woman also told of seeing him, not more than ten years old at the time, atop a load of firewood, his thin shoulders hunched against the winter wind off Little Traverse Bay. His father helped him cut and split the wood by hand but the boy drove the team to town where he unloaded and stacked it for 50¢ a cord.

Although Prinz and Koenig were not matched thoroughbreds, Papa gave them rubdowns and combings and at Christmas time he braided their tails and fitted their harnesses with sleigh bells. They responded to his tender loving care in kind, standing patiently while he piled the wood and collected from his customers. They waited without moving while he loaded the stone boat with rocks from the fields. They pulled the plow through the root-tangled new ground without protest and they gave him time to swing around the heavy plow at the end of the furrow.

In those boyhood years while he was doing the work of an adult, he began to dream of the barn he would build to replace the log shed built by the man who had homesteaded the farm. It would be a great, hip-roofed structure like the ones farther south he had seen from the train. In the basement it would have five horse stalls, two for young draft horses, one for a buggy horse and two for Prinz and Koenig when they were too old to work.

And there would be enough stanchions so he could build up a dairy herd of ten, also space for calves and pigs, all enclosed by the thick stone foundation banked with ground to keep the animals warm in winter and cool in summer. Above the stable there would be a heavy plank floor, strong enough to hold a loaded wagon and a team of horses as well as the hay and straw mows on either side. There would also be storage space to shield the farm implements from the rain and snow, and a granary for the wheat and oats and barley.

He saw it all in his mind before he began to make simple drawings of the magnificent barn which would rise majestically near the row of black walnut trees which he had helped his father tend.

In his mid-teens he started cutting down the choicest hard wood trees on the back forty, maple and oak for the timbers and planking. Later he cut hemlock and pine for the vertical siding and the roof boards. From a neighbor's swamp he got cedars for the shingles in exchange for digging fence post holes. The biggest rock outcroppings in the fields he snaked to the foundation site during the summer evenings after the farm work was done. During the winter days he hauled the big logs to the McManus Mill on Bear River in Petoskey where they were sawn to the proper length and thickness, then rough planed.

And when he was eighteen, a barn builder was engaged to help him draw the final plans and drive the stakes for the great 30' by 60' foundation, also to show him and his brother Albert how to set and mortar the huge rocks for the basement walls which must be straight and strong and true.

The following summer the barn-raising day arrived, the master builder having made ready the timbers which would be hoisted into place by the men and boys of the neighborhood. Papa made several stipulations: there was to be a generous supply of nails on hand and the builder was to make certain that for every spike ordinarily used in a supporting member, two must be used as the barn was to stand strong and tall for many generations; also, the kegs of beer which were carefully hidden would not be opened until the day's work was done—men who were drinking were apt to bend over nails or even fall off the roof.

The barn built, it was time to begin thinking about a bride. A kindly soft-spoken grocery clerk at Fochtman's Store, had been left a widower with five daughters. He worked from 6:00 A.M. until 6:00 P.M. on weekdays and was always in church on Sunday morning for 8 o'clock Mass. From afar Papa had been admiring one of the daughters for months but now he asked her father for permission to take her for a buggy ride.

Papa's idea was a leisurely Sunday afternoon trip to the town's miniature zoo which had some of the animals native to the region, bears, wolves and foxes, also some monkeys and tropical birds. However, the young lady's idea was to attend a night-time barn dance, to which he reluctantly agreed. For one thing, he didn't know how to dance and for another, night-driving was hard on an old horse.

Learning to square dance was not as simple as the girl had assured him it would be and the other fellows seemed to be much better at "dosidosing" and swinging his partner than he was. Also it began to look as though the careening around would go on until dawn. So, promptly at midnight by the pocket watch he had bought for the occasion, he announced that it was time for him to take her home.

This did not sit well with the exuberant young lady who was an excellent dancer and was having a wonderful time. However, she agreed to meet him at the door, saying, "Go, get your horse and I'll dance another set."

It was a sleety night in October and Papa removed the horse blanket he had draped over old Prinz and brought his rig to the sliding door entrance, there to wait and wait and wait while both he and his horse shivered in the cold. "She must have danced two or three more sets or whatever they're called," he told me many years later when I asked him about his brief courtship with Mamma's Cousin Celia who was to be my first teacher as it happened. "I had a notion to just go home and leave her there," he added. "That's what some fellas would've done but I'd promised her father I'd bring her home safely, so I did. But it was awful hard on my horse, never saw such a night for sleet!" Those were very strong words for Papa who didn't like to criticize anybody. Apparently that sleety night had been "awful hard" on him also.

Probably Cousin Celia would not have gone out again with such a serious-minded young man if he had asked her, which he didn't. At sixteen, she had no intention of getting married and settling down—first she wanted to become a teacher, read lots of books and see a bit of Michigan. However, some months later, she did arrange a buggy ride with him for her Cousin Gertrude and this time the young couple went to the animal zoo instead of to a barn dance.

Next, Papa took Mamma to see his beautiful new barn and to meet his family. By now he had a sleek-limbed buggy horse, Lady by name, and a rubber-tired buggy which was the talk of the neighborhood. Apparently Mamma was sufficiently impressed by the magnificent, hip-roofed structure, and as she was deemed acceptable by his family his next move was to haul his new gasoline engine and the wood-buzzing contraption he had put together to her parents' home on the other side of town, there to demonstrate the ease with which he could cut up a year's supply of firewood.

The gasoline engine, however, did not displace horse

power. Hitherto, he had cut wood to size by hand with a buck saw or with a cross cut saw for two. The demonstration was met with awe and admiration and helped to give the young suitor the courage to ask Mamma's father for her hand. They were then considered properly engaged and had their picture taken, Papa with a rose from the chapel garden in his lapel and she with her engagement watch pinned to the yoke of her modest, high-necked dress.

It was to be another year until the wedding took place on June 5, 1906, the bridegroom at twenty-one, the bride at nineteen. Small farmers could still do fairly well and during the intervening months, Papa had built up his dairy herd from four to seven and he had several heifers soon to mature. Also he had acquired another team of horses to do the heavy work. And, until they died from natural causes, Koenig and Prinz were put to pasture literally. It was no more than right, Papa always said, that those who had worked hard all their lives, should be respected in their old age.

As was then the custom in many households, the young couple shared the living quarters with the original family, their only privacy for several years being a bedroom on the second floor which at least had a chimney hole for a heating stove when needed. Mamma had grown up with seven brothers and sisters so she was accustomed to crowding and confusion. However, she was taken aback by the amount of time her father-in-law spent at his prayers.

Instead of helping with the milking, morning and evening, he was in the chapel, ringing the steeple bell and saying the Angelus. He was there again at noon, keeping the family waiting while the food on the table was getting cold. True, he was giving the big new barn a second coat of paint but the job would have taken half the time, had he been content to paint it a solid red—but no, it must be artistic, he must paint all the battens white, thus necessitating moving the heavy ladder around the barn twice. And, although he was willing to hoe milk weeds and Canada thistles out of the corn and potatoes, he could have done the job ten times as fast with the double-row horse cultivator.

Also, she couldn't understand his disdain for the English

language and she refused to believe that he couldn't understand a word of it after more than a quarter century in America. If he wanted to cling to "old country" speech and folkways, if his native land had such a wonderful culture, why in the world had he left it?

One day to test him, she asked, "If you find out that God doesn't know German when you get to heaven and hasn't understood a word of your prayers, what will you say and will you say it in German?"

By the look on his face and by his subsequent added aloofness, she was quite sure that he had understood every word she said. However, Grandpa's loyalty to his native tongue came to be recognized even to the third generation. The summer before he died when my sister Madeline, not yet two years old, was playing in her sand box and needed an implement to make her mud pies, she knocked on the kitchen door and when it was opened, she said, "Spoon." But when she saw it was Grandpa, she switched to the German, "Loffel."

Papa preferred to humor his father, reminding Mamma that the old man was still hankering after the Hessian countryside of his youth which he would never see again.

So gentle and good-natured was Lady, the buggy horse, that she responded to orders in any language. Once when Grandpa was leaving the chapel, he found her grazing contendedly near his newly planted rosebushes. "Geht du heim," he thundered and Lady, with a nod of her head and a flick of her tail, sauntered off toward the barn rather than offend the old gentleman.

But Lady was not to remain in the family forever. Past middle age when purchased, she found it increasingly hard to make the round trip to town and one morning Papa found her dead in her stall. Some would have sold her carcass to a local fox farm but Papa spent a day digging her grave near those of Prinz and Koenig.

Daisy was to be our next buggy horse, light-footed enough for the road, yet strong enough for the field. Much to Papa's consternation, she was to run away with Mamma at the reins and again, to his humiliation while he was driving to the cemetery for a graveside service. However, she did produce two colts who grew up to be well-behaved horses and were named King and Prince after Papa's first loves in the horse world. They continued in unspectacular service until the late 1930's when thoroughbred draft animals became affordable because of displacement by tractors. Papa then retired Daisy's offspring and bought a handsome matched team which remained his pride and joy until he died.

When automobiles made their debut in our neighborhood, Papa was highly skeptical. Oh, they might be all right for doctors during the good weather months when there were a lot of house calls to make or for mailmen with their long routes. But for farmers, who already had hay and grain, "Horses couldn't be beat, you bet your boots!"

Even in summer there could be problems with the newfangled contraptions. On the road bordering our farm, a Model T couldn't make it to the top of the steep hill if it was low on gas. The fuel tank was under the front seat and since there was a gravity feed, the car would chug to a halt half way up the hill. The driver then had the option of letting his car roll back to the foot of the hill, turn it around, and try again backside forward. Or, if fearful of backing up the hill, he could call on Papa to tow his man-made machine over the summit.

Occasionally a late night visitor to a moonshine still several miles to the East would get mired in the mud if he zig-zagged off the road and it was Papa to the rescue. Once, a befuddled driver who was checking his gas tank with a lighted match was thrown bodily into a water-filled ditch with his whiskers ablaze. Hearing the explosion and the cries for help, Papa was able to save the toper but not the Model T.

Sometimes Papa was paid a tow fee and sometimes he wasn't but he always seemed to get a great deal of satisfaction out of proving that horses were superior to the gasoline guzzlers which were trying to take over the roads. Horses could maneuver in almost any situation, they were self-supporting, they consumed but a small quantity of the food they helped to produce and what they did eat could later be put back on the soil in the form of manure.

Tractors were even more of an abomination than cars, to Papa. They were alien to the land, they had to be fed

something which came from far away and who knew when the oil wells would go dry, better to ration what gasoline there was for work not fitted for horses, like powering a buzz saw. And they were dangerous on steep hillsides like those in Northern Michigan, they toppled over backward pinning their drivers underneath them. They had no love, no feeling for their masters, they did not renew the soil, they made the land dependent on chemicals which in time would ruin the good green earth.

Like the Bismarck his father had talked about, Papa considered the tractor a false god of bigness and greed, one which had no heart. Those who wanted tractors wanted them so they could farm more acreage, not because they truly loved the soil. Not satisfied with 80 acres which was enough for any one farmer to till and tend, they hankered after more and more. But what would it profit a man if he gained a whole section of land but lost the natural goodness of the soil?

As a child, I liked horses, too. I have pleasant memories of riding to town in the buggy or the cutter—it took about an hour to get there at Topsy's easy pace. There was no noisy motor, just the pad, pad of the horse's hooves on the sandy road or the crunch, crunch on the frosty snow. There was time to talk about the past and the future as well as the present.

For the most part, Papa liked to tell stories handed down from his father about life across the sea. The one I remember best was about the hungry wolves which had followed a family travelling through the Black Forest snapping at the horses' feet and snarling at the children. Papa didn't tell us the folk-tale version, with a child thrown off the sleigh to appease the ravenous wolves, rather it was one of the horses, a true hero, which was sacrificed to save the family.

There were also stories about the wars in the "old country" when so many men on both sides were killed that their bodies were never taken back to their villages but were buried in a common grave. And he told us about the beautiful cloister which had stood for many generations near Obertifenbach where Grandpa was born, but which was destroyed in a battle, all but the foundation stones. And now another was being fought overseas and there was more death and destruction. We children should get down on our knees at night and pray that the world's people would learn to get along together and that included *us!*

On the quiet rides with Mamma, her talk was mostly about plans for the future, about redoing our bedrooms with flowered wallpaper, about making some new curtains for our windows, about getting our empty fruit jars filled for winter, about some special recipes for Christmas cookies.

After Mass on Sunday, Papa would sometimes take us to the zoo, or animal park as he called it; it seemed to be his one special recreational attraction and later when the Zoo was abandoned, it was the fish hatchery at Oden which he liked. Then, after Sunday dinner, he usually took a nap, a luxury he couldn't afford during the work week. Mostly we didn't begrudge him this seventh day of rest but occasionally we coaxed him to take us fishing at Conway on Crooked Lake. It was about three miles from the farm and Carl often hiked there with a friend but we girls were not allowed to go places without adult supervision. Papa said it was because Carl was older but we thought it was because he was a boy and boys were permitted more liberties.

As we started for home one time when Papa had given up his nap to take us fishing, a neighbor with a newly purchased automobile blew his horn and pulled up alongside our buggy and shouted, "Do your kids want a ride home?"

Carl was quick to jump over the buggy wheel to accept the offer and Madeline got permission to accompany him. Colette waited to see what I was going to do but I was torn between taking advantage of the wonderful opportunity and loyalty to Papa. While I hesitated, the Model T was driven off in a cloud of dust.

"Didn't you want to go?" Papa asked me.

"I like the horse and buggy best," I told him, something which I was beginning to doubt a little.

"I do, too," four-year-old Colette chimed in. "Cars are too noisy."

By now I was feeling very noble for not having deserted Papa and Topsy. After all, we'd had a wonderful time, we had a string of fish to take home, and we girls had even been permitted to go wading near the shore—although not at the public beach—all because Papa had given up his nap for us.

I could see that he was pleased that we hadn't left him to make the trip home by himself and he rewarded Colette and me by retelling one of our favorite stories about his boyhood—how he was afraid to run away from the boarding school because the snowbanks on both sides of the railroad tracks were so high he feared he couldn't climb over them if a train came roaring toward him. How lucky we were, I thought, that we had never been sent so far from home like that. But still, an automobile ride would be nice!

However, there came a time when loyalty to Papa and Topsy began to give way. By then we were the only family in the whole neighborhood going back and forth to town in an old-fashioned top buggy which seemed to signify that we were too poor to buy an automobile. Sometimes I had a dream about walking up the aisle at church in my bare feet while all the other girls were wearing shiny black patent-leather slippers and now I was beginning to feel the same way about our horse and buggy.

While in the 8th grade at the parochial school in town, I was embarrassed to be seen riding behind a horse. If I chanced to see any of my classmates, I turned my head the other way, hoping they wouldn't recognize me. And once, a boy from the public school taunted me for no reason at all, "Cat-licker, horse-licker!" I felt like yelling back "Pup-licker" but I didn't want to make a spectacle of myself. Yes, there was something demeaning about dawdling behind a horse and being left in a cloud of dust by every automobile streaking by.

A church-related fund-raiser was a possible way out of our dilemma. The Knights of Columbus was raffling off a car, a beautiful, upstanding Chevrolet which was on display in the churchyard. Papa was asked to buy a book of chances and although he didn't buy a whole book, he did buy one chance since it was for a good cause. The thought that we might win that gorgeous black sedan with a self-starter instead of a crank was enough to set our young hearts thumping and our prayers wafting heavenward.

Oh, how we prayed, at least Colette and I did, not only on our knees in the evening but while washing dishes, weeding in the garden, picking berries, whatever. And if our prayers were answered and we won the Chevrolet, it would be clear to Papa that God approved of the automotive invention—"Thy will be done!"

On the evening of the raffle, Madeline went to bed at the usual time, telling me to call her if we won the car, but Colette and I continued to kneel by the window, fingering our rosaries and reminding God of our need for better transportation. We prayed on into the night until sleep overtook us but the next day we learned that a resorter had won the Chevrolet and he already had a Pierce Arrow!

Papa said that praying for something like a car was a mistake, if we wanted to ask God for a special favor we should pray for rain which would benefit not only us but all the farmers as the corn was beginning to get shriveled and yellow, although barely tasseled out. Mamma said that anyone who already had a car should have turned it back and

Carl claimed he'd rather have a Packard anyway. As for Madeline, she said she'd had a good night's sleep.

Rather than prayers, it seemed that what was needed was the purchase price of a car so we began to save the nickels and dimes we earned by doing extra work. We girls picked wild berries which Mamma sold for us in Bay View, Carl did odd jobs for one of the neighbors who had no children, we pooled the birthday dollars we got from one of our aunts—but we didn't mention our secret cache to Papa.

I see it now as rather devious behavior, but since efforts to achieve our objective by honorable prayer had not been successful, another tack would have to be tried. So it was that we older children entered into an underhanded pact, nothing illegal of course, rather it was like trying the back door when the front door is locked. One of our uncles was the service manager in a garage in Grand Rapids and a letter was secretly dispatched to him, inquiring as to whether he knew of any good-running, second-hand cars at a reasonable, low price.

Already I was instinctively aware of the needs of the male ego so my letter was laboriously composed, with the early drafts submitted to Carl for his approval as he was to sign it. Also, the letter must seem to be a very casual but serious inquiry so that Papa would not be aware that we had initiated the action and on top of that, it must appeal to Uncle Joe's sense of importance and his generosity.

We were delighted when the reply came with no mention whatsoever of the inquiry. It was an uncle-to-nephew letter which included a paragraph in which he said he was considering selling his 1922 touring car and buying an enclosed sedan, and that he was driving to Petoskey the following weekend. If the family was interested, he would sell his Chevrolet to us for $100 cash.

Carl forgot all about preferring a Packard and we began a six day promotional drive to win Papa's approval of the deal, both ideological and financial as we had barely half enough money to swing the transaction. We used every conceivable tactic that might persuade our reluctant father to say "yes"—a car would make it possible for us to attend the Wednesday evening church service as well as Sunday Mass, the newly graveled State Road replacing the old sand track was hard on Topsy's feet, the car was in fine shape because Uncle Joe knew all about mechanics, there would probably never be such a bargain again etc. etc. Furthermore, we would contribute our hard-earned personal savings for something which would benefit the whole family!

By Friday we had Papa nearly convinced that perhaps, after all, a car would serve a useful purpose at least during the good weather months. By Saturday, we had him almost thinking that it was his idea in the first place. Our strategy was working.

Papa, Mamma and the younger children were at church when two Chevrolets came rolling into the yard on Sunday morning—the '22 touring car and the '23 sedan which Uncle Joe was thinking of buying from his friend who was driving it.

"Pa says it's okay, Pa says it's okay," was Carl's greeting as Uncle Joe jumped out of his car and shook hands.

"Wait 'til Papa sees it," I cautioned, wanting the inspection and the final decision to seem to be Papa's alone.

"I'll leave it here and come back this afternoon after your dad gets home," Uncle Joe told us as he left the marvel of engineering ingenuity in our care. It was beautiful but rather dusty so we set about washing it so as to make it look like a brand new car. The wash job made it glisten but when it was wiped dry, it was a dull, second-hand looking black and it was then that Carl bethought himself of the oil which Papa used to keep the horses' harnesses supple and shiny. This we applied liberally to the body of the Chevrolet and also to the spokes of the wheels, giving the whole automobile a glossy, liquidy look. It didn't occur to us that metal, unlike leather, would not absorb the oil and that on our first venture on a country road, the oil would attract dust like flypaper attracts flies.

Topsy seemed not to notice the beautiful, black behemoth on display in our front yard when she came trudging home after church. Perhaps she was tired and hungry after the trip to town in the August heat and no doubt, Papa kept her on a tight rein, looking the opposite way from her replacement.

That was the beginning of the decline for flesh and blood

horse power on our farm. Carl, now in his mid-teens, kept up a clamor for a tractor and was finally able to persuade Papa to buy a second-hand Fordson. With the zeal of a teen-ager, he quickly mastered automotive mysteries and was able to keep both the car and the tractor in good repair. Very proudly he demonstrated that the Fordson could do in a day what it took the horses a week to do.

Occasionally Papa would use the tractor but his heart wasn't in it. And as Mamma noticed, when he did use it, he was careful not to let his horses see him doing so, for fear it would hurt their feelings. And until his dying day, he maintained that horses would stage a comeback; cars and tractors were man-made, they had no real place in the natural scheme of things, their rusty carcasses were dumped into gullies and creek beds where they were an eyesore whereas horses returned to the earth from whence they came. He didn't go as far as saying that horses had souls but I am quite sure that he thought they had a role to play in heaven. Although man could make a machine only God could make a horse and surely He would reserve a place for His own.

Daughters of Eve

THE first picture in our *Bible History for Children*, the one with Eve luring Adam into trouble with an apple, set the tone for the moral philosophy which held women responsible for the waywardness of men. Papa seemed to subscribe to this school of thought pretty much although his credo had a positive side as well. "Man is neither good nor bad but woman makes him so" would have more or less summed up his thinking on the subject. At least he was willing to give credit to womankind, if and when credit was due.

He may have considered it something of a trial and tribulation that the Lord had presented him with mostly daughters, four out of six. And what made his cross especially hard to bear was that they were coming of age at a time when the morals of the country were going down hill lickety-split, like the devil on a bobsled. Women, having gotten the vote, were flaunting their newfound freedom. Rather than setting a good example to young girls, they were out-doing the men in shameless behavior; they were drinking in "speak easies," they were lighting up cigarettes on the streets, they were using foul language.

No longer did they know their place in the world, no longer did they take their "Kirche, Kindren und Kochen" duties seriously. Now they were playing golf on the Country Club course on Sunday morning instead of going to church, now they were sprawling on the beaches instead of washing diapers, now they were playing "Mah Jongg" and bridge instead of baking bread.

The scanty dress styles gave wanton witness to the tenor of the times: hemlines above the knee-caps instead of below the ankles, plunging necklines instead of chaste, chin-high guimpes, narrow skirts which crept upward as the wearers climbed into rumble seats. Indeed, it was a time to try a father's soul!

And as for the underclothing shamelessly displayed in store windows as well as in the Sears Roebuck Catalogue, it was a disgrace to womankind. What had been unmentionable was now put on display for all to see. Even the names of under-garments were intended to be seductive, such as "step-ins." And the skintight, so-called bathing suits were such that no self-respecting woman would be seen in one. What the styles were coming to, was more than Papa cared to imagine.

He tried to stress the positive. The girl who dressed simply and neatly and modestly would not be subject to whistles and catcalls and in the end, disrespect. The girl who learned to cook and clean and sew would attract a good husband in due time who would give her a comfortable home and who would love and cherish her until death did them part. To reward them along the way, God would send them many children—children they must teach to follow in their footsteps.

And not only should a girl consider the benefits of virtue to herself but to others as well. Each side of our family had a clean record and we must keep it that way. Papa didn't spell out exactly what he meant but eventually it became clear that he was referring to untimely weddings or certain occurrences out of wedlock. There must be no daughters' sins visited upon their parents nor on future generations.

Modesty in dress was the foundation of virtue. As babies it was permissible that both sexes wear the same type clothing; all six of us wore the long Grandmother-made baptismal gown with its profusion of tucks and lace inserts and hemstitching. But once the early childhood years were over, boys must dress like boys and girls like girls. A woman wearing trousers was as outrageous as a man wearing skirts. Yet some females were beginning to do that very thing, strutting around in broad daylight with bulges in the rear as well as in the front!

In our country school, dress length had to do with age. Teacher and the teen-agers wore their skirts to the ankles whereas we younger girls wore ours halfway between our knee-caps and our high-topped shoes which were either buttoned or laced. We all wore black cotton stockings.

But the short skirt craze which came in soon after the passage of the 19th Amendment, rocked the foundations of modesty. No longer did young girls yearn for ankle length styles, no longer did teen-agers consider long dresses the sign of maturity. Now, the shorter the dresses, the more removed from parental restrictions were the wearers.

Although I wasn't anxious to grow up since it would mean leaving the family nest, I thought that long dresses had a dowdy, countrified look. As I stood on a stool while Mamma pinned up my skirt hem, I knew exactly where I wanted the hem to be. However, Papa had quite a different notion as to where propriety left off and impropriety began. Poor Mamma was caught betwixt and between, as to where she should put the pins.

My sisters and I finally hit on a way to out-maneuver Papa—we perfected the art of hunching. By letting the shoulders droop a little, by expelling as much breath as possible, by holding in the stomach tightly, and by bending the knees a bit, one could end up with a skirt which was shorter by several inches than his prescribed length. Mamma didn't seem to catch on to our strategy, and if Papa later pressed her for an explanation, she would venture the guess that we were going through a stage of rapid growth.

However, the most satisfactory solution to the problem was to opt for the two-piece dress or the blouse and skirt with an elastic waistband. This made it easy to adjust the length as the situation required. At school we could hike up the skirt several inches and at home or at church we could lower it, thus keeping peace in the family, as well as keeping up with the style.

Then there was the matter of sleeves—sleevelessness of course was "Verboten." Papa was strong for the wrist length but Mamma preferred the elbow, reminding him that long-sleeved dresses had to be washed more often. He was willing to make a compromise half way between, but unfortunately for us, three quarter length sleeves were not in fashion.

The neckline, however, was not a matter for compromise. For any dress with an unacceptable cut, Papa's answer to the problem was the guimpe. It would cover a multitude of deficiencies—necklines which were too low, necklines which were too loose, necklines which were too revealing. The guimpe, be it known, was a high-necked shirt waist, usually white or cream-colored, which was designed to be worn under a jumper or a pinafore or, as Papa insisted, under any kind of dress which exposed too much of the female anatomy.

I despised the guimpe—to me it seemed to be a left-over style from ancient times when my parents were young. It could make a gorgeous frock look positively frumpy but, especially when we went to church, it was an absolute requirement for any dress which did not meet Papa's specifications. I remember a lovely pink taffeta bit of finery with a slightly low neckline and short puff sleeves—a hand-me-down from a resorter acquaintance. Mamma said it was a party frock and not right for school; Papa said it wasn't right for church either but finally agreed to let me wear it with a long sleeved guimpe under it. That would have spoiled the whole effect so I never got to wear it at all and it was the only really elegant dress I ever had.

Fleece-lined union suits or Long Johns were another mortification of my girlhood. In the country school everybody wore them—even the teacher—and they did keep us warm. After ploughing through the snowdrifts we would sit around the stove drying off our long-legged underwear and our stockings until the bell rang. But once in high school, I did not find warmth and comfort the chief consideration. During my Freshman year I struggled along through part of the winter, folding and refolding those bunchy union suit legs, trying to achieve a smooth uncountrified look.

Finally, one February morning in an agony of thick-legged shame, I hacked off the offending parts even though I might freeze my lower limbs walking to school from the farm. And the next to go, a short time later, were black-ribbed cotton stockings. Flesh-colored hose were now being worn by my classmates.

After that, Papa had to retire from the field to re-group his shattered guidelines but he was never able to hold any new fall-back position for very long. On one style after another he had to give way: knee length skirts, guimpeless dresses, short sleeves, high heels. But on one precept he held his ground—his daughters were not to wear the new skin-tight bathing suits.

In those days beach garments had skirts, they had backs and there were no bare midriffs but even so, they were a far cry from Papa's standards of decency. Not that he had occasion to see many bathers in person as he certainly spent no time on the beaches. However, in the course of making a living and while minding his own business, he once came face to face with a modern Jezebel.

Cordwood was one of our main sources of income along with garden and dairy products. We considered fireplaces old fashioned but resorters seemed to like open fires, despite the dust and smoke, even when they didn't really need them for warmth. There was no accounting for the tastes of rich people but we were glad to have a market for our wood. Most people in Petoskey had switched to coal which they burned in big, nickel and ising-glass trimmed stoves which needed firing only twice a day.

At any rate, most of Papa's customers were Bay View cottagers. Mamma would take the orders during the summer and Papa would fill them during the late fall after the crops were harvested. By that time the resorters had gone south for the winter, having paid for their fireplace logs, sight unseen, before they left. They knew that Papa's wood was as good as his word.

As it happened, one summer a customer needed an extra supply so Papa obligingly took time off from the fields to deliver the order. When he arrived at the cottage, there seemed to be no one around, so he set about unloading the logs and piling them under the back porch as usual. Halfway through the job, the "lady" of the house came "sashaying" up from the beach, clad only in a bathing suit and a wet one at that.

"Been out for a dip, the water's great," the woman exclaimed as Papa told Mamma later. "I hardly knew which way to look," he added within my hearing.

After she had dried her bobbed hair—and I could tell by the way Papa said "bobbed" that he disapproved of her hair as well as her costume, she said she was going in to have a drink and did he want one? It was a hot day and Papa said he wouldn't have minded a drink of plain cold water but not whatever she had in mind and this right during Prohibition, too!

"No," he said he told her. "I've got to get this wood unloaded and get home as it's hot here for the horses standing in the sun."

"Well, then, I'll help you," she offered and despite his protestations that it was no job for a woman, she insisted that she needed the exercise as she was trying to lose weight. "And she sure needed to lose some, big strapping two hundred pounder. . . ."

"Oh, I don't think she weighs that much," Mamma interrupted.

"Legs like stovepipes, big, fat hussy," Pappa sputtered.

I could hardly believe my ears. Papa never said unkind things about anybody.

"Women like that don't have enough work to do, no wonder they get fat, just beachin' around," Papa wound up somewhat lamely.

Fortunately for Papa's scandalized state of mind, the "hussy" had dropped a log on her toe and after a bit of profanity disappeared into the cottage, there to remain while Papa hastily finished the job and took off without waiting to be paid for the wood. It was left for Mamma to collect at a later date and to somehow explain her husband's abrupt departure. Thereafter, during the summer when there were calls for fireplace logs, Papa had an excuse handy, he delivered wood only during the off season.

"Tights" was the disparaging word which Papa used for the scanty costumes worn by trapeze performers. Carl said it was because of the half-naked tight-rope men and women, that Papa didn't want to take us to the Circus which came to town every summer. Several times, however, he did take us to see the animals being unloaded from the box-cars and to watch the elephants pick up the huge tent poles and hoist them into place—and all this was for free.

We kept up a barrage of begging and Mamma said that every child should be able to attend at least one big tent performance, so at last Papa agreed to take us. It was before we had our car and we all piled into the buggy, except for Mamma and the baby. On the way to town Papa told us a story that had come down to him from his father about a tailor in the "old country" who had poked a needle into the flank of an elephant as the circus parade went by the open window of his shop. The elephant did nothing that day but the next time the circus was in town, the animal who never forgets blew a trunkful of water into the tailor's shop, ruining all his expensive fabrics.

For me it was a toss-up as to whether Christmas in December or Barnum and Bailey in mid-August was the most soul-stirring. The clowns going through their antics, the horses marching in tune to the music, the lions jumping through fiery hoops, these were as exciting as opening the presents which Santa Claus brought us.

I didn't care much for the trapeze performers as I was afraid they might fall and break their necks but I could understand why they didn't wear more clothes. "What should they wear then?" I asked Papa after suggesting that bulky costumes might get in their way and cause them to lose their balance.

"They shouldn't wear anything—anything like those indecent outfits," he added hastily as I waited nervously to see whether a female performer would make it into the arms of her partner, halfway across the top of the tent. It was evident that Papa thought that "tights" were in the same class as bathing suits.

But we girls weren't interested in tights for tights' sake or in skintight swim suits either. What we wanted was an opportunity to go bathing in a "genuwine" Michigan lake. Black sateen bloomers and old middy blouses had served our needs adequately during our brief adventures in Carl's home-made swimming pool and we were willing to make-do with them if only we could get Papa to take us bathing in a sizeable body of water.

"You can take your baths right here at home," he told us.

It would be more discreet, we decided, to downplay the bathing part of the outing and stress the picnic end of it in our promotional efforts. "We can take some wieners and marshmallows and roast them on the beach," we coaxed, knowing how much he liked these store-bought delicacies.

"You can blacken them up just as well in the kitchen, just take off the stove lid," he countered.

But we kept at him, emphasizing the family togetherness of our project and pointedly adding that most fathers took their children on occasional outings. Gradually we wore him down and he finally agreed to take us on one condition—he always hooked a condition onto every concession—he would not take us to a public beach and to this we consented although with a pretended show of reluctance. It was not wise to act as though Papa had lost the battle completely, better to let him think that we were forced to give ground also.

As a matter of fact, we preferred not to go to a beach where all the other girls would be wearing store-bought bathing suits as we did not relish being seen in our makeshift swimming gear. All we really wanted was the pleasure of frolicking in a body of water with more length and breadth than Carl's ill-fated heated pool.

To accustom Papa to the idea that we had a little more in mind than just the food, we made occasional casual remarks like, "Of course, before the picnic we'll go in wading and so on." Whether he tumbled to the meaning of "so on" was unclear, but I think he was beginning to accept the fact that we were reaching an age when he couldn't count on our abiding by all parental rules if they were too stringent.

We were in a tremble of anticipation when the great day arrived. The sun was shining beautifully, the cloudless sky was a lovely Northern Michigan blue and the temperature was perfect for our purposes. In addition to the wieners and marshmallows, we were taking many homemade goodies including cream puffs which we seldom had at our house because they took a lot of eggs—five for the puffs and two for the filling. Whipped cream would not do in the hot weather as it might get sour. During the summertime when she had orders from her customers, Mamma was rather stingy with her eggs, rationing them carefully for family use. She tried to talk us into a one-egg applesauce cake but since it was a very special occasion, she relented and let us splurge "this one time." The puffs turned out perfectly—feather-light, golden mounds which we slit and filled with vanilla custard, one for each of us.

Sunday afternoon was Papa's time to catch up on his rest after six days in the fields, and we had suggested that we go on our picnic on a week day but he wouldn't hear of it. "Beaching around" on a work day would shock Joe Gallagher. Joe had some frontage on Pickerel Lake which was too wet for cropping but it served as a pasture and watering spot for his cows. It was several miles farther away than Crooked Lake but apparently Papa figured that the Gallagher swamp would not be infested with resorter-bathers.

We had our second-hand Chevrolet by then, so after church we loaded it with market baskets of food and jugs of lemonade. Papa gave his horses some special Sunday treats and we set off to take our first plunge in an honest-to-goodness lake. Joe heard our car as we pulled into his yard and came out to greet us and after he and Papa exchanged comments on the weather, they went on to discuss various matters of mutual interest—the comparative yields of Alfalfa and Timothy hay, the high cost of farm implements as against the low price of farm produce, the relative nuisance of grasshoppers as compared to that of potato bugs, all this while we girls fidgeted in the back seat, wondering if Papa would ever get to the point.

Finally, after a nudge or two from Mamma, he came out with it, "The children here, they want to have a picnic or something, thought maybe if it's all right with you, we'd sort of use your lane to get down to the lake," Papa explained rather lamely.

"Oh sure, sure! Tisn't much of a place for women folks though—chuck holes, cow piles, mosquitoes—but go ahead if that's what you've come for," he boomed, obviously pleased to indulge in generosity so cheaply.

"And, oh yes," Papa added. "They want to start a little fire to cook something, but we'll be careful."

"Wet as it is down there, you can't hurt nothing. I'll open the gate—the cows won't bother you none and we got no bull," he told us.

With a kind of mirthless laugh, Papa thanked him and off we started down the lane with Joe calling after us not to go all the way to the lake with the car or we'd get stuck. Honest as Papa was, he hadn't said a word about "sort of using the water."

The ground began to get a little oozy just as we caught sight of Pickerel Lake and Mamma urged Papa to stop the car and let us walk the rest of the way. Gleefully we piled out, each of us grabbing something to carry. I took charge of the cream puffs as I didn't want anything to happen to them after all my hard work and all those eggs. Carl was not with us that day, he had eaten his cream puff at home, pronouncing it "yummy" and gone somewhere with a friend.

As we neared the lake there were hoof prints, some of them partly filled with water, but we saw no cows and after we found a comparatively dry spot, we put down our baskets, tossed off our outer garments and in our bloomers and middy blouses, we made for the water. Near the shore the bottom was mucky and sucked at our feet but once we were out a few yards and away from the slime and the weeds, the sensation was glorious and we began splashing and romping with great abandon.

"Hope there's a place like this in heaven," Colette called back to Papa who may not have found the idea amusing. He was having a hard time trying to find enough dry sticks to build a fire, and Mamma was busy swatting mosquitoes and chasing away flies which had scented the food, and two-year old Giles was begging her to let him get into the big wash-tub, too.

But for us girls, the next hour was pure ecstasy as we plunged and wriggled and frolicked, trying to make up for all the years of privation. Despite the thought of the delicious food awaiting us, we were loathe to return to shore but, hoping that good behavior would win us a repeat performance, we obeyed Papa's call promptly.

Mamma had set up a makeshift tent with a blanket where we changed into dry clothes in record time. Papa had some sharpened sticks ready for the wieners and we were soon standing around the fire "blackening" them up as Papa called it. There wasn't a good place to sit down, the mosquitoes were biting us, the flies were determined to get a share of the food but no matter, the wieners were juicy, the baked beans were bacony and even Papa seemed to be enjoying himself. We gave him the extra wiener.

We were about to start toasting our marshmallows when, like a streak of lightning, it happened. From another cove, not over fifty yards away, dashed four or five teen-age boys and they were bare naked but all I can remember noticing was the horrified look on Papa's face. After his many efforts to keep the situation under control, his precautions had been for nothing. It was like a sign from Heaven that the Lord was displeased.

With his mouth full of the last wiener, he told us to get back to the car and he began slamming food and dishes into the baskets.

"But they're in the water now, can't see anything but their heads," Mamma protested, adding "Let's finish eating first."

But Papa wasn't taking any chances and we were hastily herded in the opposite direction from the rollicking teenagers. In the rush, one of my sisters stepped into a fresh cowpile and I scratched my leg on a prickly bush but Papa kept us going without mercy. Fortunately, we were able to slow down a bit and get our breath when he remembered the bonfire and had to hurry back to douse it.

It was the muck which foiled a quick getaway. In his haste to turn the car around in the narrow lane, Papa managed to mire it axle-deep and there, within viewing distance of the male intruders, he had to leave us while he went to borrow Joe Gallagher's team for a tow.

We were much more interested in the dessert than we were in the boys. The marshmallows were salvageable but the cream puffs were a mess; they were all squished out of shape in a sea of custard as Papa had jammed the bean crock on top of them in his haste to gather up our things.

When Papa got back with Joe's horses, he had a hard time

hitching them to the car which had spun itself sidewise in the narrow lane. Also, the balky creatures were not responding properly to Papa's "Gees and Haws" and I was almost certain that I heard him use his one expletive under his breath, "Bastards!" Since he could not handle the reins and steer the car at the same time, he finally let me have a go at the wheel, something I had never before been permitted to do, and eventually we were able to get free of the muck. All in all, except for what happened to the cream puffs, it had been an exhilarating day.

At times it appeared to Papa that we girls were succumbing to Eve's bad influence but in the long run, he seemed satisfied that his daughters had heeded his admonitions. At least we were never known to "sashay around" on the beaches and there were no untimely trips to the altar.

Bad Books

It all began with *The Michigan Farmer,* a conservative, non-sensational weekly which dealt mostly with agricultural matters. For the menfolks there were articles about crop rotation, the butterfat content of milk from Jersey cows as compared with that from Guernseys and Holsteins, the market price of hogs on the hoof and such like. And there were advertisements for cream separators, mowing machines, manure spreaders, hay rakes and grain binders.

For the womenfolks there were recipes for pickled pigs' feet, head cheese and cucumber chow chow. There were instructions for ways to get rid of cut worms, chicken lice and tomato blight. There were patterns for patch quilts, maternity dresses and baby clothes. And to sweeten the pot for any farm wife who had any spare time in her busy life—although there were few such ladies in our neighborhood—the paper was running a novel in serial form, *The Hunted Woman* by James Oliver Curwood, the Wolverine State's very own author.

For want of something, just anything, to read, I occasionally thumbed through the farm paper even though by the time I was ten years old, I had decided that I was not going to be a farmer's wife. I aspired to something which did not involve pulling weeds in the garden, washing milk pails, picking up potatoes—humdrum, earthy jobs, I thought. For the time being I was willing to do what had to be done but in the distant future I wished to be spared from such unimportant work. Also, I did not intend to pinch pennies, cook cull beans and make one-egg cakes.

My interest in extracurricular reading began through something of a fluke when I was in the third grade. My head had become infested with lice which, apparently had emigrated from the boy who sat behind me. The two girls whom I had considered good friends made a big to-do over my predicament, declaring they were not going to play with me any more. So, rather than be humiliated in the schoolyard at recess time, I chose to sit at my disk in splendid isolation and read a "libary" book.

We didn't have much of a selection on our book shelf—mostly there were out-of-date geographies and upper grade readers with missing pages, but I managed to find one which seemed to be a grown-up type of book—it had no pictures, it had small print, it was fairly thick and it was one long story in chapters. It was *Tom, the Bootblack* by Horatio Alger and I set about reading it with as scholarly an air as I could muster. At every recess for weeks, I would keep at it and as my classmates came trooping in when the bell rang, I would riffle through the pages which I had read, proud of what I had accomplished while they were playing childish games in the schoolyard.

The hero in my "libary" book is not one to waste his time romping around with kids his own age, he works hard at his shoe-shine job, he is careful with his money, he supports the old man he lives with who is too sick to work. Tom plies his trade in front of the Astor House which sounded something like one of our hotels in Petoskey, and I could imagine him shining the shoes of the guests who sat on the long porch of the Cushman House across from the Railroad Station.

What Tom does not know in the first chapter is that his dead father had left him a lot of money but an evil guardian had stolen it and hired the old man to take the boy off his hands. Quite by chance, Tom shines the shoes of the villainous guardian and in another "quite by chance" (there are a lot of them), our hero finds a yellowed document which is legal proof of his guardian's wrongdoing.

In chapter after chapter, Tom pursues the evasive villain. The pursuit takes him to Cincinnati and while on the train to the Queen City, he chances to protect from harm another passenger, the young and beautiful Bessie Benton, whereupon he secretly vows to ask her father for her hand once he has retrieved his rightful fortune.

In the next "quite by chance," Tom gets a job in the firm his father had once owned, then goes on to study law in night school so that he can win his case in court. And in the final chapter we learn that he regains the family fortune, marries the beautiful and virtuous Bessie Benton and is elected to a seat in the U.S. Senate. The moral of the story is very clear. While other boys his age are playing around and having a good time, Tom is hard at work but in the end he reaps his reward.

There are no love scenes during Tom's rise from rags to riches, nor were there any in *Tom Sawyer*, the book my first teacher had read aloud to us—oh, there was mention in it of Tom's engagement to Becky but that was just kid stuff. However, the *Hunted Woman* was no kid story, it was listed in the farm paper as a novel, a NOVEL, how I relished the grown-up sound of the word.

In the first chapter the heroine is speeding across the continent on the Canadian Pacific Railroad and I imagine myself travelling with her, marvelling at the spectacular scenery from the train window—the foothills with their jagged outcroppings of reddish rock and the snow-capped mountains in the distance. And I tremble with her as we hurtle through black-as-night tunnels and cross raging rivers on narrow dizzying trestles. I had never been out of Emmet County before except to Kingsley for my Uncle Albert's wedding when I was very young so the trip through the Rockies is a new and romantic experience.

On the same train are "hordes" of roughneck men on their way to extend the rails in British Columbia which I looked up in a geography and found to be half the world away. Also on the train are some heavily rouged young women who are tittering at the coarse jokes of the men.

But through it all our heroine, Joanne Gray, sits demurely, her tinted silver veil drawn lightly over her delicate face— indeed, there is something about that veil which sets her above and apart from the giddy, giggling girls to the rear of the coach. Later, when she lifts it with a modest sweep of her dainty gloved hand, the reader learns that her eyes are the deep blue of the mountain violet, her cheeks the pink of the wild rose, her skin the softness of flower petals and her hair like lustrous spun gold.

My seat companion is on her way to investigate a rumor that her husband is dead. She married him at the bedside of her dying father who did not wish to leave her alone and undefended in the cruel, hard world. However, she does not love her legal husband nor has she ever lived with him so she certainly has a problem since she does not believe in divorce.

As the passengers leave the train at Tete Jeune which is Joanne's destination, she is accosted by a beefy tavern keeper who mistakes her for one of the painted women. It is then that John Aldous steps forward to save her from a fate worse than death and it was then that I stepped back from what was to be a developing romance. Oh, I followed events from afar but I felt that Joanne and John deserved a little privacy.

The farm paper came on a Saturday and I could hardly wait from one installment to the next to find out how things were proceeding in British Columbia. I tried to beat Carl to the mailbox because it seemed to take him forever to check the paper for any new idea in the way of farm equipment—he was always hoping to find a labor saver which he could build—with modifications if necessary.

Mamma didn't seem to catch on as to why I had suddenly taken such an interest in *The Michigan Farmer*. She knew I liked to read and there wasn't much else in reading matter around our house. Carl took note however, and threatened to tell on me—as if reading a love novel was a sin or something. I told him I had a good one to tell on him and he knew what I had in mind. At the time he was trying to make some dandelion wine and Mamma was deathly opposed to wine. Not only that but Carl had used some of her canning sugar!

In the Far West the romance is really getting heady. Our hero, it turns out, has written many famous novels and wonder of wonders, Joanne has read and loved them all. The great novelist lives in a simple rustic cabin and he offers to show Joanne where his books have been written and of

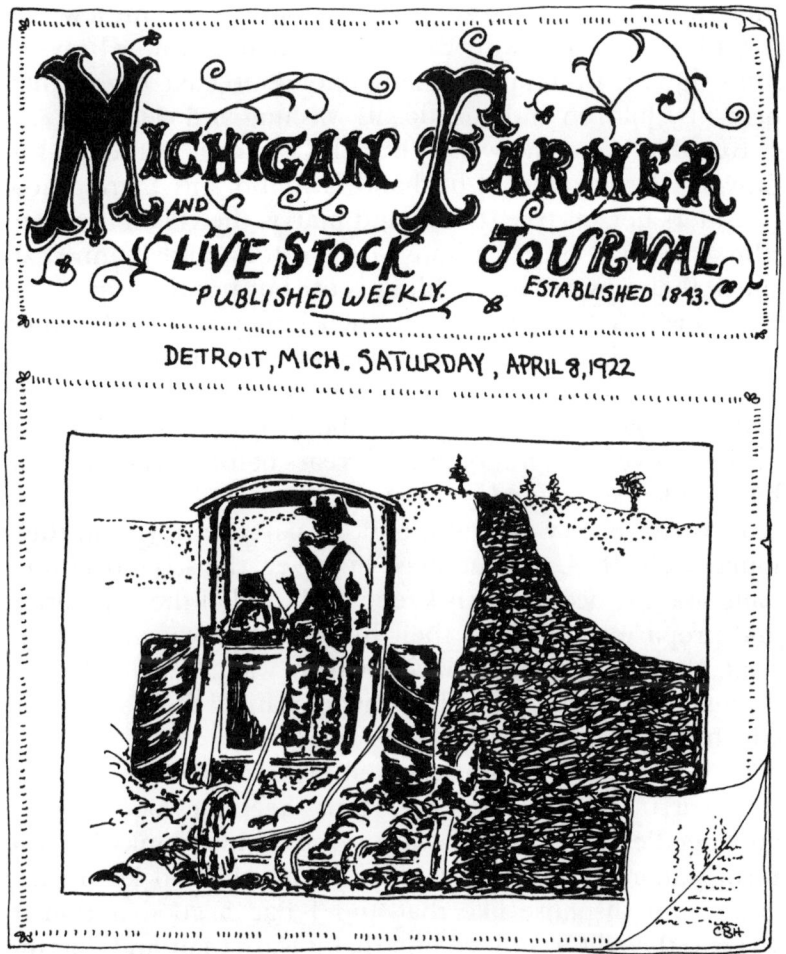

course she is thrilled at the opportunity and asks if she can cook a meal for him in appreciation.

After he shoots down a partridge on the wing she pins a tea towel over her crisp pink gingham dress and proceeds to bake some biscuits to go with the tasty bird, this while our hero relaxes in his easy chair and smokes his pipe in great contentment. He is beginning to realize that Joanne has all the qualities he has been seeking in a wife including the ability to cook!

With a husband like John Aldous, I couldn't help thinking,

there would be no need for a girl to aspire to become a writer (I had been toying with the idea of writing a novel myself some day). It would be fulfilling enough to bake his biscuits, bear his children and yes, do his washing and cleaning.

But all is not going well in British Columbia. Although the grave of her scoundrel husband is found and Joanne now considers herself free to love and marry, the villain turns up (the grave had been a phony) before John and Joanne can speak their vows. The wedding is off but not the trip to the Yukon which was to have been their honeymoon. John must collect material for his next novel and conveniently there is a chaperone handy—an old man who knows the Yukon well and is hankering to get back to the Province where he had buried his young wife some forty years before, also where he had hidden some gold.

In great secrecy our hero and his party set forth on their journey North. Unfortunately, however, the scoundrel husband and the beefy tavern-keeper get wind of the expedition and prepare to follow in their hunt for the woman and the gold. Now at last, I knew why the novel was called *The Hunted Woman* but I wasn't sure which villain wanted the woman and which one wanted the gold.

The end of an installment always seemed to come at the worst possible moment, thus keeping me on pins and needles for a whole week. One would think that the farm paper people would know better than to keep their readers in suspense like that and I had a good notion to write to the editor and tell him that it wasn't fair and that the paper would get a lot more subscribers if it changed its policy.

From Tete Jeune to the Yukon there is a narrowly averted catastrophe in every chapter but John and Joanne and the old miner manage to outwit and outrun their pursuers. Weary and worn, the young couple reach their destination, their honor unsullied, and their chaperone finds the grave of his beloved—it is under an overhanging rock and, wonder of wonders, the bible of the deceased wife is still intact among the wild flowers growing on her resting place.

But hark! Hoof beats on the trail are heard approaching, the villains are again at hand and preparations must be made for what will be the final conflict. John has no wish for violence but he must again safeguard Joanne's virtue.

Our hero insists that our heroine remain safely inside the sturdy log cabin where once the miner had lived with his bride. John gets very little help from the old man so he must almost singlehandedly try to repel the assailants. Why, I wondered, didn't the two defenders hole up in the cabin with Joanne instead of trying to act so brave and manly by making a stand in the open? But maybe that was the way men were, they had to prove their courage instead of using common sense.

A dreadful scene ensues, horses whinnying in terror, gunshots resounding in the clearing, blood being spattered all around. When it is over, the bad guys are dead and our hero is mortally wounded or so it appears. Joanne and the old miner carry him into the cabin and lay his motionless body on the bed and do what they can to stanch the flow of blood. And there, with the mountain breezes stirring the ruffled curtains, still crisp and white after forty years, John makes a marvelous recovery, a recovery no doubt hastened by Joanne's tender, loving care. His head is pillowed on her golden tresses while she keeps vigil, kneeling by his bedside.

As John opens his eyes, his first whispered words are, "Joanne, my sweetheart, now you are free!"

Since his wants are few and he has decided to live out his few remaining years near the grave of his beloved, the old miner has no need for the precious nuggets which he had hidden under the cabin floor. So it is that he entrusts the bag of gold to his young friends with the request that they use the proceeds to help the poor and needy, that is, the *deserving* poor and needy—something which John Aldous has already been doing for years with the profits from his books.

That was the last installment of *The Hunted Woman* although I had hoped for many more. However, I was certain that even without benefit of clergy and without chaperone, our hero and heroine would get back to civilization honorably. And I was also certain that John Aldous would write many more great novels, that Joanne would bake many more delicious biscuits and that the couple would live happily ever after.

I was rereading one of my favorite chapters, the one about the partridge dinner, when Mamma's mother who was visiting us asked me, "What are you reading, child?"

Sensing trouble, I closed the weekly hastily and answered casually, "Oh, just *The Michigan Farmer*."

"Let me take a look," she said and what could I do but hand it to her. I could tell by her face and her voice that she was scandalized. But except for a "humph" or two she didn't say or do anything as she scanned the much thumbed pages.

But that evening I chanced to overhear her talking to Mamma in low tones—low tones usually meant something which would be worthwhile to hear. As I stood outside the kitchen door I could hear almost every word. "She's just like your cousin Celia, always with her nose in a book when she was that age," Grandma was saying.

"Yes, I know she does like to read," Mamma said rather proudly I thought.

"I took a look at that *Hunted Woman* thing in your farm paper and it's nothing but trash—a woman visiting a man in his one room cabin!" And there, Grandma interjected one of her disapproving "Humphs."

"Oh, it's just a story," Mamma said. "I glanced at it a couple of time but didn't take time to read it."

"Well, that sort of thing's not fit for a child, what is she now, ten or eleven? And one thing leads to another—Celia always read everything she could lay eyes on, that's how she picked up a lot of crazy ideas," Grandma went on.

"But Celia's heart's in the right place, I'll say that for her," Mamma insisted.

"I'm not talking about her heart, I'm talking about her head, she filled it up with the wrong kind of thing, Socialist stuff and like that. She voted for that man who's in jail, Debs, I heard her say so myself."

"But he didn't kill anybody, it was just that he was against the war," Mamma explained.

"Well, the Socialists are all against religion and they want to divide everything up, even if you've worked hard and saved."

"Prices what they are, I don't see how anybody can save

anything these days, at least not farmers," Mamma said, trying to change the subject.

But Grandma didn't want to talk about farmers and farm prices, she wanted to talk about Cousin Celia and me. "She calls herself a free thinker, got that from some of those books she's been reading, next thing you know it'll be free love," Grandma said, sort of sarcastically.

"Oh no, no, you've got her all wrong. One of these days she'll be settling down and having a family—she won't have time for any kind of books then!"

"Well anyway, you'd better keep an eye on that girl of yours, keep her away from bad books. If she's got to read, I'll see that she gets some good ones."

I didn't want to hear any more of what Grandma had to say about me or about my first teacher. Grandma made reading sound like some kind of a disease that was catching. Before this I had always liked her—she made wonderful gingerbread men and she sometimes brought us oranges as a special treat; she told us stories about Ohio and the War between the States and how bad things were then. All she got for Christmas one year was a lump of brown sugar! Her mother had died when she was only six and I was still sorry about that, but just because Grandma was old, she didn't know everything and no matter what she said, I wanted to read a lot of books.

And I did begin to get a great many, a regular deluge which Grandma found somewhere and they were mostly Father Finn stories and Lives of the Saints for children, very dull and childish after *The Hunted Woman*. I read them all but I fear they didn't have the intended effect—they merely whetted my appetite for what Grandma considered bad books.

In my irritation over the state of affairs, I decided to look up a book which my brother and I had glanced over one time when we were checking an out-of-the-way shelf to see if we could find something interesting. There were two books really, one a Medical Guide which had illustrations of human organs such as the lungs and the kidneys, and a couple of the entire body which weren't especially revealing—you couldn't even tell whether the people were he's or she's.

It was the other one which I wanted to find, a bright red volume with the title in white letters, *Socialism, The Nation of Fatherless Children*. Carl had thumbed through that one, too, but there wasn't a single picture in it so he tossed it aside and at the time it didn't appeal to me either because it had a lot of fine print. But if Socialism was what people got from reading hard books, I wanted to find out for myself what it was. Also, as I remembered, there was a chapter heading in it, "Free Love" which hadn't interested me much when I was young.

But now, with my taste for forbidden fruit suddenly stimulated, I couldn't find either of the books. Because of what Grandma had said, perhaps Mamma had hidden them away somewhere or maybe, in a fit of housecleaning, she had burned them up just when Free thinking and Free love had become tantalizing topics.

Since I no longer trusted my brother on serious subjects—he always pretended to know about everything but I had found that it was mostly "disinformation"—I decided to go directly to Mamma. One day when we were shelling peas in the back yard and the baby was asleep so there weren't likely to be interruptions, I asked her flat out, "What's a Free thinker?" If I got a satisfactory answer to that one, I might go on to Free Love.

"What makes you ask that?" Mamma wanted to know.

"Oh, I just wondered," I replied as innocent-sounding as possible. "I was thinking about Cousin Celia, that's what she is, isn't she?"

"Well, some of her ideas are sort of . . . different," Mamma admitted.

"Is that because she reads bad books?"

"I wouldn't say she reads bad books . . . but she does do a lot of reading," Mamma hedged.

But I pursued the matter doggedly. "How can you tell when a book's bad? One time Carl said it was when it's got pictures of women with hardly any clothes on." For the sake of modesty I had inserted the word "hardly."

"Carl doesn't always know what he's talking about. You're right to come to me when you've got questions," Mamma told me.

"Well, what is a bad book than, you tell me." I insisted.

After a little hesitation Mamma did the best she could to give me an answer.

"I guess it's when it gives people the wrong idea about something. Like Prohibition, some say it's a bad law because it takes away people's freedom but it's really a good law because it keeps men from getting drunk, spending their grocery money and beating up their wives and children. So I'd say that a book which wants to do away with Prohibition is a bad book, it doesn't tell how much good Prohibition does."

"What about Free Love?" I ventured to ask since Mamma seemed willing to discuss grown-up matters with me.

"I don't know where you pick up such ideas," Mamma answered rather nervously I thought. "You're too young to be talking about things like that."

"But is it something bad?" I wanted to know, determined to pin her down if I could.

"Love is something good but nothing is free in this world." And with that she grabbed up the dishpan of pea pods, some of them not yet shelled, and said it was time to start dinner.

I wasn't altogether satisfied with her answers but there wasn't much that I could do but put my curiosity on hold. For the time being at least, a "free thinker" was what I was planning to be and if Free Love meant being free to marry someone like the hero of *The Hunted Woman* instead of just a plain, ordinary Michigan farmer, then I supported that, too.

From the Gold Fields to the Stockyards

THE notion of wanting to be an actress or an opera singer or a ballet dancer never occurred to me as a girl. We children had heard about movies but the only pictures we ever saw on a screen, the screen being a bed sheet tacked on the wall, were some biblical scenes projected by a magic lantern which was lighted by a small kerosene lamp. The gadget had belonged to Papa's schoolteacher uncle whose idea of an appropriate program for the last day of school was a showing of "The Creation to the Resurrection" with captions in German and English.

Our town cousins told us about the wondrous sights to be seen at the Palace Theater in Petoskey—the bravery of Rin Tin Tin, the antics of Charlie Chaplin and the rescue from drudgery of Mary Pickford in *Cinderella*. We hankered to see pictures of dogs and people actually moving around on stage but the Palace was four miles distant, an hour trip each way by horse and buggy. Also Papa wasn't at all sure that movies would have a wholesome effect on us whereas Mamma had other uses in mind for any spare nickels and dimes.

Opera and ballet were unheard of in our household but there was an all-inclusive general term for women who displayed themselves on stage in abbreviated attire or who "screeched like barn owls" instead of singing hymns, and the term was "opry dancers." Also in this category were trapeze artists who swung around like monkeys in circus tents wearing skin tight costumes. There was something vaguely indecent about all such women—they weren't "our kind of people."

My early aspirations were always along more soulful lines, like converting the heathens from their godless ways, like rescuing drunkards from the gutters, like ridding the world of war-makers. I must have been born with a crusading instinct as I frequently found myself with a tremendous urge to save somebody from something, whether in faraway lands, in Emmet County, or wherever.

But there came a time when the urge to save became sidetracked by the urge to write. I had read and reread *The Hunted Woman* and now that I was thirteen and in high school, I was eligible for the kind of library card which entitled me to enter the "sanctum sanctorum," the adult stacks. And there I found more of Curwood's books, including *The Flower of the North* and *God's Country and the Woman*. From James Oliver Curwood I went on to John Fox Jr., Peter B. Kyne and Zane Grey.

The elderly librarian sometimes looked at me with a jaundiced eye as I checked out these love stories two at a time, the limit allowed. I was now staying in town with an aunt during the school week which Mamma thought necessary to provide me with the time and energy to do my home work instead of walking the eight-mile round trip each day. There were no school busses in that time and place. Aunt Mamie didn't pay any attention to what I was reading—I think she thought it was required for my courses at school and I didn't enlighten her. Reading late into the night as I did, must have increased her electric bill but she didn't complain, no doubt considering it one of the costs of getting an education, something which she sorely missed.

Be it known that what I was gorging myself on was not at all like the steamy stuff on the bookstands and magazine racks today. It was as chaste as the mountain dew and pure as the driven snow. True, there was an occasional brief embrace or a light kiss upon the brow of the beloved but that was about it. The romance lay in the hazardous adventures on the way to the altar which led across rushing rivers, up mighty mountains, down treacherous trails and over arid deserts.

For my purpose, the scenery in Northern Michigan left much to be desired. I had overheard resorters talking about the million dollar sunsets over Little Traverse Bay but they were pale and pallid in comparison with those of the Far West where the scarlet sun sank like a colossal crimson coin slipping slowly over the ruby red rim of the horizon.

Resorters also made much of the beauty of the Inland Route to Lake Huron by way of tree-lined streams and a chain of lakes. They called it picturesque but even though I had never traveled the Inland Route by boat, I knew that it couldn't compare with the roaring rivers and rushing torrents in the books which I had read. And as for the wooded hills of Emmet County, they were scrubby and insignificant alongside the majestic mountains of the Rockies and the snow-capped peaks of the Cascades.

One of the chief farm crops in our region was potatoes and what could be less romantic than a potato patch for a secret tryst? Instead of purple sage and flaming cactus flowers, we had only milkweeds and Canadian thistles. And what could be less worthy of adjectives than a dinky cow pasture hemmed in with a barbed wire fence while on the Great Plains, the huge herds of cattle could roam free and unfettered?

The dull and monotonous scenery in our area would simply never do as a backdrop for a stirring romance—for that, one must have a magnificent sweep of open spaces, a setting of greatness and grandeur. Only then could there be daring deeds and romantic rescues!

The urge to write came during summer vacation when library rules prevented me from checking out any books without charge since I was a rural resident. So if I couldn't read a novel, I would write one. Anyhow, I had been dying to dip into my growing supply of lovely adjectives which would be laughed to scorn in my own family if I tried to use them in ordinary conversation. I couldn't even work them into my themes for English class as the teacher insisted that we write on the subjects she assigned. And how could one make use of exotic words in describing anything or anywhere in Emmet County?

The last library book I had read during the school term was Zane Grey's *Riders of the Purple Sage* and I decided on a similar setting but as for the plot and the characters, my novel would have an ingenious slant, perhaps something in the way of the noble renunciation. For one of my book reports I had read *Uncle Tom's Cabin* and found it very moving so by combining the romantic with the tragic, I could give my readers the best of both genres.

And like John Aldous, the author hero in *The Hunted Woman*, I would give generously of my earnings if I became a successful writer. Of course I would have to retain adequate funds for my personal expenses and put something aside for my old age but anything extra would be used for worthy purposes, possibly to help struggling young novelists. Curwood's hero had lived in a simple rustic cabin but for myself I would need a little more space, hopefully a place provided with some of the modern conveniences such as the electric icebox which was just coming on the market in the mid-20's.

What I really had in mind was a comfortable cottage like those in Bay View, one with an upstairs porch where I could sit quietly above the clatter of the street and the chatter of the passers-by while I constructed unusual plots and dreamed up interesting characters. Later I would betake myself to my downstairs studio and type my manuscripts—surely by then I would own a typewriter.

Somewhere I had read that many great poets and authors had started their writing careers amid cobwebs in a garret. We called the space under our roof an attic but the only way to get to it was through a trap door in the hall ceiling and that required a ladder. Knowing my brother, Carl, all too well, I could imagine him removing the ladder while I was hard at work, leaving me no way to get down except by jumping. Also there was no window for light and air so the garret idea had to be abandoned.

I didn't have a room which I could call my own—I had to share it with my sister Madeline who was always running in and out, looking for something like a safety pin or a barrette for her hair or sometimes just to annoy me, as she knew I

wanted no interruptions. I felt I deserved some privacy after I got my household and garden chores done, and done properly, without her barging in on me every little while. But of course, she claimed she was within her rights as it was her room as much as it was mine and I didn't need to act so high and mighty just because I was making like an author!

But for the time being I would have to do the best I could under difficult circumstances. In our bedroom there was no desk, therefore no place to put my feet if I tried to write at the dresser or the commode. Thus I was reduced to lying on the bed on my stomach which was not my idea of the proper position for serious creative writing. For materials I had some looseleaf notebook paper and several pencils with good erasers—I would have liked to have a pencil sharpener like those at school as there was something about a freshly sharpened pencil with its smooth clean wood and its lovely sharp point which was inspirational. As it was, I had to keep running down to the kitchen to use the paring knife. But never mind, when fame and fortune came my way, things would be different.

Now at last, Chapter 1 began to take shape. I didn't know what sagebrush was exactly but when the sun slanted through it, apparently it looked like purple fire and the cactus flowers were supposed to be gorgeous scarlet blossoms against the azure blue of the sky. But I did know that western cattle were not a all like the raw-boned, heavy-footed cows in our barnyard—they were sleek-limbed creatures of tawny gold. And the mustangs were swift, half-wild steeds which only a fearless cowboy could ride, not at all like our plodding, sway-backed horses even though ours were supposed to have broncho blood in their veins through "Daisy" who had been purchased from an out-of-town livestock trader.

As for the plot and the characters, I decided that a feud between two old ranchers would be a suitable setup for what I had in mind. Rancher A, the father of our hero, has been tricked by Rancher B, the father of our heroine. Through a legal maneuver Rancher B has gotten title to the waterhole which the herds of both men had used in prior years. With a shotgun B stands guard to keep A's cattle from the water they must have or die of thirst in the desert sun.

Rancher A is broken in body and spirit after a long and exhausting court battle and as he lies with the dew of death upon his brow, he calls his only son to his bedside and whispers, "We have fought the good fight but we have lost. You must not take the law into your own hands now."

"But Father, our herd must be saved and I must avenge the wrong which has been done you," the son cries out.

"No, my son, you must go far away and start life afresh. Promise me this so I can die in peace!" (He does not realize what he is asking since he does not know that his son is secretly in love with Rancher B's daughter.)

Our hero who had planned to use his shotgun if necessary to get access to the disputed waterhole, must now make a decision. He asks for an hour to think over his father's request and in that hour he keeps a tryst with his beloved.

"You must honor your father's dying wish," our heroine tells the hero. "You must do what I have done in keeping the promise I made to my mother that I would stand by my father as long as he lives even when he's in the wrong," she adds with tears rolling down her petal-soft cheeks.

"It will mean that we must part and that I must go many miles away," he tells her sadly.

"But you will kiss me once before you go," she whispers. And so it is that he folds her to his heart and kisses her lightly on her alabaster brow as a fond farewell.

And as the scarlet sun sinks slowly over the horizon like a crimson coin, our hero hastens back to his father's side to tell him of his heart-wrenching decision.

"My son, my son," the old man cried. "Now I can die in peace!"

I thought the first chapter was rather good even if I did write it myself, but I was having a little trouble figuring out how best to proceed with my novel. I liked the idea of the noble renunciation but on the other hand, it would be painful to keep the ill-starred lovers apart forever. I was thinking seriously of having Rancher B conveniently die of natural causes after being thrown from his broncho while trying to head off a wild stampede, when my career as a writer came to a disastrous halt.

It is said that pride goeth before a fall and it was true that I considered that the style and content of my novel compared favorably with those of the popular authors of the day. I had noticed that my brother seemed to be chortling over something as he came to the dinner table one Sunday and, as it turned out, he had my unfinished manuscript in his pocket. When he was through eating, he pulled out my sheaf of notebook paper, stood up and between fits of laughter, he began to read my most passionate passages.

I was behind the table against the wall with a sister on either side and I couldn't get out fast enough to wrest my precious novel from him—also, I was half paralyzed with embarrassment over the way Carl read the farewell scene—he made it sound stupid and silly! I couldn't understand how he had gotten possession of my manuscript as I thought I had it well hidden. Could it be that Madeline had been bribed? And why had she blocked my way from the table?

My sisters were all giggling and Mamma was sort of half smiling but all she said was "Pass the jello please." However Papa, who was just starting on his dessert, jumped up from the table and went into the kitchen where I heard the pump go into action. Some men cuss when they're angry or upset but Papa always washed his hands.

A fledgling author needs encouragement not ridicule. And not only did my brother make fun of what I had written but when he finished reading, he tossed the looseleaf pages across the table toward me and some of them landed in the chicken gravy.

However, it was something of a relief to get the ill-starred lovers off my hands. I now realized that the dramatic build-up had peaked too soon and no matter what I had happen next, it would be a kind of anti-climax. Besides I had found that writing novels was not the easiest job in the world, especially under difficult conditions. But some day when I could work in peace and quiet and have access to an author's practical needs, I would resume my interrupted career.

Thereafter I began to lose interest in James Oliver Curwood, John Fox Jr., Peter B. Kyne and Zane Grey. I had read most of their books anyway and while they were all right while they lasted, maybe they were a little silly. Furthermore a serious-minded person like myself ought to be concerned about the social problems of the times.

It was some months later that I came upon *The Jungle* which was realism not romance. Oh, I had read about dreadful conditions before, like *Oliver Twist* set in England in the mid 1800's and *Uncle Tom's Cabin* written in pre-Civil War days, but they were about times and places which were long ago and far away. They were about evils which had been exposed and corrected, about wrongs which had been righted.

But *The Jungle* by Upton Sinclair was about 20th Century America, it was about the city of Chicago at the other end of our own Lake Michigan. It was about European immigrants who had come to our shores to find a better life. But, unlike my own grandparents who had settled on farms, they went to work in the meat-packing industry and to live within sight and smell of the stockyards.

No writer could have imagined the conditions in *The Jungle* if he had not seen them with his own eyes. And having seen them, no writer would have failed to be shocked and shaken. And no writer could have walked away without vowing to try to do something about them.

The American system of meat-packing was thought to be a marvel of efficiency. The hogs climbed up a six story chute on their own power to the killing beds and in due time, the carcasses slipped or fell or rolled their way through various processes to the first floor where they came out as smoked hams and pork chops and sausage links. "Everything was used but the squeal" it was said—the bristles for paint brushes, the blood and bones for fertilizer, the fat for lard and soap.

But it was not upon these marvels that Sinclair dwelled. He had gone behind the scenes where the workers sloshed around in the blood of the pigs which had been stuck; he saw the boiling lard tanks into which a person occasionally fell and was sizzled to death; he saw the sweepings and rat droppings being dumped in with the meat scraps and plenty of seasoning to make the sausage edible. He stood in the lines on pay-day where the immigrants were cheated out of some of their earnings, but because they were unschooled they could not protest.

But it was the description of the homes of the workers which sent chills down my spine as there were houses like them in Kegomic, a tannery company-town near Bay View. Here, too, there were immigrants from Eastern Europe living in small, identical frame houses, probably thin-walled like those in *The Jungle,* which gave little protection against the crunching cold of our winters and the icy blasts off Little Traverse Bay.

Sinclair's Lithuanians had lived in thick, mud-plastered huts which were warm in winter and cool in summer. And in the "old country" they had plenty of fuel from the forests while here they had to buy coal or send their children out to pick it up along the railroad tracks. There, they had frost free pits to store their cabbages and potatoes while here, they had to buy everything they ate.

For Jurgis and Una, everything goes wrong in the stockyard jungle. Although they both work, Jurgis in the fertilizer section and Una wrapping hams, they can barely make enough to live on. For fear of losing her job and being black-listed, Una submits to the advances of her boss and when Jurgis finds out, he almost kills the rapist and is sent to jail. When he gets out he finds that the family has been evicted, Una dies in childbirth. Jurgis is in despair and if he had not found some hope in the Socialist movement, he might have gone on to drink himself to death.

Until now I had never given much thought to the people of Kegomic but *The Jungle* awakened in me a feeling for those who were less fortunate than we were. We were poor, yes, we didn't have heat in our second floor bedrooms but we had plenty of patch quilts and in the morning we could dash downstairs and, while the menfolks were milking, we could wash and dress in front of the kitchen range with the oven door open for extra warmth. And there was always enough to eat although we sometimes complained about too many beans and cakes with only a dab of frosting on the top.

But in some places like Chicago, even in our own Emmet County, there were people who were cold and hungry. I began to piece together bits and fragments of other things I had read and heard, poems and passages which my first teacher had quoted and what Grandma has said about Cousin Celia being "a Socialist or something." I thought about the plight of the slaves in *Uncle Tom's Cabin* and that of the workers in *The Jungle* and found them equally bad. I was determined to find out more about Socialism and whether it would really help to make the world better. The book *Socialism, The Nation of Fatherless Children* which I had glanced over briefly as a child, might have some answers to the problems which were bothering me.

I was embarrassed to remember how much time I had wasted on silly romances and ashamed to recall that I had once tried to write similar tripe myself. My brother still twitted me about "purple fire in the brushpile" and "kissing her on her plaster brow." But that was adolescent stuff and like playing with dolls as a child, all that was behind me—I was beyond such frivolous nonsense now and forever.

There were still many wrongs to be righted, there was much work to be done and it was time that women take a more active role in the world, not like Carrie Nation with her hatchet but more like Harriet Beecher Stowe with her pen or Jane Addams and her peace ship. Eventually, I would see what I could do!

Fatherless Children

MY ancestors were not a scholarly lot from what I have been able to learn. My paternal grandfather took up woodworking in the "old country" and hoped to become a maker of fine violins but the Iron Chancellor wanted to make him into a soldier. Although Grandpa had served willingly in the local militia, he did not care to take orders from the Prussian Junker, Otto Von Bismarck, so he left Hesse rather hurriedly for America. However, he was to find that there was not much demand for good music and hand-crafted instruments in the backwoods of Northern Michigan so he had to settle for farming, an occupation for which he was not well suited.

As for my paternal grandmother, she was also foreign born but came to the new world as an infant and was left an orphan as a child. The only thing she knew about her forbears was that her grandfather had stayed on in a German province after Napoleon's retreat from Russia, hence her French maiden name, Boyer. She was apprenticed to a seamstress in Baltimore and it was her skill in needlework which helped to pay the bills on the family farm near Petoskey.

On my mother's side, three Quivileau brothers emigrated from France to Canada in the mid 1800's. One was a Jesuit who spent the rest of his life as a missionary among the Indians in the Quebec area. Another brother found his way to Detroit where he bought a farm on its outskirts with the money he had earned in the lumber woods of Ontario. The third brother, also a woodsman, stayed in Canada until the early 1870's when he and his family went by boat to Cheboygan, Michigan, thence by ox team to Emmet County where he homesteaded a farm.

Ill, a widower and childless, the downstate settler went to the northern part of the state to die, leaving his Wayne County property to his brother's family, its name now Americanized to "Coveyou". Several years later, a couple of lawyers appeared at the Emmet County farm, saying that the downstate acreage was becoming very valuable and that the heirs were entitled to a sizeable fortune provided they signed some papers. They signed but that was the last they heard of their fortune until another lawyer turned up, offering to retrieve for them what was rightfully theirs if they signed some more papers and paid some of the fees in advance. By this time, however, the confidence of the Coveyou heirs in the law profession was nil and thus was lost any claim to wealth.

Mamma's maternal grandfather, Samuel Draper of English ancestry, was something of an adventurer. Born in Tennessee, he never lived very long in one place. While in Upper Sandusky, Ohio, his wife died leaving him with five young children. He left four of them with neighbors and headed for California with his oldest son, promising to bring back gold to pay for the other children's keep. But when he returned several years later, he brought neither gold nor son—the boy had died with a fever somewhere along the way.

I would like to think that my great grandfather had some of the genes and some of the talents of the historian, Lyman Draper, who wrote of pioneer days in Tennessee and border states but it is highly unlikely. Samuel, apparently, could never sit still long enough to put pen to paper and he died in St. Ignace, Michigan after several other moves which proved unprofitable.

Thus, neither fortune nor scholarliness was anywhere to be found, at least not in my immediate ancestry. The closest thing to anything like fame or immortality is my father's surname carved in stone in the center aisle of the Cathedral in Limburg, Germany. A great, great uncle is buried there

but since he was a Catholic bishop, he left no descendants or possessions.

All this by way of explaining why there was no library in our farmhouse, no leather bound volumes, no paintings or other signs of culture. Grandpa had some music books in German with the four line staff which might be collector items by now but they were stored in our attic after his death and when the mice began to shred them, they were disposed of as a fire hazard. Mamma had little use for anything German anyway.

However, other than school books we did have one hardbacked volume which apparently had been considered a scholarly treatise, at least judging from the number of footnotes in fine print. It was bright red and the title stood out in chaste white letters, *Socialism* with a sub-title, *The Nation of Fatherless Children*. The authors were David Goldstein and Martha Moore Avery who were ex-Socialists and claimed to know everything there was to know about the Red Menace.

Most book peddlers shied away from neighborhoods like ours where the houses were far between and the roads were sand tracks in summer and snow ruts in winter. And almost anything from Watkins Vanilla to lightning rods would sell better than reading matter. Also, most farmers roundabout would have been insulted if anyone should think that they had enough free time to sit down and read regular books. Books were for the teachers and for the idle rich.

But one time at least, a book had been sold at our house, or rather bartered for two meals, a night's lodging, plus hay and a stall for a horse. Mamma didn't really favor the exchange, she told me later, she disliked nothing more than a pushy peddler with his foot in the door. Besides, the book agent had eaten non-stop for an hour at both supper and breakfast and talked non-stop at the same time. But Papa felt sorry for the itinerant and especially for his horse which had a lame leg and needed a good night's rest and some attention to its injury.

As an inducement for the trade, my parents were told that the book would keep them and their children from being infected by the deadly virus which was then sweeping the country. Eugene V. Debs, the Socialist candidate for President in 1912 had just garnered a million votes and God and Country were in mortal danger. The book would serve as an antidote to the poison which was flooding the land and make them and their offspring immune from the pestilence which had entered the body politic.

I doubt that Mamma ever read more than the chapter headings—she was not one to waste time on non-bread-and-butter issues, especially those promoted by a loud-mouthed peddler who not only devoured a whole glass of raspberry jam but awakened the baby asleep in the next room. I wonder now that she didn't pitch the book out as she had very little shelf space and only one closet in the whole house. But keep it she did, and my brother and I had stumbled on it one time when we were rumaging around, but it didn't appeal to either one of us at the time.

However, after reading *The Jungle* and recalling the title of the bright red book, I wanted to learn more about Socialism and how "The Fatherless Children" fitted into the picture. I had overheard one of my grandmothers calling my first teacher a "Socialist or something" and if all Socialists were like my idol or like the Socialists in *The Jungle,* I might consider becoming one myself. If Mamma hadn't thrown it out, I would inform myself on the subject before making a decision as to my political future.

"Where's that book about Socialism?" I asked Mamma one day when I was looking for something meaningful to read. Had I been able to get to the Public Library, I might have found some enlightenment there but it was vacation time and I had no summer card—also it was a chore to get to town.

She gave me a puzzled look as if she didn't know what I was talking about but then she finally said, "Oh, that! But I don't think you'll find it very interesting." However, she told me where it was, no doubt recalling that it was supposed to be the antidote, not the poison itself.

She was right about the first few chapters which were so dull and dry I merely skipped over them—"Dialectical Materialism, The Communist Manifesto," things like that. But then there was one on Evolution and that was more enticing as there had been a lot of talk the previous summer about the Scopes trial in Tennessee. Also, I'd read some of the articles on the case in the Detroit papers which Aunt Martha had given us for starting fires.

Personally, I couldn't see why anyone would want to claim relationship to the monkeys. From what I'd seen of them in the town zoo, they were always picking their noses or hunting for lice on each other. But the Socialists, one and all according to the book, rejected the biblical account of the Creation. They believed that the world had been in existence for millions of years—however, they had no answers as to how it came to be created in the first place.

And they believed that man had descended from monkeys

instead of from Adam and Eve. It was true, the authors suggested, that Socialists often acted like monkeys and barnyard animals but that didn't prove that evolution was true. What it proved was that they were trying to replace the Bible with the so-called scientific theory which had no basis in fact.

I now remembered that the defense attorney in the Scopes trial was Clarence Darrow and he was thought to be a Socialist, at least he had defended a lot of Socialists in years past. But he had lost the Scopes case, evolution was disproved and could no longer be taught in the schools. If the Socialists were wrong about evolution, were they wrong about other things, too?

And then I remembered something else, the "Bobby Frank thrill slaying" in Chicago and Darrow had defended the slayers. Everybody seemed to think that he had taken the case because of the money involved—if Loeb and Leopold had been poor and unable to afford a high priced lawyer, the killers would have gotten the "chair"—instead, they were sent to prison and would probably be paroled when nobody was looking. What kind of Socialist was that?

People in our area were especially interested in the trial because young Loeb was the son of a Sears Roebuck millionaire who owned a showplace dairy farm near Charlevoix. Before the slaying there had been open house at the Loeb place on certain Sundays. It was at a time when farmers in our neighborhood were beginning to get automobiles and although joy rides per se were frowned upon, going to see the Loeb farm made a good excuse to try out their horseless carriages.

We didn't get to make the trip—we had no car at the time—but I remember hearing descriptions of the Loeb showplace, partly in awe and partly in ridicule. The dairy staff wore white uniforms and I heard one woman remark that if Mrs. Loeb had to wash all that white stuff, she'd have the help wearing blue overalls like everybody else. And another one said that you'd think it was a bakery instead of a barn, it was so "unnatural clean." But some of the men were more respectful—the Loeb cows gave so much milk that they had to be milked three times a day and it was done with sterilized gadgets clamped to their udders. Each cow had a special drinking fountain and its food was carefully weighed. Each had a chart where its output was recorded, and each cow had a number—there was no nonsense about names like Molly and Milly and Mandy.

But what everybody in our neighborhood talked about at the time of the trial was what someone who had worked at the farm had said about the Loeb boy when he was around ten years old, "It was none of my business but the kid was always hanging around the breeding pen and one Sunday he offered me ten dollars to let the prize bull out into the crowd to see what would happen—I think he hoped somebody would get gored. Too much money, that was what was wrong with that boy!"

And about Darrow, many were saying, "What could you expect from a man who helped to get that Socialist guy off, that fellow who was always running for president?" As for Papa, he said it wasn't right to sentence anyone, rich or poor, to death. It was up to God to be the judge. But he did say that if Loeb and Leopold as boys had chores to do like milking cows the regular way—not with those new fangled gadgets—they wouldn't have had time to get into trouble.

What I couldn't understand about Darrow, if he was a Socialist like they said he was, why did he take the case of the thrill slayers, why didn't he stick to the cases of the poor and the underdog—those who couldn't afford to hire a lawyer? And why did he want evolution to be taught in the schools—it made people think he was against God and religion.

The chapter on atheism in the book claimed that all Socialists were godless and being godless themselves, they didn't want anybody else to have the comfort of religion—which they said was the opiate of the people as it told them "You'll eat pie in the sky when you die." With them it was war to the knife against the churches—tax church property like everything else, deny the bishops the right to be landlords, close the parochial schools.

The school issue had been a hot one in our area—in Michigan a law had been proposed to make every child attend a public school, following the lead of one state which had already passed such a statute. A man who had come to town to speak on the subject and call for the measure, was met at the railroad station with a barrage of rotten eggs and placards reading, "Bolshevik, go home!" and "Go back to Russia!"

It was all very confusing. From the footnotes which were mostly quotations from Socialist writings, it did seem that there was a bias against the churches, with claims that the clergy was mostly on the side of the wealthy who could make big contributions. But in *The Jungle*, Jurgis had heard a Socialist lecturer who had referred to Jesus as one who knew sorrow and pain, who was the friend of the poor and the sick, who had driven the moneychangers from the House of God. He had preached the brotherhood of man and peace among nations and because the rich and the powerful feared Him, Jesus was called an agitator and a disturber of the peace—and this was why he had been put to death on the cross.

Now, what was I to make of such differences?

Then there was the chapter on Capitalism versus Socialism. According to the authors the Socialist leaders didn't have any money except what they could get by passing the hat at their meetings, so they wanted to divide up everything—the factories, the mines, the railroads—the big businesses as well as the little ones like the grocery stores, the farms and the blacksmith shops.

Papa had to shoe his own horses now as there weren't any more blacksmiths nearby but that was because cars and tractors were taking the place of horses. But I could just imagine what he would say if a Socialist tried to take away our farm, and I knew what Mamma would do—she'd meet him at the door with a broom!

The authors claimed that even if all the wealth was divided up equally it wouldn't stay equal very long as some would spend theirs foolishly instead of making wise investments. And anyway, according to the Bible, "The poor ye will always have with you." We had the best system on earth and if the workers, when they got their pay envelopes, would put some money in the bank each week instead of stopping at a saloon or a pool hall, they would be surprised how quickly their accounts would grow. It was by being regular in their savings and wise in their spending that everybody could get ahead under capitalism.

They seemed to be saying that people were poor because they didn't work hard nor spend their earnings wisely. Now that I knew was not "right reason," which they said was the basis of their book. After all, neither Papa nor Mamma ever spent a dime for anything foolish. Papa didn't drink, not even before Prohibition and he didn't play pool. I thought about him making a box out of clean scrap lumber to save the expense of buying a coffin for our dead baby sister and I thought about Mamma going without dentures for a whole year because there were so many other things we children needed more. And I thought about the stockyard workers in Chicago and the tannery workers in Kegomic and I decided that David Goldstein and Martha Moore Avery didn't know everything!

But then I read the last and the longest chapter in the book, "Free Love" and what that meant, the authors said, was free lust and it was all caused by free thinking. Socialists didn't believe in the sanctity of marriage, "til death do us part" and all that—couples just lived together until they got tired of each other. Thus in a Socialist society, the offspring of these temporary unions would be scattered around hither and yon—fathers would take no responsibilities for them and there would be "A Nation of Fatherless Children!"

Socialists all believed in Woman Suffrage which they said was necessary if women were to have a say in the affairs of government and to get equal pay for equal work. But God had never intended that they should compete with men in government and the workplace—their place was in the home, there to keep the hearth fires burning and to take care of the needs of their husbands and children, so said the authors.

Since the book had been written, the 19th Amendment had been adopted and things hadn't gone to pieces. And another thing, if Martha Moore Avery practiced what she preached, what was she doing co-authoring a book with David Goldstein who wasn't even her husband? Not that I thought that women shouldn't be writers, I might even try being one myself some time, but she had no business telling other women to do something she wasn't doing herself.

I closed the bright red volume with mixed emotions. I

certainly didn't think that the authors' views on woman suffrage and poor people were "right reason," but on the other hand I didn't like some of the things about the Socialists either such as their ideas about evolution and churches and free love. After all, I wanted a home of my own some day and a husband who wouldn't take off with some free-thinking woman and leave our children fatherless.

For the time being I would reserve judgment—I would do more reading and more thinking before making up my mind about such matters—it was better to be safe than sorry. I remembered Papa's story about the old farmer whose barn was struck by lightning. Enraged at seeing his beautiful hip-roofed barn going up in flames, he shook his fist at the heavens, shouting, "God, if there is a God up there, go ahead and strike the house, too!" and God did.

Historians Are Made

HISTORY was not my favorite subject when I was in high school. In my Junior year I took both European and American History, not through choice exactly but for academic reasons. For the most part I found the courses rather dull and repetitious—one empire after another, one war after another and all with numerous names and dates and places to be remembered. Was nothing ever learned by what had happened over and over again?

Also, it seemed to me, that history was mostly about men, written by men intended for the glorification of men. Oh, a woman was mentioned now and then, usually not because she had played a meaningful role in human affairs but because she was the wife or mistress of some important man. There were few queens who had wielded much power and if they did, it was because they had acted like men in their quest for more territory.

Nor was there much about the lives of ordinary people throughout recorded history, how they lived and worked, how they felt about their leaders and whether they had gone into battle willingly. Those who made the history books were men who wanted to make their countries bigger, not about those who wanted to make the lives of their countrymen better.

Most of the war-makers were bully boys in my opinion—the Ceasars, the Napoleons, the Bismarcks and the Kaisers—they had won immortality by orgies of blood-letting although, of course, they maintained that they were acting for

God and country. Sometimes wars were defensive but all too often they were fought over territory which neither side could rightfully claim. And did the historians condemn such criminal behavior? No, they seemed to take for granted that wars were what history was all about—without them what would they do for material!

Sometimes when I was studying my assignments, I was reminded of a feud between my brother, Carl, and a neighbor boy, Tom, which started over an eagle's nest. At the time the state was paying bounties for the predators such as weasels, foxes, woodchucks and chicken hawks which were preying on farmers' crops and poultry. Carl was perpetually in search of money-making schemes in order to buy a more powerful gun so as to be able to shoot bigger game, including bears and wolves whose tracks he claimed to have seen.

Eaglets were rarely seen in our area even then, but Carl insisted that he had discovered an eagle's nest and had noticed the parent birds circling over the nesting tree. Although he didn't care to take on the full grown creatures, he figured that the eaglets would bring him a sizeable sum in bounties.

Carl made the mistake of boasting about his find to Tom, but he refused to disclose its location. This apparently made his friend suspicious since Tom's uncle owned some acreage adjacent to our woodlot and when he, too, spotted the nest he laid claim not merely to half the baby eagles but to all of them when they hatched. It was then that Carl enlisted the aid of Madeline and me to help him move the nest to a secret spot.

"Tom is trying to cheat me out of a lot of money," he told us but not until we reached the nesting site did we realize that he had misrepresented the facts in the case—the tree was actually on Tom's uncle's side of the line fence although some of its branches extended over our property.

We girls didn't care to get mixed up in a border dispute which involved breaking the law but Carl insisted that fences had nothing to do with wild animals which meant that it was a case of finders, keepers. We were also concerned about what the mother eagle would do as we had heard tales about these giant birds swooping down and picking up children as

well as chickens—in fact Carl had been the source of the tales. However, he assured us that we were now much too big to be carried off by an eagle and if there was any danger, it would be to his ears and nose. As a reward for our help, we would each get the proceeds from one of the eaglets as he was expecting a hatch of ten or twelve.

We were to stand watch and sound a warning if either of the parent birds was seen approaching, also if Tom or any of his relations put in an unexpected appearance. Then, with a stocking cap pulled down over his ears, a scarf tied around his head to shield his nose and a market basket strapped to his back, he began his upward climb. His strategy was to detach the nest, put it in the basket and lower it to the ground on a length of binder twine where we were to guard the precious eggs from any marauders, human or otherwise.

It was a half dead tree—for some reason both crows and eagles seemed to prefer them that way—and some of the limbs began to come crashing down as Carl began his ascent. We begged him to give up his plan for quick wealth; however, he was an expert at climbing and was able to get to the nest without mishap or miss-step.

"Only two eggs" he shouted in furious disappointment. He had been counting on a dozen or so as was the custom with Mamma's setting hens. Under the circumstances he decided to abandon his plan to move the nest which was larger and more complicated than he had imagined—a contraption built with sticks and bark firmly attached to the topmost fork in the tree. Also, it would take more time than he was willing to risk in his exposed position.

"Darn stingy eagles," he complained. "Only two eggs so I'll bring 'em down in my back pockets instead of the basket." Because of the circumstances, he decided to alter his plans. We would keep the eggs warm in our hands until we got to the section of the chicken coop where Mamma had her setting hens and let one of them take over the hatching job.

This was easier said than done. We had a phrase "mad as a settin' hen" and I found the hen to be very mad, indeed, as I tried to give the eggs to the prospective stepmother. She seemed to think that I was trying to steal one of her own eggs instead of adding to the dozen she was already guarding. Her feathers would rise up on end every time I made a move toward her nest and she had a vicious peck. Finally, by my pretending to be reaching under her from the front, Madeline was able to slip the eggs under the rear end of the hen. Carl had turned the job over to us as we were better at that kind of thing "bein' girls an' all."

Again Carl couldn't resist a bit of boasting but his brags proved to be premature as when the baby chickens hatched a week or so later, the mother hen pushed out the eagle eggs as counterfeit. Tom was certain that the eaglets would have hatched if they had been left in his uncle's tree whereas Carl was certain that the eggs had been abandoned before he removed them. "After all, whoever heard of an eagle botherin' to set on just two eggs," he said. But Tom maintained that his eggs had been stolen and so the feud continued, fueled by charges of other instances of theft and treachery.

Yes, their little scrap was similar to bigger ones in the history books, with rulers warring over territory and markets which neither side could rightly claim. There was no question about it in my mind—it had something to do with the male of the species—boys liked to roll up their sleeves and show what big bulges they had in their upper arms. The boys who grew up to be kings and generals—and yes, even presidents—liked to flex their political and military muscles. And once having made their brags, they often had to back them up on the battlefield. But they sat back and let their soldiers to the fighting and the dying.

And it wasn't just the soldiers, the women and children suffered, too. In our own Civil War, for instance, William Sherman who was described as "perhaps the greatest military genius of the Union Army," hadn't spared the civilian population and their homes and their livestock. There was a song, *Marching through Georgia* with a rousing tune which we had sung in the country school. Fifty thousand strong, his army marched to the sea from Atlanta which had been burned to the ground, and even though there was little resistance because the Confederate men were all off fighting somewhere else, a swath was cut through the state, leaving scarcely a building or a stalk of corn standing.

Aunt Rose, Papa's sister, brought a friend with her one summer who had grown up in the South, and she filled me in on her version of the behavior of another Union General, Philip Sheridan. His regiment rode through the Shenendoah Valley, leaving a wasteland behind and Sheridan bragged that "Even a crow flying over the countryside had to carry his own rations!" And these were the generals on our side which was supposed to be the right side! These were the men who were supposed to be fighting in a great and glorious cause—to free the slaves. These were the leaders of the men who sang as the marched:

> *Hurrah, hurrah, we bring the jubilee*
> *Hurrah, hurrah, the flag that makes you free.*

"Free, fiddle de-dee!" my aunt's friend scoffed. "Look, how they treated the slaves after the war, look how they treat them now!" And it seemed that she was right.

On the question of slavery, I had done some thinking about it after reading *Uncle Tom's Cabin* and it was certainly wrong according to our Declaration of Independence which stated that "all men are created equal and are endowed with certain inalienable rights including life, liberty and the pursuit of happiness." But the same document also included the right to dissolve the political bands which have connected them with another—so why couldn't the southern states secede just as the colonies had separated from England?

Thus each side had a point, so it was a case for arbitration and compromise. Why didn't representatives from the North sit down with their counterparts from the South and try to resolve their differences peaceably? If the slaveholders had been offered the market price for their slaves or even ten times the market price, the cost in dollars would have been far less than the cost of the war, to say nothing of the cost in lives. That would have been the common sense thing to do, the woman's way to do, and if women on both sides had been consulted the war might have been avoided.

But, it seemed, when confronted with common sense arguments, men tended to fall back on such noble sounding notions as honor and bravery and patriotism and the leaders took advantage of this. But what was honorable or brave or patriotic about killing half a million people and destroying much of the country they were supposedly trying to save?

In the eighth grade I had learned a poem which must have been written by a woman and it went something like this:

> *Under the sod and the dew*
> *Awaiting the Judgment Day*
> *Under the one the blue*
> *Under the other the gray*

> *These in the robings of glory*
> *Those in the gloom of defeat*
> *All in the battle blood, gory*
> *In the dust of Eternity, meet.* . . .

What about the soldiers of the blue and the gray, indeed? In the "dust of eternity," what would those in "the robings of glory" be saying to those in "the gloom of defeat?" Would they be saying, "There must have been another way?"

If a woman were president now—and it was possible since women had gotten the vote at last—I would expect her to get down to brass tacks in a hurry; she could call the politicians and the generals together and say, "Look, fellows, we're making some changes around here, no more big guns and battleships, no more messing around where we have no business to be, we're going to concentrate on the problems of our poor and needy."

"But the Bolsheviks will take over," some general would say.

"They've got their hands full as it is," she would tell him.

"But there have always been wars and rumors of war, it says so in the bible." That would be some Protestant politician—they were good at quoting the bible, chapter and verse.

"But somewhere in the Bible it also says, 'Thou shalt not kill'!" I would say. That ought to be enough to quash his argument.

However, a woman wasn't President and there wasn't much likelihood that there would be one any time soon despite the passage of the 19th Amendment. It was still a man's world and historians were all men. A woman had a better chance of having some influence on human affairs as a poet, it seemed to me.

Child labor was common at the time; laws to prohibit it had been struck down as unconstitutional by the Supreme Court, composed of nine men. However, included in *Contemporary Poetry* (edited by a woman) which we studied in English Class (taught by a woman) were some poems (written by women) which I learned by heart. One was *The Flower Factory* by Florence Wilkinson and some of its lines were:

> *"Lisabetta, Marianina, Fiametta, Teresina*
> *They are winding stems of roses, one by one,*
> *Little children who have never learned to play*
> *They have never seen a rosebush or a dewdrop in the sun*
> *Let them have a long, long playtime*
> *Lord of Toil, when toil is done*
> *Fill their baby hands with roses*
> *Joyous roses of the sun."*

Men, or most men anyway, would have been afraid to be considered sentimental if they wrote a poem like that. And they might have been afraid of being called an agitator and told to go back to Russia if they wrote a poem like *God and the Strong Ones* by Margaret Widdemer. Two of its first stanzas went like this:

> "They are stirring in the dark said the strong ones
> They are struggling who were moveless like the dead
> We can hear them cry and strain, hand and foot against the chain
> We can hear their heavy upward tread. . . .
>
> They will trample us and bind!" said the strong ones
> We are crushed between the blackened feet and hands
> All the strong and fair and great, they will crush from out the state
> They will whelm it with the weight of pressing sands. . . ."

And the final lines were:

> "Ye have held the light and beauty I have given
> Far above the muddied ways that they must plod
> Ye have builded this your lord, with the lash and with the sword
> Reap what ye have sown!" saith God.

Why was it, I wondered, that it took women to write poetry like that? Men who had the courage to face death on the battlefield tended to be timid about facing up to the evils in our society. Yes, poetry was the thing that I would write. . . .

But then something happened. I was called to the Principal's office and asked if I would like to represent Petoskey High School in an upcoming academic contest which was being held at Central Normal College in Mt. Pleasant. The schools had been criticized for putting too much emphasis on sports and too little on academic excellence. Michigan, along with several other states, was holding academic contests that year—however, the idea was abandoned shortly thereafter.

I had never cut much of a figure in extracurricular activities, never been in a play nor on a debating team, never been elected to a class office, never gone to a school dance but now, at last, my scholastic ability was being recognized. English was my favorite subject and I always got A's on my themes.

"I've talked to both your history teachers," the principal said. "And they tell me that you qualify for both American and European History."

"History," I sputtered. "But I thought. . . . I mean. . . . I'm better in English."

"It's like this," he explained. "We can't afford to send more than five students and we think you can represent Petoskey High School in two subjects."

I could already foresee a problem—by splitting one's energies, one's chances for a first place would be diminished, but I promised I would do the best I could.

"Fine. The contest is three weeks from now so you'll have plenty of time to prepare for it. You'll all go in one car and one of the teachers will be driving."

I could have said something about the school sending a whole bus-load of boys around Northern Michigan to play football but I didn't—I was overwhelmed by the honor I had been given and the heavy responsibility which had been placed on my shoulders.

That evening I took stock of the situation. After a good look at the two textbooks and after counting the entries in the index of each one, (I had been told that the tests would probably be the multiple choice type which were then becoming popular), I decided to concentrate on American History. And so began a one-subject blitz—I reread all the material we had already covered and the chapters we had yet to study. I then used the index for review until I could give a definition for every entry from the ABC Papers to the XYZ Affair. I could list the Presidents backward as well as forward, I knew the date and place of every battle, the name and rank of every officer—I was a walking encyclopedia. I was again annoyed by the scarcity of women's names but never mind about that now.

By the time we left for the contest, I felt fairly confident that I knew everything there was to know about American History. I had purposely neglected European History—it would have been impossible to cram anything more into my bursting skull. The Physics teacher was proudly driving a new Essex and since it was the first trip out of Emmet County for several of us, he pointed out some of the geographical attractions. But I couldn't have been less interested—at that point geography and history didn't mix.

For supper we stopped at Clare. Eating a meal in a restaurant was another first for me. Being price conscious, I ordered the least expensive thing on the menu, salmon loaf and baked potato—the others ordered steak. However, it being Friday, I was glad I hadn't ordered meat and I expected to be rewarded with help from heaven the next day if I needed it.

We three girls were taken to a dormitory where each of us was put under the wing of a "big sister." As I followed mine down a long hall and up a stairs, I heard her say "Charleston" and ask whether I was familiar with it. Glad to oblige, I proceeded to tell her that it was the town in South Carolina where Fort Sumpter was located, the fort which had been fired on, April 12, 1861, this being the first hostile act of the Civil War. I was about to tell her more when she burst out laughing and said, "Oh, I meant the dance!" which she then proceeded to demonstrate, scuffing around on the slick tile floor in a way which seemed most unscholarly for the first college girl I had ever met in person.

When we got to her room, she showed me the bed which would be mine—her room-mate had gone home for the weekend and then came my first real culture shock. After looking up and down the hall surreptitiously, she closed the door, opened the window part way, whipped out a cigarette pack and offered me one. I was speechless with horror but there was more to come.

"I'd like to show you around the campus," she said between puffs but my date is coming for me at nine o'clock—if you like I can fix you up for the evening!"

I was aghast when it dawned on me what she was suggesting. Here I was, a serious-minded student, in town to represent my high school in an academic contest—and I was being propositioned for a blind date with someone I'd never even seen before!

I drew myself up to my full 62½ inches and clasping my history book to my breast and with all the disdain I could muster, I told her flat out, "I'm not that kind of a girl!"

"Have it your way, just thought I'd ask!" she giggled. "But now I've got to run." With that she crushed out her cigarette on a pin tray, dumped the ashes in a wastebasket and took off with a flippant "Toodle-do."

I was relieved that she had gone and after checking the wastebasket to make sure there wouldn't be a fire, I tried to get back to my history index. For a time I was too shaken up to concentrate—cigarettes, blind dates, a silly dance, was this what went on in an institution of higher learning? Even if I hadn't had history on my mind, even if the thought of going out with a total stranger hadn't been repugnant, I would have been fiercely loyal to a certain someone back home. Not that we were officially going together or anything like that but we walked home from school occasionally (as often as I could casually manage it), and we exchanged views on the important issues of the day. With infinite tact I had sounded him out on the causes closest to my heart such as war and peace and found most of his positions acceptable—several could be corrected with time.

However, I wasn't distracted long and I set about to review the index for the last time. I found my score perfect and I crawled into bed and turned out the light just before midnight when my so-called big sister was due back. I did not care for any more conversation with a person of her moral standards or lack of them.

I was at the proper place promptly at nine o'clock the next morning, ready to disgorge the names and dates and places which I had been regurgitating for three weeks. The first page of the multiple choice test was easy enough but on succeeding pages there was some ambiguity or so it seemed to me. For example, how should I check this one?

George McClelland was:
    ( ) An officer in the Revolutionary War
    ( ) A graduate of the Naval Academy at Anapolis

( ) A candidate for President in 1864
( ) Removed from command for insubordination

General George McClelland was not an officer in the Revolutionary War, he was not a graduate of the Naval Academy, he did run for President against Lincoln in 1864 and he was removed from command but was it for insubordination? He had been tardy in following General Lee across the Potomac but would that be considered insubordination? I pondered long and hard over that one and several others, the time got away from me and when the bell rang, I had not even begun the last page. In distress I looked around the room and all but one of the other contestants had gone, apparently having finished all five pages. I knew now that I had failed in my effort to win first place.

I was heartsick—I had done the best I could but it wasn't good enough. It would have been great to win for my school, to say nothing of winning for myself. But I was relieved that the ordeal was over. I had been flattered to be asked to represent Petoskey High but history was not for me, never had been, never would be. The experience had taught me a lesson:

Say not the struggle naught availeth
The labor and the wounds are vain. . . .

We had each been given 50¢ to buy our lunch and I got a hot dog and a double dip cone. With what was left I bought some scenic postcards and a 29¢ box of chocolate covered cherries for Mamma for Mother's Day (I liked them, too!) I ate my lunch on a campus bench, taking stock of my life, almost forgetting that I had another test to take. It turned out to be partly multiple choice, partly essay type questions which I finished on time. And on the way back to Petoskey, I enjoyed the scenery.

Several weeks later I was again called to the office. Memories of the ill-fated contest had mercifully almost left my mind along with the hodgepodge of material I had crammed into my head, "Congratulations!" the Principal said. "You've won a first place for Petoskey High! I'll announce it tomorrow during the Friday morning assembly program so be prepared to come on stage and receive your award."

I was flabbergasted, beautifully flabbergasted. Could it be a mistake? Was I dreaming? I washed and set my hair that night so as to look my best for the occasion. But another shock was in store for me, "First Place in European History" the Principal said as he handed me a gold pin on a velvet cushioned card. How could that be, I wondered as I returned to my seat amid the wondrous clapping of 500 or more of my fellow schoolmates. And then I remembered my blast at the stupidity of the Hundred Years War and the woman professor—she probably recognized in me a kindred soul!

So now, I had some re-thinking to do about my future. Perhaps after all, History should be my field. If I became a historian, I could do justice to women after the long centuries of neglect. Instead of glorifying the war-making men, I would glorify the peace-making women like Jane Addams who rated only one dinky paragraph about the Peace Ship expedition she had organized during the World War. There was a wonderful phrase, "Changing the Course of History—now, that was a worthy goal for an eleventh grade girl!

Tit for Tat

I'M Madeline, the one referred to as "Mary" in one of my sister's tales. She has me lazing around trying to get out of work while poor Martha is slaving over the dishes in the kitchen. Well, that's her side of the story and now I'm going to have my say. Fair is fair!

Just because she was twenty-two months older, she took for granted that she could always make me see things her way, do things her way and even think things her way. And if I didn't go along with her ideas, she would try to make me feel guilty for shirking my family obligations or of bringing shame to those "near and dear." She claimed to be the dutiful one, the goody-goody one and I was the lazy laggard. She was always sacrificing herself for others while I was selfish and stubborn! That wasn't the way it was at all!

"Do it for Mamma's sake" was the way she'd put it but my idea of necessary work was more like Mamma's than hers. "Take good care of the baby" was all Mamma would ever say as she left for town, leaving us in charge of the house and the younger children. I say "us" as she never named Martha as her deputy—I shall call her Martha for the time being since she dubbed me "Mary." But as soon as Mamma was out of earshot, she started bossing me around.

Sure, the dishes had to be done, the milk pails washed, the beds made but Martha's notion was to go tearing through the house like a tornado raising dust—moving the furniture every which way, dumping out drawers, re-arranging everything to *her* liking, not Mamma's!

As an example, every blooming container had to be taken off the kitchen cabinet shelves, the contents removed, the container washed, dried and refilled, then returned to the shelves with fresh newspaper on them—this every Saturday! And she expected me to fall in with this kind of nonsense and say "Yes, Martha," or "As you say, Martha," or "Right away, Martha!" Where she got her overbearing ways, I don't know—she was the one who must have been adopted!

And every week or two, she'd think of some extra job which should be done, "for Mamma's sake" as she'd put it. But when she started wanting to do things "for Papa's sake" too, that was taking matters too far—like the time she decided that we should clean out the cellar. There were some apples left over from winter and they had gotten rotten and mushy. "Let's surprise Papa and carry them out to the manure pile," she said, real sweet-like.

"Let Carl surprise Papa," I told her.

"Carl's helping Papa in the field. Besides I can never get him to do anything," she said.

But she thought she could get *me* to do whatever she wanted. Well, she had another thing coming, I wasn't going to be her fetch-and-carry sister forever. "I'm not going to touch your old smelly apples," I answered, and we were still arguing about the job when Papa came back from the field to get the potato sets for planting. He saved the day for me that time by scooping up the apples on his silo-feed fork and putting them on the back of the wagon, saying he would dump them on the manure pile as he went by.

"See what I mean," I told Martha. It just took him a couple of scoopfuls and you wanted to make a big job of it—you must like to work and make others work!"

But then there came a time when I really put my foot down and put it down hard. We were expecting company the next day and I knew that was why she wanted to get everything slicked up extra special. On top of all the other jobs she had lined up, she wanted me to help her straighten up the woodshed which was a little messy but the company didn't have to go poking around where they had no business to be. So I up and gave her a piece of my mind and then took off for self protection.

When she found me she was the one who started throwing things so I fired back with a rotten egg—it was the only thing handy. Then she threw a hunk of coal as big as a baseball at me and I figured that if she'd had better aim, she could have knocked me out. So what if I did smear a little coal-black on my temple and scare her half to death—it served her right! After that she had a little more respect for me.

Oh, she still tried to make me see things her way. I was never so embarrassed as I was one time in country school and it was all on her account. Teacher always gave each of us a present the last day before Christmas vacation but one year the older girls talked her into letting us also draw names for a gift exchange. I drew Freddie's name. He was a boy in my class whom I liked a little. Before he did what he did, that is, but it was all my sister's fault.

Store-bought gifts for something like that were not an option at our house but my brother Carl had a bag of marbles which he didn't play with any more so he agreed to let me give them to Freddie. But when Martha came home on Friday—she was in high school then and staying in town through the week—she made a big fuss about giving away those marbles which, she said, looked brand new and now that we had a baby brother we should save them for him. Besides, the marbles had been a gift from Uncle Raymond who had no children of his own and he would feel terrible if he found out that the marbles had been given to someone outside the family.

That's the way Martha was, she could always come up with some noble reason for whatever she wanted done. And that was the way she talked Carl into reneging on the marble business so I had to think of something else to give Freddie, an eleven year old boy, and there wasn't much time.

Martha had learned to make French knots and daisy stitches that winter and she was embroidering some sofa pillow covers to give as Christmas gifts. One of them had a dog on it and this, she suggested, would serve as a suitable present for Freddie.

"But he's a boy, he won't like that," I protested.

"It's a boy's kind of pillow cover, with a dog's picture on it," she told me. "It even looks like his dog except for the ears."

I couldn't see any resemblance to Freddie's dog, in fact it didn't look much like a dog at all. I thought it was just a pillow cover she'd made some mistakes on and she wanted to push it off on me. Besides, I still thought it was more for a girl.

"Well, he can give it to his mother if he doesn't like it. And anyway, he won't know who gave it to him. That's the way it works when you draw names," she told me.

I couldn't think of anything else to give Freddie, the time was getting short and since he wouldn't know I was the giver, I finally agreed to let her wrap it up for me and tie it up with some of her red and green embroidery floss. And when I wrote his name on the package I made it look like the writing of someone else.

I had Freddie's gift in my muff when I took it to school, hoping to get it mixed up with the other presents while Freddie wasn't looking. He was playing with another boy by the front steps and in my haste to get the door open, the darn thing fell out of my muff. I grabbed it up in a hurry but I was on pins and needles all day for fear he had noticed that fancy embroidery floss bow—nobody else would have one like that. I was mad at Carl for backing down on the marble deal, mad at Martha for talking me into giving a boy a sofa pillow cover even if it did have a dog on it and I was mad at myself, too, for not standing up for my rights.

When classes were over and it was time to pass out the gifts, I suggested that we all wait until Christmas to open them but the boys said "Naw, let's open them now." Freddie squeezed his package and said, "I bet it's mittens 'cause it's soft." Then he pulled off the wrapping and took one look at the pillow cover. "This can't be for me, it's gotta be some girl," so he smoothed out the tissue paper, looking for the name.

"Holy Cow," he said and threw the pillow cover, the wadded tissue paper and the bow in my lap.

"You two gonna set up housekeeping?" one of his friends giggled, and of course everybody laughed, all except Freddie and me. "I'll get even with Martha for this," I was thinking, but nothing which came to mind fit my purpose.

Save the marbles, save the best pieces of chicken for the company, save everything. Once when I wanted to open a small jar of wild raspberry jam for my toast because we were out of butter, Martha grabbed it away from me before I had a chance to take off the parafin. "It's for winter, it's for winter," she screeched.

"But I helped to pick the berries," I told her.

"Not near as many as I did, half the time you were sitting in the shade," she fibbed. I had sat down only a little while because it was so hot I was afraid I'd get a sunstroke.

But Mamma sided with Martha who marched off with it and put it back on the jam shelf in the cellar. Both of them wanted to fill up every single glass and canning jar and not open a one until after snow fell.

She even wanted to save my innocence or something. When she came home from school in town with *The Prisoner's Song* which she had just learned, she sang it like this:

> *"Oh, if I had the wings of an angel*
> *O'er the top of these walls I would fly*
> *And I'd fly to the arms of my mother*
> *And there I'd be willing to die."*

Off to the country school I went, proud that I knew a hit song. But one of the girls scoffed at me saying, "Dummy, it's 'to the arms of my darling!'" When I demanded an explanation from Martha, her answer was, "Well, there are two ways to sing it. "It's 'To the arms of my mother' for children, but when you get older you can sing it the other way!"

Yes, she was always wanting to save something or somebody—for awhile it was the heathen in China. It happened like this: one of Mamma's brothers was a member of a Missionary Order and in 1928 he volunteered to work among the Chinese. While learning the language in Shanghai, he wrote letters to the family, describing the dreadful conditions there, where poverty and disease were widespread. Every day the bodies of people were picked up on the streets and hauled away on carts drawn by "human horses." In April of the next year, we got word that Father Walter and two other priests had been waylaid by bandits on their way into the lawless Interior, and had been robbed and murdered. It was a great shock to all of us, of course, and although the bodies were found, they were never brought home.

About the same time, Martha learned that she was to be the valedictorian of her class and she decided to speak about China instead of the usual farewell kind of thing. Suddenly Saturday cleanings came to a halt, they were no longer of supreme importance—the speech was the thing! She checked out *Roget's Thesaurus* from the Library and sounded out colorful verbs and adjectives by the dozen. At last she had found an ideal way to combine creative rhetoric with crusading.

As the speech took shape laboriously, the history of China was likened to a drama (the first "a" to be pronounced like "ah", not the "a" in cat) with three Acts. Act I was China Past, Act II was China Present and Act III was China Future and the title was "The Curtain Rises on the Walled Kingdom." And every scene had action instructions like, "At this point take one step forward" or "Take two steps back" or maybe it was sidewise. There were directions for the hands also, "lift the right hand slightly" or "lift both hands vigorously," and for the eyes, "Cast them downward" or "Raise them upward." It was to be a very energetic performance.

Cheerio, Carry On

I switched from general to academic courses when I was a sophomore in high school so that when the time came, I could choose whether to go or not to go to college. The decision seemed far in the dim and distant future but, in the meantime, I was amassing a vast body of knowledge. If I did go away to school, it would be largely to brush up on whatever details I had forgotten, and if I did not go, I could shore up the knowledge I had acquired and go on with my reading at home. After all, the Bronte sisters were not college graduates—however, since I had a social conscience, anything I would write would be more like *Uncle Tom's Cabin* or *The Jungle*.

In my case, of course, there was the matter of funds to consider. Small farmers were already being squeezed to the wall in the so-called boom times of the 1920's. There was no community college in our town and as far as I knew, no grants or student loans or scholarships were available. Furthermore, I was not at all sure that I wanted to give up the security of family and home.

Although Mamma insisted that I stay with an aunt and uncle during the school week, I always headed for the farm on Friday afternoon no matter what the weather or what extra-curricular activities I would miss. And on Sunday evening I would stay up until everybody had gone to bed, not wanting to face up to the fact that the week-end was nearly over.

I would even try to keep from sleeping away the last few

precious hours at home. Sometimes after I dozed off, I would dream that I was already walking back to town and when I roused, it was a wonderful feeling to know that I was still in my own bed and still had part of the night to enjoy at home.

One time, I remember, when it was at least 20 degrees below zero with a strong North wind, my aunt said as I left after lunch, "Don't try walking to the farm after school—you'll freeze to death on the way."

"Not if I can't get a ride," I told her although, of course, I'd have to be on the road to be offered a ride.

Not much was done to clear the roads in those days. The farmers who had cars put them up on blocks for the winter and used their horses. If the snow was too deep in a cut, a temporary road on the ridge which had been blown almost clear of snow was used.

Sometimes in the late afternoons, logging sleighs would be homeward bound after a trip to the saw-mill but by the mid-20's there were few big logs to be hauled and that day there was no one on the road, neither man nor beast. By the time I gave up on a ride, I didn't want to turn back.

In town I had been somewhat sheltered from the wind, but as I got out into the open country, it came howling and swirling across the fields, covering up any tracks with fresh snow so that I could scarcely tell whether I was still on the road. I tried walking backward to protect my face but that had its perils and a number of times I found myself floundering in a drift. Dusk turned to darkness and I was only half way home. Once, thinking I could get a rest and get warm, I started toward a farmhouse but a big dog came rushing at me and I changed my mind.

The cut on Crooked Hill was full of fresh snow so I took to the ridge and there the wind almost knocked me off my feet which felt like clumsy clods. I couldn't go on without a little rest so I lay down in the lee of a drift with my head on my book bag and my numbed legs tucked under my coat. I began to feel warm and drowsy but then I remembered that people who were freezing to death got sleepy so I gave myself ten seconds more by slow count, then got up and kept going.

That was when I was a freshman but after that experience, I pulled on a pair of long woolen socks over my overshoes and thin-stockinged legs as soon as I got out of town. I didn't want to go back to fleece-lined union suits but on the other hand there was such a thing as amputation for frozen limbs. However, I never missed a weekend at the farm—it wasn't that I was unhappy at school, it was just that I was happier at home.

It was not until a few weeks before graduation that I realized that time was getting short as to a decision about college. I no longer had the lack of funds as an excuse as an aunt had offered to lend me the money she had saved during years of dressmaking . . . $500 which, she said should cover tuition and books for a couple of years and I could work for my room and board.

What I half-way wanted to do was to remain comfortably at home and go on reading a lot more books and some day try my hand at writing one. Also, I might consider combining a literary career with marriage and have the best of both worlds. On the other hand, could the valedictorian of her class turn down an opportunity to go off to college somewhere and make a notable scholastic record?

Had a certain boy shown an interest in anything other than platonic conversations as we walked home from school occasionally, I would have taken that into consideration. As it was, no hope seemed to lie in that direction so one evening I sat down and wrote what I meant to be a sonnet but it turned out to have too many lines. However, I did not submit it to the school paper as I did with my editorials and other meanderings. It went something like this:

> *Long I lingered, long I listened*
> *For your step upon my threshold*
> *For your knock upon my door*
> *For your kiss upon my forehead*
> *For your whisper in the twilight*
> *That you'll love me ever more.*
>
> *Long I waited, long I wondered*
> *If your love would bud and blossom*
> *Like the lilacs by my door*
> *Like the lilies in the valley*
> *Like arbutus in the forest*
> *But you're silent ever more*

Now, 'tis too late, so come not now
What I had hoped is not to be
My tears are dried, my dreams are dead
I've locked my heart and lost the key.

It was Mamma, always practical and forward looking, who tipped the scales. She heard of a Detroit family, summering on Crooked Lake, which needed a nursemaid. In Detroit there was a University. . . .

She talked me into applying for the job and went with me for the interview. The upshot was a job for the summer and a place to work for my room and board while attending the University of Detroit. I had my credits forwarded and I was accepted by its College of Commerce and Finance, the only one then open to women in the Jesuit School. I wasn't the least bit interested in commerce or finance but there were courses in Journalism offered and I did like to write editorials.

My employers were pleasant, their children were well behaved, and their cottage was lovely. Having access every day to a lake should have seemed a wonderful opportunity but now that I was expected to live with the family for the summer, the water lost its allure. I felt cheated, being able to go home only for Sunday afternoons, and soon I would have to leave for months. I had a good notion to chuck it all.

The cottage was next to the Conway Inn where a college student was waitressing that summer. The young woman was Harriette Simpson, later to be Harriette S. Arnow, author of *The Dollmaker,* a powerful story of an uprooted farm family transplanted in war-time Detroit. Our paths must have crossed as I often took my charges for walks around the hotel grounds. At the time she was beginning work on her first novel *Mountain Path,* but we did not meet until many years later when we were both deeply concerned over the folly of underground shelters as protection against nuclear war.

As a mother's helper I was expected to leave Petoskey in late August, almost a month before registration at the University of Detroit. Our day of departure arrived and I spent my last hours at home packing, with tears running down my cheeks. To have to leave was bad enough but to have to leave long before it was necessary was a cruel trick of fate.

We left on an evening train, the children and I in one of the Pullman staterooms, which should have been an exciting experience but it held no joy for me. I had to hide my feelings while helping the children get undressed and telling them bedtime stories, but when at last I could get into my own berth, I wept homesick tears into my pillow. I wanted to go to sleep quickly so as to be one night nearer Christmas vacation—114 days and nights by calendar count.

But the rumbling of the wheels, the whistling at the crossings, the coupling and uncoupling of the cars, plus the realization that every mile took me farther and farther from home kept me awake most of the night.

We arrived at the Fort Street station early in the morning but already the trolley cars were filled with passengers and the streets were clogged with rush hour traffic. Automobiles were weaving in and out on the wide thoroughfares, their horns honking, their brakes screeching—it was a noisy confusing bedlam. And to the East in the clearing mist I could see the skyscrapers which I had been told were a sight to behold. They didn't impress me at all.

I had gotten the impression that the place where I would be staying was near the University—and perhaps as big cities go, four miles is considered near—not that taking a bus was the way to get there. Nor had anyone told me about boarding zones and bus stops, so on my first experience with public transportation I tried to flag down a bus and was ignored. However, it stopped a block or two up the street and took on several passengers there. I tried a second time and that bus went barreling by also. Could it be, I wondered, that country folks were discriminated against in favor of Detroiters? I tried to run for it the third time but the bus pulled away with a big puff of exhaust just as I reached its rear end. To heck with it, I thought, I'll walk and save the 10¢ fare, after all I had walked four miles many times at home.

My board-and-room house was in a pleasant, tree-shaded residential area but on the bus line only a few blocks away, there were warehouses with dirt-encrusted windows, rambling factory buildings belching smoke, streetcar diners,

tent-like fruit and vegetable markets, boarded-up deserted old houses—these interspersed with shiny-faced branch banks and realty offices. Not a tree or a blade of grass anywhere—it was not a fun place to walk.

As I neared Six Mile Road, the landscape changed on Livernois Ave. There was a bustle of new construction, much of it related to the new University of Detroit campus and there was grass, also young trees. The streets running off Six Mile to the west were bordered by hundreds of boxy little houses with slight variations as to front entrances and the color of the bricks, but the chimneys were all in a straight line across the roof tops like fence posts in a row.

There were only about a dozen girls as compared to twenty times that many boys in the School of Commerce and Finance Freshman class. A newsman with a camera rounded us up in our white tennis shoes, long red stockings and red and white beanies (the Sophomore girls' idea of hazing) and took our pictures in the big new stadium. The picture was atrocious and the story in one of the city papers was even worse—"a gaggle of co-eds in a herd of fellows" or some such derogatory description and I was not amused. Also, I thought that hazing was childish although I was thankful for the tennis shoe dictum as the long walks on cement sidewalks were harder on the feet than the dirt roads at home.

Journalism was to be my major but to my chagrin, I found that courses in that subject were not open to Freshmen so I signed up for European History, American Government, Mathematics, Economics and English which, insultingly, was mostly a review of grammar—nothing creative. I began spending my time between classes in the Library which was very well stocked, compared with the Public Library in Petoskey at the time. I was much taken with the novels of Stanislaus Reymont, the Polish Nobel Laureate, especially by his four volume epic, *The Peasants,* also by some of Emile Zola's novels. And when I was offered a job "reading stacks," I jumped at the chance. At 50¢ an hour, I could earn between eight and ten dollars a week and with this I could get a room which was really "near" the campus, buy enough food to keep me alive and start saving money for my trip home at Christmas time. Except for my tuition of $175 per semester, I had used nothing from my aunt's loan. Books and a few new clothes I had bought with my summer wages.

In October of that year, 1929, the Great Depression hit and within a week or two, almost all the fast-paced construction around the campus came to a halt. Foundation walls were left several blocks high, window openings remained unglazed and on the residential streets "For Sale" and "For Rent" signs appeared.

Perhaps because of the crash, I was able to get a room within a few blocks from the University for $2.00 a week and the food I ate cost very little. I had an orange and a couple of cookies for breakfast, an apple and a 5¢ White Castle hamburger for lunch and when I went to my room after Library hours, I took a pint bottle of milk which I drank with some doughnuts or cookies. After mid-November, my biggest problem was keeping warm in my lodging place.

A section had been partitioned off in the attic of one of the boxy houses on Prairie Avenue but it had never been plastered—the 2″ by 4‴s were still exposed. It did have a heat duct, a ceiling light, a single bed, a table and straight chair and some open shelves, with nails on the wall for hangers. The landlady was a widow with three teen age children who were always squabbling so I kept to myself, using the bathroom on the first floor only in the evening and the early morning before I left for school. Mamma sent me a heavy patchwork quilt so I spent most of my rooming-house time in bed, studying, reading library books or sleeping.

Except for my job and my extra-curricular reading, I liked nothing about my new life but, never mind, each hour brought me closer to Christmas vacation on my mark-off calendar. And when the great day arrived, I had all my belongings packed, including my books and some gifts for the family, everything except the bulky quilt which Mamma had sent me.

"Are you coming back?" my landlady asked, eyeing my two suitcases and a bag under each arm as I was about to go out the door.

"The semester isn't over until late January," I told her non-committally.

"Then I'd like the rent now, I need it for groceries," she said.

I knew she was having a hard time and although I was sure she had been snooping in my room and cutting down on what little heat there was at night, I paid her the rent for the vacation weeks. For once I was in a magnanimous mood.

I had written home that I was taking the Pere Marquette on Friday evening and the train was getting in at 5 o'clock in the morning but what I hadn't realized was that I would be transferring to the Pennsylvania line in Grand Rapids. I was so excited that I couldn't sleep, also the coach was chokingly hot in comparison with my attic room, so I kept my nose on the cold window pane. But I enjoyed every minute of that long December night as the snowy miles took me nearer and nearer the home I loved. I would find Papa awaiting me at the station with the horse and cutter and Mamma would have a hot breakfast ready for us, perhaps pancakes and some of her wonderful homemade sausage.

But Papa wasn't there to meet the train—so many times I had imagined that long awaited homecoming and he hadn't come to get me—I felt hurt and abandoned, then fearful that something had gone wrong, someone was sick. . . . After the other passengers had been greeted and taken away by their families, I started walking with a heavy heart, two big suitcases and a couple of paper bags under my arms.

As it happened, Papa and my sister, Colette, had gotten up at three o'clock that morning and were at the Pere Marquette Station waiting for me there. By the time they realized the error and had driven to the other station, I had already left. But they caught up with me just beyond the edge of town and it was a good thing they did as I would never had made it otherwise, not with all that baggage. And Mamma did have a pancake and sausage breakfast for us— my first hot meal in months. Aside from the one snafu, every moment of every day of that vacation was wondrously happy until on New Year's Eve, Mamma asked me when I would be leaving.

I broke down then and told her that I didn't really want to go back. I disliked everything about Detroit, I didn't care much for my courses, I hated my rooming house, the only thing I liked was my library job.

But Mamma, ever practical, reminded me that Christmas fun would not last forever, also that since I had been lent tuition money, I should at least finish the semester. "And if you do come home then, be sure to bring that warm woolen quilt," she reminded me.

Back at school, without the prospect of approaching holidays, the time dragged interminably, even the library job had somehow lost its appeal now that I was not shopping for family gifts out of my lush earnings. And then one day when I did not go out for my usual hamburger because of the weather and was sitting alone, munching on an apple, I was invited to join another freshman girl who was sharing a brown bag lunch with her upperclassman brother, majoring in Journalism. From him I learned that a cub newspaper woman would not be entitled to sit at a desk and write editorials and syndicated columns! I would be expected to go chasing around the city in all kinds of weather to the scenes of accidents and murders and to hang out at police stations, firehouses and the like. I must have seemed a provincial babe in the woods and perhaps aroused a protective sentiment in him.

"Where you should be is in a Liberal Arts College if you're interested in Creative Writing, not in the rough and tumble newspaper world. Try the University of Michigan next year, the tuition is a lot less there, too," he urged. I also learned that he was working several part-time jobs and had no time for social life. "It's tough," he said, "but I've got to carry on for a few months more, just hope I can find something in my field then."

Now I found myself taking a brown bag lunch every day and deciding to stay at the U. of D. for the rest of the year. I was even finding my attic room a fit place for composing romantic poetry.

A week or two after the second semester started, the Journalism Major told me that he had been assigned to write an article about me for the college paper. Remembering the dreadful one about the "gaggle" of Freshman girls, I was a little apprehensive but when the story appeared, I was ecstatic, not only because of what it said about me but what it said about the writer himself.

As I remember the headline it was, "Old Frosh Cabbage Head Theory Disproved," and it went on about the top grades in the school. The final line was something like this, "But fellows, you haven't heard anything yet, the freshman is a girl!" Now, there was a boy who wasn't upset if men were sometimes upstaged by women, here was someone who was unlike the typical U. of D. male student who dated girls at the nearby Women's College—girls who left the business of Commerce and Finance to men where it "properly belonged."

But then, a short time later, my dreams which had been abuilding, came crashing down. From the boy's sister, I learned that her brother was sick, had been spitting blood and was dropping out of school on doctor's orders. He had been working too hard, getting too little sleep, eating irregularly and had been worrying about things at home because his father was out of work. A week or so later, she told me that he had been admitted to a State T.B. Sanatorium.

I sent a note to him but he never answered although he did send a verbal message through his sister, "Cheerio, Carry on" but then she, too, dropped out of school and I never heard from either one again. But, several years later, someone who had been at the Sanatorium at the same time, said he thought he remembered the name but was quite sure the young man had died.

I did carry on after a fashion, I kept my job at the Library, I remained at school and my social conscience was reawakened. I began to look around and see what I had formerly read about in books.

The Motor City had become not only a drab but a fearsome place. Hundreds of thousands of people were out of work and many were being turned out of their homes— I saw furniture piled on the sidewalk after an eviction. There was no unemployment insurance, little public welfare, nothing but family help or private charity to keep people from starving.

On the street corners there were able-bodied adults selling apples and pencils, a way to camouflage the fact that they had been reduced to begging. In the outdoor markets there were women in babushkas hunting for cabbage and turnip bargains. Men with hopeless, hangdog looks stood at the factory gates stamping their feet in the cold, before being turned away. And waiting to be served at Salvation Army kitchens were the same unemployed men, with their collars turned up against recognition by their friends and neighbors.

The Great Depression held the city in its grip. The "Five dollars a Day" slogan which had brought many peasants to work in our automobile plants had back-fired. Here, as in the stockyard area in Chicago, people were cold and hungry and homeless. In the "old country" there had been wood from the forests for fuel, and cabbage and turnips and potatoes in their frost free pits. Fear was in the air, so all pervading that one could almost feel it, taste it, smell it. Now I knew what real trouble was. . . .

I went back to the farm in June a wiser, humbler person—

I had begun to scale down my expectations. Life would not be a "bowl of cherries" in the words of a popular song—it was grim and hard for many people, perhaps for most of the world's people. One had to hope and work for better days, one had to "Carry On" and carry on, I would somehow.

A Brush with the Law

IN the 1922 family car, driven by our brother, Carl, my sister and I arrived in Ann Arbor on a hot day in mid-September, 1930. We had come from our farm, some 265 miles away, in just under nine hours, good time for an old Chevrolet. Because the headlights had gone bad, Carl wanted to get to Grand Rapids before dark where he planned to spend the night with relatives.

On the corner of Ann Street and Observatory, he stopped the car and unloaded our baggage. "It's got to be right around here, it says University Hospital." We had been told that our pre-arranged rooming house was next to Hill Auditorium on Thayer St. but there he left us on the sidewalk with two heavy suitcases, two boxes tied with binder twine, our winter coats and an umbrella. "Don't want to get stopped for no lights" were his parting words.

It had taken a little arm-twisting to get Madeline to transfer to University High School for her senior year. Although I had been offered a tuition scholarship, I had decided not to go back to the University of Detroit and spend another lonely, homesick year in what I considered a godforsaken city and I did not want to major in Journalism, not after learning what would be expected of a cub reporter. But I did not want to quit school either—I knew now that I knew very little and I was embarrassed to remember my former youthful arrogance.

Since we'd always had differences of opinion and frequent squabbles, I couldn't openly admit to Madeline that I wanted her companionship and the feeling of family while far from the security of home. The way to handle the situation, it seemed, was to stress the advantages to her if she made the transfer. "You'll be all set for admission to the University of Michigan—it's one of the greatest in the nation, you know," I told her.

"What do you mean, all set?" she asked, ignoring my plug for an institution I had never seen at the time.

"Well, being right in the same town, knowing the ropes—no problem of adjustment, I can help you with that. And the tuition is only $50, we can easily make enough for both of us—get good jobs!"

"What kind of jobs and how much an hour?" she wanted to know. She was a stickler for details.

"Oh, like reading stacks in a library at 50¢ an hour, maybe more," I told her. She was earning a measily 25¢ as a mother's helper in Petoskey that summer.

"Well, I'll think about it," she said. And as she thought, I bombarded her with more advantages, imagined more than real as it happened. But after the decision to make the transfer was settled, I made it a point to caution her that we would have to be very careful spenders.

The careful spending began the very afternoon we arrived in Ann Arbor. "Where's Hill Auditorium?" I asked a passerby.

"Four or five blocks from here," the stranger said, with a wave of his hand in the direction from which we had come.

"We can't carry all this stuff that far," Madeline complained, as I started picking up our belongings. "There's a taxi, let's get that."

"Taxis cost a lot of money—I told you we've got to be careful spenders," I said to her sternly. She might as well get used to doing without luxuries.

"Careful spenders, you mean tightwads," she muttered, a comment I was to hear several times the next hour and many times during the next three years.

It was sticky hot, the bulky coats were awkward under our arms, the binder twine was sharp to the hands, and one of the suitcases bulged itself open on the corner of Huron and

Forest. There we had to stop and tie it up with a piece of twine to keep it from disgorging some of our clothes.

By resting every half block or so, we managed to proceed westward toward Hill Auditorium but somewhere we made a wrong turn. There was a confusion of University Avenues, North, East and South, so we had to be redirected, this time across the Diagonal, thence back to Thayer Street and the Auditorium.

Perspiring and exhausted, we finally reached our destination, a large red brick house where Mamma had arranged a room for us through a teacher who had been summering at Bay View. Miss Bennet taught Math at nearby Ann Arbor High School and rented the upstairs flat, subletting all but a combination living room-bedroom which she kept for herself. In addition to our room there was one occupied by a middle-aged lady working on her doctorate, and in another room plus a kitchen there were several nurses. We all shared the same bathroom.

Our landlady knocked on our door as we were unpacking. "I'm going out to dinner shortly and I'll show you girls a nice moderately priced place to eat," she offered.

"Oh, we're not hungry right now, just tired," I told her, giving my sister a meaningful nudge. "Moderately" probably meant 50¢ apiece and we could buy a lot of groceries for a dollar. Besides, we had some cookies and apples left over from the lunch which Mamma had packed for us.

In those days, undergraduate women were required to live on campus or in approved houses under the supervision of house mothers. Miss Bennet had agreed to act in that capacity and no doubt she considered it her duty to see that we were eating properly. Eventually however, she gave up asking us to go out to dinner with her as she could never catch us when we were hungry. True, I knew her knock and was usually able to get to the door first as I could never be sure about what Madeline would say.

We had learned that there was a list of part-time jobs for students in the Dean of Women's office and there I went the first thing the next morning. Alas, there were no cushy library positions but I was able to get a job doing housework for a faculty family at 50¢ an hour for twenty hours a week on the average, and for Madeline I got one baby-sitting on weekends. She also got work in the high school cafeteria which in addition to her noontime meal and 25¢ an hour in wages, she was permitted to take home any leftover food which would not be edible the next day.

Unfortunately, the food was usually left over for a reason—it hadn't attracted too many takers, it was macaroni with too little cheese, or creamed fish that was too fishy or jello that was so rubbery, it bounced. However, it was filling and it was free. We didn't have any refrigeration but we did invest in a 98¢ hot plate which made some of the food more palatable. Once, I remember on a Friday Madeline brought home a half gallon jar of the fish dish. It was all right that evening and fair the next day, but on Sunday it gave off a terrific odor when we heated it for dinner.

Hastily we tried to waft the fumes out the window with our bath towels but we weren't entrirely successful—our next door roomer made a loud, pointed remark as she went down the hall, not the kind of remark one would expect from a doctoral candidate. However, our house-mother made no complaints, I think she preferred to have us do a little cooking in our bedroom to having us die of starvation on her hands.

Despite the Depression, there were still football fans coming to town for the games. For the Minnesota home game that year, a larger crowd than usual was expected and we heard that the Sugar Bowl needed a couple of extra waitresses. We applied because as it happened, we were both free that afternoon and we were hired at 50¢ an hour from noon 'til 9:00, plus tips, mind you!

Turkey was on the menu, turkey with all the trimmings including pumpkin pie with whipped cream. After the game started we were asked by the manager if we wanted to eat and I answered promptly for both of us, saying we had just had lunch before we checked in—at $1.50 each, the price of the meals would make quite a dent in our earnings and besides it was true that we had eaten macaroni and cheese in our room.

The other waitresses all seemed to be gorging on the

savory turkey and sage dressing when Madeline, refusing to take notice of my cues, asked if there was a reduced rate for the help. "Reduced?" one of the girls said with a laugh, "It's on the house!"

Suddenly I, too, became ravenously hungry and we both went back for seconds. It was a lovely meal, almost as good as Mamma's chicken dinners at home.

Except for selling my student tickets which were included in our tuition charge, sports events were of no interest or concern to me or my sister. That evening an over-exuberant alumnus at her table apparently decided to have some fun at her expense. "Tell me, young lady, what team did Michigan play today?"

Notwithstanding the fact that the town was plastered with "Beat the Gophers" signs, Madeline in all innocence replied politely, "I don't know, Sir, but I'll go find out."

Although Prohibition was still the law of the land, there were those who ignored it, especially at football games. "She'll go find out, she'll go find out," her questioner boomed in a voice loud enough to be heard in the whole restaurant. Poor Madeline, she didn't know what she had said to cause such a burst of merriment not only at her table but at others also. However, her embarrassment was forgotten when she got a $5.00 tip—mine were all less than a dollar. "With this," she told me, "I'm going to have something better than macaroni and cheese for a whole week. She didn't say "we."

I was a full time student but sometimes it seemed that I was sandwiching my classes between full-time jobs instead of the other way around. I was taking Literature and History courses but the one which made everything else worthwhile was the one in Creative Writing. The class met every Wednesday evening for three hours at which time some of our papers would be read aloud by the professor, Carlton Wells, who was a true teacher—he made each of us think we had something unique to contribute. Instead of "Publish or Perish" his goal seemed to be "Inspire or Perish," and to each of us he devoted a half hour of individual consultation every week. Now, instead of working for grades, I was interested in writing something which he would consider worthy of being read at the evening session.

Ann Arbor, still a quiet, tree-shaded college town, was somewhat insulated from the Great Depression which was raging all around it. The cities had been hit first but the upstate towns and rural areas began to hurt as the economic crisis deepened. Business enterprises were floundering, teachers were not being paid or being paid in script, farmers were unable to sell their produce so were giving away apples and potatoes or dumping them on their fields as fertilizer. There were many things to write about—either the happy times of my childhood or the troubled times of the day.

Something was wrong, terribly wrong, that much I knew from what I had seen first hand in Detroit. It did not make sense that in a country with tremendous natural resources and with millions of people willing and able to work, there should be unemployment and hunger. There were as yet no soup kitchens in Ann Arbor—faculty members were not as vulnerable as were many Americans. Their salaries, although never high, were still being paid and the wives of full professors could still afford part time maids and the wives of instructors could afford to have baby sitters occasionally.

Madeline and I were therefore able to get as much work as we could handle and by "careful spending," we not only earned enough for our modest expenses but put aside a hundred dollars to be used for a 25th wedding anniversary present for our parents. It never occurred to us to buy something in silver; furniture for the living room on the farm was what we had in mind.

First we tried a furniture store in Ann Arbor but at the time, we were as much interested in quantity as in quality. Perhaps in Detroit, we could find both in good used furniture—accordingly on a Friday afternoon following classes, we were able to get a ride with a graduate student who was commuting from East Detroit. We had checked with the telephone directory and learned that there were a number of second-hand shops on Michigan Avenue and it was there that the lady driver dropped us off with raised eyebrows but no comment.

Although I had lived in the University of Detroit area the previous year, I knew very little about the rest of the city. Michigan Avenue turned out to be a street of cheap movie houses, greasy restaurants, porn book shops—and yes, second hand stores. In and out of them we dashed, but we could find nothing suitable for an anniversary present. In one dingy, dimly lit place, I remember, there was a fairly nice looking mohair suite but on close inspection, there was evidence of moths at work. "Just get one of those fancy dolls with a big skirt and nobody'll ever see the bare spot," the proprietor suggested.

By the time we gave up on the second hand stores, it was too late to check for repossessed furniture in the department stores farther down town. "Let's wait until tomorrow," I told Madeline. Neither one of us had jobs until noon the next day and staying over would be simpler and cheaper than returning another time. An aunt and uncle lived in Allen Park but getting out there and back would also be a problem. The upshot of it was that we decided (later my sister said that *I* had decided) to spend the intervening hours at the Michigan Central Railway Station, also on Michigan Avenue.

To put in the evening and to satisfy Madeline, we got a 35¢ pork chop dinner and went to a 10¢ movie which turned out to be a disgusting waste of money. By eleven o'clock, we were sitting quietly in the big, noisy station minding our own business, after calling our landlady so she wouldn't worry. We still had our books with us as we had left directly after classes, and I was reading a play in my one volume *Complete Works of Shakespeare* for a course I was taking from a blind professor. I recall thinking that the fine print in my book plus the lights on the high ceiling were enough to make anybody blind.

By midnight we were both getting very sleepy, probably dozing off at times, when a lady whom we had noticed at the Traveler's Aid booth approached us, saying, "You girls have been here quite a while—are you waiting for a train?"

Taken aback by the unexpected question, I answered "Yes" since that was what she seemed to want to hear.

"What train?" she asked pointedly.

"Er—well, the one from Grand Rapids," I replied. I hadn't the slightest idea whether or not there was such a train or what lines the station served but I had to say something and we did have relatives in Grand Rapids, that much was true.

"What time is it due in?" was her next question and I thought I detected a there-I-caught-you look on her face.

I was in so deep now that I might as well stick to my story.

"Around 2 o'clock," I told her, nerves causing my hands to get sweaty.

"Hm . . . well . . ." and with that she left us.

"We'd better get out of here," Madeline warned. "I didn't think much of this idea in the first place—some more of your tightwad stuff."

"But where can we go now, it's so late!" I recalled the shuffling, destitute looking men we had seen on our second-hand store tour and I preferred to sit it out. After all, we had done nothing wrong.

"Maybe we should go out to Allen Park after all," my sister suggested.

"We can't ask Uncle Frank to come and get us this time of the night, besides he may have let his car go back, now that he's out of work."

"Then, let's take a taxi," Madeline insisted.

We were still debating the matter when two strapping women in police uniforms came marching toward us. One sat down beside me and the other one took Madeline a short distance away, apparently to grill her separately.

"Now what's this about a train from Grand Rapids, there's no such train," my inquisitor asked.

By now I knew that we were in for big trouble so I tried to explain our predicament which meant admitting that I had fibbed about the train and that all we wanted to do was to wait in the station until the stores opened the next morning. "It's like this," I told her. "Our parents' 25th wedding anniversary is in June so we came over from Ann Arbor. . . ."

"You live in Ann Arbor?" she interrupted.

"We have a room there, we really live in Petoskey, that is on a farm near Petoskey but we're working our way through school and we saved this money. . . ."

"You're working your way through school, it's your parents' wedding anniversary, you saved this money . . ." her voice was very skeptical.

"Yes, and we're looking for some good furniture, not like

that moth-eaten stuff we saw on Michigan Avenue so we thought we'd stay the night here!

"Michigan Avenue, don't you know it's not a safe place for young girls?"

"We thought we could get a better bargain there, everything is so expensive in Ann Arbor—a hundred dollars is all we have to spend." I went on, trying desperately to make her understand the situation.

"Humph, you've got that much money on you right now?"

"Oh yes, I've got it right here and enough to get back to Ann Arbor on the bus by noon tomorrow—we've both got jobs then."

There was another loud "Humph" and she then signalled her partner who had been grilling Madeline. It was probably a mistake to tell her about the money but it was too late now and besides, Madeline had probably mentioned it also. The two police women consulted with each other in undertones but we were able to hear a few phrases, "All that money . . . runaways probably . . . furniture for a present, my foot. . . ."

"We'll have to take you girls in and check out your stories (what had my sister been saying, I wondered) so pick up your books and let's get going" we were told. And with that, they marched us out to their cruiser, parked near the front entrance. They didn't put handcuffs on us but they had vise-like grips and I was pushed into the front seat while my sister was under guard in the back seat. Away we went with sirens sounding to the Women's Detention Home.

As we reached the building with its barred windows, the metal garage doors went up as if raised by an unseen hand and once we were inside, the doors went down with an ominous clank. By now we were both thoroughly alarmed—supposing we were kept incommunicado, how would we let our employers know we couldn't get to work as planned? Supposing the police got in touch with our parents and told them we were in jail? Supposing they took our hard-earned cash, thinking we had stolen it! Supposing they tried to pin some terrible crime on us, what would we do for a lawyer! Supposing, supposing, supposing, supposing. . . .

On an elevator we were taken to an upper floor where a middle-aged, kind-faced woman was seated behind a desk. She looked up inquiringly.

"We found these girls at the Michigan Central Station, first they lied about meeting a train from Grand Rapids, then they told us some cock and bull story about coming to buy furniture for their parents with money they earned working their way through school. They say they have it on them—a hundred dollars!"

The woman at the desk waved them to silence and turned to us, "Now you girls tell me what this is all about," she said in a calm, quiet way.

We were both close to tears but we managed to get the story out and this time it was the truth, the whole truth and nothing but the truth—unlikely as it may have sounded.

When we had finished, she turned to the police women and said, "I believe these girls—nobody could make up a story like that!" Then she asked us if we had any relatives in the area where we could spend the balance of the night. We told her about our aunt and uncle, she dialed the number and handed the phone to me.

Half asleep, my aunt answered the phone, saying, "Sure, you can come out but how will you get here and what are you doing in Detroit this time of the night?"

I assured her that we could arrange transportation, that we would take a taxi and would explain everything when we got there.

The police women were directed to drive us to our destination and this time they both sat in the front seat. "Free taxi ride!" my sister whispered as she nudged me.

"Please don't stop right in front of the house with the porch light on," I asked. They obligingly did so and we heard their car pull away as Aunt Viola opened the door. "You can tell me what this is all about in the morning," she said. "It's time to get to bed!" and to this we heartily agreed.

Early the next day we tiptoed down the stairs, leaving a scribbled note saying we had to get back to Ann Arbor for our jobs but we would explain everything later. It was later, quite a few years later, before we could bring ourselves to tell her or anyone else about our night on the town.

After having suffered through such an experience, we weren't going to give up on our project, so we were at the entrance of a small but respectable looking downtown store when the door was opened for business. The proprietor took us in hand and for our hundred dollars, he sold us a three piece mohair suite, almost new, and threw in a walnut dining room table with enough leaves to accommodate a threshing crew. He also agreed to have the furniture crated and shipped at his expense. We left the store and the city feeling very pleased with ourselves in spite of our brush with the law.

In September of the next school term, we were able to find an apartment or what passed for an apartment in that time and place. It was one of the five units on the second floor of an old frame house near the campus, all of us sharing a bathroom. The landlord and his wife lived on the first floor and since the set-up was satisfactory to the Dean of Women, we were given permission to live there. Our unit was the only one to have a complete kitchen, that is, it had a four burner gas stove with an oven, a sink, a cupboard, table and chairs but no refrigerator. It opened on a screened porch with two single beds and a rod with hangers—that was it. Now, at last, we could cook regular meals and wash dishes without running to the bathroom for water.

On the coldest night of that winter, we couldn't keep warm on the porch so we dragged our bedding into the kitchen and spent the rest of the night on the floor after lighting the burners and the oven for a quick thaw. Fortunately our alarm went off early for an eight o'clock class as the stove was unvented.

At the University I was finding most of my courses interesting, I was continuing with my writing, and I was becoming more and more concerned about social issues. The mood in the country was now becoming angry—President Hoover was being blamed for the ills of the nation, it was said that although he had fed the hungry of Europe after the War, he was doing nothing to feed the hungry at home. Although Ann Arbor had been spared during the first months of the Depression, it now had wolves snarling at its gates.

At reduced hourly wages, my sister and I still had jobs and we were not going hungry. Through an uncle we had acquired an old car, we were able to save on train fare, also bring produce from the farm—and we had our kitchen. We felt both lucky and guilty!

In June when we left for home, we told our landlord that we would be returning in the fall and we wanted the same kitchen-porch apartment. And when we got back in September, we had a full load of produce from the farm from potatoes to pickles. The entrance doors to the house were never locked and seldom the doors to our units, so we proceeded up the stairs with as many of our belongings as we could carry and went barging into our kitchen. There, to our consternation, we found that it had been taken over by two young men who had their books scattered about and their food cooking on our stove. We stepped back in dismay, almost colliding with our landlord who kept nervously repeating, "Your room is down the hall, down the hall, down the hall...."

"But what about the kitchen?" Madeline wanted to know.

It didn't have one, except for a two burner plate and some open shelves in a cubby-hole—no oven, no sink and no cool porch to store our apples, squash and potatoes. As we later learned, fearful of not being able to rent all the units in the worsening economic times, our landlord had decided to rent on a first-come, first serve basis and the two male teachers, back to earn advanced degrees, had not been interested in any of the other units.

But what could we do? We hadn't signed any lease, we hadn't made any advance deposit and the landlord claimed that he thought we'd like a front unit better, there wasn't time to look for other quarters and Registration was the following day. And besides losing our kitchen there was another problem—mixed housing was verboten in those days.

With fear and trembling I stood in line the next morning and when the fateful question was asked, I answered as casually as possible, "Same as last year." To my relief the word "Approved" was stamped in the proper place on my registration form and I proceeded to coach my sister as to what had worked for me, so she too, was able to pass muster.

Had the Dean of Women gotten a run-down on the variety of renters on the second floor at 513 E. Jefferson that term, I think she would have had my sister and me expelled for deceit in deliberately violating her housing rules. In addition to the two male graduate students, there was a middle-aged gentleman who turned out to be an alcoholic, an elderly lady who felt the need to shoplift small items at the grocery stores, and a practitioner of the oldest profession who was later evicted after one of her clients with a wooden leg fell down the stairs and the purpose of his visit admitted.

However, it was one of the male students, recognizing me as one of the girls down the hall, who gallantly offered to share his raincoat with me during a sudden downpour as we were returning from classes one afternoon in October. One thing led to another and the following July we were married and have continued to share the same roof ever since. But that is another story.

Forward, Turn Forward
An Epilogue

On his 71st birthday my father died in the farmhouse bedroom where he had been born on Sept. 16, 1884. He had undergone exploratory surgery, cancer of the pancreas was discovered, and it was recommended that he remain in the hospital for pain control. However, he insisted on going home, there to spend his last days in familiar surroundings and within sight of his horses grazing contentedly near his window.

Until the last afternoon of his life, he was able to withstand the pain without medication but when it became excruciating and his own doctor was unavailable, another physician, Dr. Blum, was willing to make the trip to the farmhouse to ease his passing. He died that evening, his rosary entwined in his fingers, his daughter, Eileen, and his wife of 49 years at his bedside.

My mother survived him by eight years and although those of us who did not live in the area hoped that she would spend time in our homes, she preferred to remain on the farm with her memories and await our frequent visits. She was especially pleased when any of her thirteen grandchildren came to be with her for week-long stays.

The most vivid recollection I have of her last years was of the day she received her first Social Security check. It was almost $500 for the prior year and a third, the monthly payments being the minimum amount, approximately $30. She held the opened envelope in her hands, her eyes shining and her voice trembling with emotion, saying, "Oh, if Philip could only have lived to see this!" However, I doubt that he would have shared her happiness as he did not approve of Government help of any kind. He would never apply for the Soil Bank subsidy, preferring instead to rotate his crops and use the manure pile as a source of fertilizer. "Jobs for everybody" was what was needed, not hand-outs, he often said.

Carl continued to farm the family fields until his death in 1983. Since he found it increasingly difficult to make a living on 80 acres, part of it too hilly for a tractor, he supplemented his income as a handyman. He would tackle almost any fix-it job and was usually able to come up with a Rube Goldberg solution to whatever the problem. He and his wife had hoped for a family but there was only one child, a daughter who was stillborn. Nieces and nephews were always welcome to ride his tractor, tramp the woods with him or drive his snowplow. One of his nephews recently said that the happiest days of his childhood were spent with Uncle Carl and Aunt Mabel; a niece came from Colorado for his funeral to give the beautiful eulogy she had composed.

Madeline, I must admit, outgrew her early allergy to work. After her graduation from the University of Michigan she was a social worker with the Red Cross until her marriage to a cellist in the Cincinnati Symphony Orchestra. After their two sons were of school age, she did graduate study in Education and until her retirement several years ago, was a teacher in the Cincinnati Public School System. In partnership with one of her sons, she developed a number of teaching aids: several of them including "Fun-Da-Math" and "Quizzle" have been marketed in the Midwest by Ideal School Supply.

Colette, my birthday present sister, earned her R.N. degree at the Good Samaritan Hospital in Cincinnati. After practicing for three or four years she married an Eastern Airlines Airport manager and moved to the Atlantic City area. When their four children were young she brought them to the farm each summer to their delight and that of their grandparents. After her children were in their teens she returned to nursing. Since her husband's death in 1979 she has lived in Arlington, Virginia near her daughter and son-in-law, both of whom are attorneys.

After a half dozen years in Southeastern Michigan, first as a student at Eastern Michigan University, then as a Briggs employee in Detroit, Eileen and her husband and young daughter returned to Petoskey where they went into the motel business. Widowed a few years later, she has continued to operate the Lake Breeze Motel where she accommodates many of the family members of Northern Michigan Hospital patients. It was she who was on hand on a daily basis during the terminal illnesses of our parents.

Giles struck out on his own at an early age and was with the Chrysler Corporation for many years, first in Detroit, then in Indianapolis. Having a "turn" for machinery like his brother Carl, he became an expert in micromatic honing and was featured in a *Machine Tool* publication in the mid-60's. He took an early retirement from Chrysler several years ago and now has his own business selling Amzoil products.

As for the farm itself, it is still owned by the surviving members of the Philip Schmitt family since it was our parents' wish that it be a safe haven for their children in case of need. Its fields lie fallow, its buildings are deserted but to see it pass into the hands of strangers would somehow seem a violation of parental trust.

The way of life which my father loved and envisaged for his descendants began to languish when the tractor replaced the horse and acquiring more land became necessary for survival. Coincidentally it was Bismarck with his quest for more territory which destroyed the dreams of my grandfather and it was technology which eventually destroyed the dreams of my father. But time marches on and the roots of the fourth generation are elsewhere. . . .

When we look backward through rose-colored glasses, as many of us do when we reach the bifocal age, we feel the pull of the past and the urge to preserve that which was meaningful and good in our childhood years—the love of family, the spiritual values, the belief in the future. But we must also address the awesome problems of the present; we must spur our efforts toward building a world of peace and plenty, a world with its people of many creeds and colors working together for the common weal under the rule of law, not the lawlessness of the nuclear jungle. Otherwise there may not be a future for those who come after us.

Beatrice Henshaw
July, 1986

SCHMITT-COVEYOU GENEALOGY

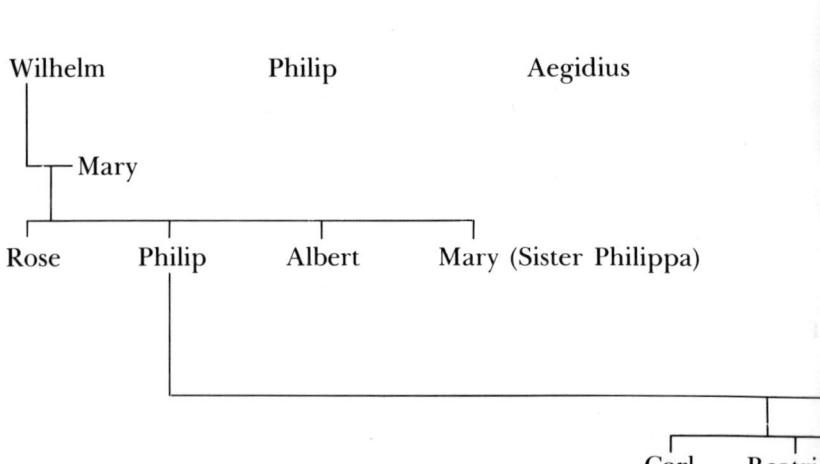